HONG KONG
SPECIAL ADMINISTRATIVE REGION
SHENZHEN
FUTIAN
LUOHU
NANSHAN
SHEKOU
DEEP BAY
(Shenzhen Wan)
LOK MA CHAU
SAN TIN
MAI PO
SHEUNG SHUI
Tsim Bei Tsui
Mong Tseng Wai
LAU FAU SHAN
TIN SHUI WAI
KAI KUNG LENG
TAI TO YAN
LAM TSUEN VALLEY
PAT HEUNG
YUEN LONG
KAM TIN
SHAP PAT HEUNG
SHEK KONG
Kap Lung
TAI MO SHAN
TSUEN KAM AU
Tai Lam Chung Reservoir
Shing Mun Reservoir
Hung Shui Kiu
Lam Tei
Nim Wan
Black Point
CASTLE PEAK
TUEN MUN
LUNG KWU TAN
Tap Shek Kok
Lung Kwu Chau
URMSTON ROAD
PILLAR POINT
CASTLE PEAK BAY
Pearl Island
SO KWUN WAT
TAI LAM CHUNG
SHAM TSENG
TSING LUNG TAU
TSUEN WAN
KWAI CHUNG
Tsing Yi
MA WAN CHANNEL
Ma Wan
RAMBLER CHANNEL
Sha Chau
The Brothers
STONECUTTERS ISLAND
KOWLOON
Chek Lap Kok
Hong Kong International Airport
YAM O
PA TAU KWU
PENNY'S BAY
Siu Ho
LO FU TAU
DISCOVERY BAY
Discovery Bay
TAI HO
TUNG CHUNG BAY
TUNG CHUNG
SHA LO WAN
TAI SHUI HANG
Peng Chau
Siu Kau Yi Chau
Kau Yi Chau
Green Island
SULPHUR CHANNEL
SAI WAN
VICTORIA PEAK
POK FU LAM
Cyberport
LANTAU ISLAND
MUI WO
SILVER MINE BAY
Sunshine Island
Hei Ling Chau
NGONG PING
LANTAU PEAK
SUNSET PEAK
Sai Tso Wan
TAI O
KEUNG SHAN
Shek Pik Reservoir
Tong Fuk
CHEUNG SHA
PUI O WAN
CHI MA WAN
CHI MA WAN PENINSULA
MAN CHEUNG PO
SHEK PIK
TONG FUK MIU WAN
TAI LONG WAN
TAI HOM SHAM
Yi O San Tsuen
FAN LAU
Cha Kwo Chau
ADAMASTA CHANNEL
Cheung Chau
WEST LAMMA CHANNEL
EAST LAMMA CHANNEL
LUK CHAU WAN
YUNG SHUE WAN
Yung Shue Wan
George Island
PICNIC BAY
Sok Kwu Wan
HA MEI WAN
Lamma Island
Shek Kwu Chau
Siu A Chau
Soko Islands
Tai A Chau
Series HM200L/E
Year 2001
km 0 2 4 6

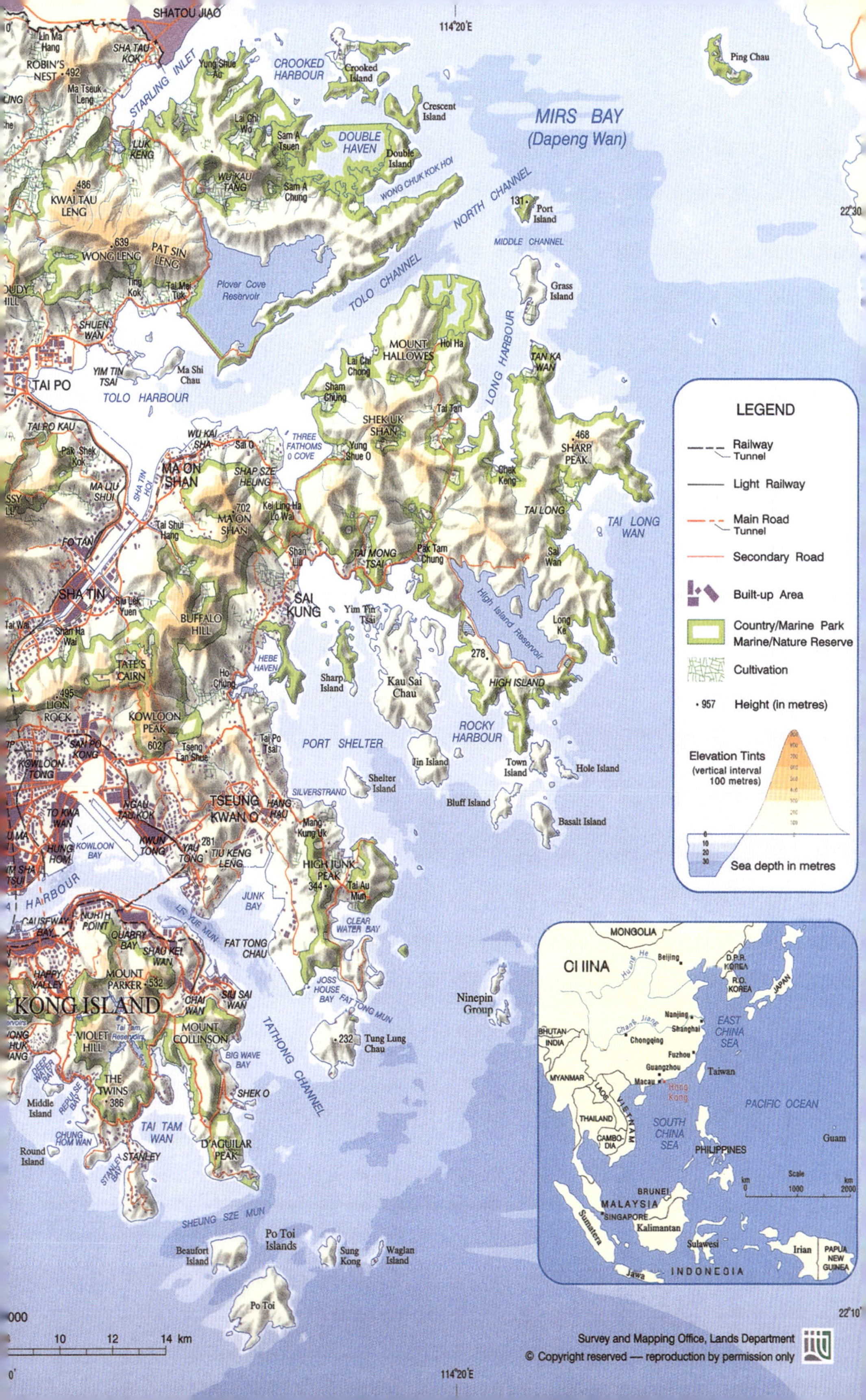

SHATOU JIAO
114°20'E
Ping Chau
MIRS BAY
(Dapeng Wan)
CROOKED HARBOUR
Crooked Island
Crescent Island
DOUBLE HAVEN
Double Island
STARLING INLET
SHA TAU KOK
ROBIN'S NEST 492
Lin Ma Hang
Ma Tseuk Leng
Yung Shue Au
Lai Chi Wo
Sam A Tsuen
LUK KENG
WU KAU TANG
Sam A Chung
WONG CHUK KOK HOI
NORTH CHANNEL
131 Port Island
MIDDLE CHANNEL
22°30'
486 KWAI TAU LENG
639 WONG LENG
PAT SIN LENG
Ting Kok
Tai Mei Tuk
Plover Cove Reservoir
TOLO CHANNEL
Grass Island
SHUEN WAN
YIM TIN TSAI
Ma Shi Chau
TAI PO
TOLO HARBOUR
MOUNT HALLOWES
Hoi Ha
Lai Chi Chong
Sham Chung
SHEK UK SHAN
Tai Tan
LONG HARBOUR
TAN KA WAN
468 SHARP PEAK
TAI PO KAU
Pak Shek Kok
MA LIU SHUI
WU KAI SHA
Sai O
THREE FATHOMS COVE
Yung Shue O
MA ON SHAN
SHAP SZE HEUNG
SHA TIN HOI
702 MA ON SHAN
Kei Ling Ha Lo Wai
Chek Keng
TAI LONG
TAI LONG WAN
Tai Shui Hang
FO TAN
Sai Wan
Shan Liu
TAI MONG TSAI
Pak Tam Chung
SHA TIN
Siu Lek Yuen
SAI KUNG
Yim Tin Tsai
High Island Reservoir
Long Ke
Tai Wai
Shan Ha Wai
BUFFALO HILL
TATE'S CAIRN
HEBE HAVEN
Ho Chung
Sharp Island
Kau Sai Chau
278
HIGH ISLAND
495 LION ROCK
KOWLOON PEAK 602
Tseng Lan Shue
Tai Po Tsai
PORT SHELTER
ROCKY HARBOUR
SAN PO KONG
KOWLOON TONG
Jin Island
Town Island
Hole Island
Shelter Island
SILVERSTRAND
Bluff Island
Basalt Island
NGAU TAU KOK
TSEUNG KWAN O
HANG HAU
TO KWA WAN
Mang Kung Uk
KOWLOON BAY
KWUN TONG
281 YAU TONG
TIU KENG LENG
HUNG HOM
HIGH JUNK PEAK 344
Tai Au Mun
HARBOUR
JUNK BAY
CLEAR WATER BAY
LEI YUE MUN
CAUSEWAY BAY
NORTH POINT
QUARRY BAY
SHAU KEI WAN
FAT TONG CHAU
HAPPY VALLEY
MOUNT PARKER 532
KONG ISLAND
CHAI WAN
SIU SAI WAN
JOSS HOUSE BAY
FAT TONG MUN
Ninepin Group
VIOLET HILL
Tai Tam Reservoirs
MOUNT COLLINSON
TATHONG CHANNEL
232 Tung Lung Chau
DEEP WATER BAY
REPULSE BAY
BIG WAVE BAY
THE TWINS 386
SHEK O
Middle Island
TAI TAM WAN
CHUNG HOM WAN
Round Island
STANLEY
STANLEY BAY
D'AGUILAR PEAK
SHEUNG SZE MUN
Po Toi Islands
Beaufort Island
Sung Kong
Waglan Island
Po Toi
22°10'
10 12 14 km
LEGEND
Railway
Tunnel
Light Railway
Main Road
Tunnel
Secondary Road
Built-up Area
Country/Marine Park
Marine/Nature Reserve
Cultivation
957 Height (in metres)
Elevation Tints (vertical interval 100 metres)
Sea depth in metres
MONGOLIA
CHINA
Beijing
Huang He
D.P.R. KOREA
R.O. KOREA
JAPAN
Nanjing
Shanghai
Chang Jiang
EAST CHINA SEA
BHUTAN
INDIA
Chongqing
Fuzhou
Guangzhou
Taiwan
MYANMAR
LAOS
Macau
Hong Kong
VIETNAM
PACIFIC OCEAN
THAILAND
SOUTH CHINA SEA
CAMBODIA
PHILIPPINES
Guam
Scale
km 0 1000 2000
BRUNEI
MALAYSIA
Sumatera
SINGAPORE
Kalimantan
Sulawesi
Irian
PAPUA NEW GUINEA
Jawa
INDONESIA
Survey and Mapping Office, Lands Department
© Copyright reserved — reproduction by permission only

HONG KONG'S JOURNEY TO REUNIFICATION

Hong Kong's Journey to Reunification

Memoirs of Sze-yuen Chung

Sze-yuen Chung

The Chinese University Press

Hong Kong's Journey to Reunification —
Memoirs of Sze-yuen Chung
By Sze-yuen Chung

ISBN 962–996–002–8 (Casebound)
962–996–020–6 (Paperback)

THE CHINESE UNIVERSITY PRESS
The Chinese University of Hong Kong
SHA TIN, N.T., HONG KONG
Fax: +852 2603 6692
Fax: +852 2603 7355
E-mail: cup@cuhk.edu.hk
Web-site: www.chineseupress.com

Printed in Hong Kong

To the People of Hong Kong

Contents

List of Illustrations xii

Foreword xvii

Acknowledgements xix

Abbreviations xxi

Chapter 1 Early Reflections 1

My First 24 Years 1

Early Education 1

Dangerous Adventure 3

My Time Outside Hong Kong 7

Work in Free China 7

English Sojourn 10

Post-war Era of Hong Kong 13

Industrial Revolution 13

My Business Career 18

Beginning of Public Service 21

"Perennial Temporary Legislator" 22

Chapter 2 Sino-British Negotiations 25

The Inception 25

Hong Kong's Future on the Agenda 25

Leading the Executive Council 33
UMELCO Debated the 1997 Question 35
The Chinese Invitation 39
Arrival of Edward Youde 43
The Open Forum 49
Advising Thatcher 51
A Lady's Place 53
The Stalemate 56
The First Encounter 56
Truth Unveiled 58
A Place at the Table 60
Battle for Hearts and Minds 63
No Time Table for Talks 67
The Breakthrough and Breakdown 69
The Councillors' Rage 70
The First Concession 72
Target: Allen Lee 74
Britain Caved-in 75
The Haggle 76
UMELCO's New Strategy 76
The Lobo Motion 78
Proclamation of British Exit 81
British Sensitivity 83
Hostile British Reception 86
Furious at Sir Geoffrey Howe 88
Public Support for the UMELCO 90
Discriminatory Nationality Act 92
Readying for Beijing 95
Hard Talk with the Supreme Leader 97
Craft of Story Telling 104

Public Support for the Beijing Trip *107*

The Joint Liaison Group *109*

Political Gambit *111*

Agreement Became Declaration *113*

EXCO's Final Mission to London *114*

Dunn's Embarrassment *116*

False Alarm *117*

The Hand Shake 118

The Commendation *118*

A Minor Rebuff *121*

UMELCO's Reaction to the Declaration *122*

On the Plane with Thatcher *128*

The Highest Knighthood *130*

Preventing Sabotage *132*

The Grand Finale *135*

Chapter 3 The Long Transition 137

Honeymoon Period 137

The Three-act Play *137*

Secret Meetings with Xu *139*

Sir Edward's Death — An Omen *146*

Sir Edward's Vision *148*

Myth of the UST Cost Overrun *154*

Basic Law Conundrum *158*

Democracy in Gestation *163*

Another Chinese Invitation *168*

Period of Distrust 170

The Shock from Tiananmen *170*

Seeds of Confrontation *176*

The Third Chinese Invitation *178*

Airport Turbulence *182*

Birth of the Liberal Party *189*

Period of Confrontation 192

Patten Realigned the Executive Council *192*

Patten's Political Reform *195*

Anatomy of a Dispute *204*

A Blessing in Disguise *207*

Patten Saved from His Waterloo *210*

Preliminary Working Committee *215*

Little Tricks *219*

British Enmity with the PWC *221*

Executive-led Government *223*

Reckless Driving *228*

Victims of the Sino-British Dispute *233*

Chapter 4 The Hong Kong SAR 237

The Preparation 237

Provisional Legislative Council *237*

The Guessing Game *241*

Bumps and Ruts on the Road *244*

Vanguard of the Hong Kong SAR *250*

Support for Tung Chee-hwa *257*

Democracy and the Civil Service *262*

The Ceremonies 268

Final Hours of the British Rule *268*

The Sovereignty Return *271*

Final British Retreat *279*

Founding of the Hong Kong SAR *280*

The Mandarin Hurdle *287*

New Era, New Honours *289*

The Threshold 293

The Paradigm Shift 293

The Initial Experience 297

The Future 302

Party Politics 302

Executive Council Reform 305

SAR's Economic Future 311

Appendixes 317

1. Chronology of Events 319
2. List of Chinese Names with Their English Equivalents 325
3. Biography of the Author 329

Illustration Credits 333

Index 335

Illustrations

Plates

Chapter 1

1.1 The author and his wife at the Diplomatic Corps Ball, 1974 — 8

1.2 The author with his family and relatives at the University of Sheffield, 1985 — 12

1.3 The author's son, daughter-in-law and two grandsons, 1995 — 19

1.4 The industrial complex of Sonca Industries Ltd., 1966 — 20

Chapter 2

2.1 Sir Sik-nin Chau leading the Hong Kong Trade Mission to the European Economic Community, in Italy, 1963 — 26

2.2 The author with Sir Y. K. Kan, 1978 — 33

2.3 The UMELCO and Foreign Secretary Lord Carrington during his visit, 1981 — 38

2.4 The UMELCO and Lord Privy Seal Humphrey Atkins during his visit, 1982 — 40

2.5 The author with Sir Y. K. Kan, Mr. T. K. Ann and others in Japan, 1978 — 42

2.6 The Swearing-in Ceremony for Governor Sir Edward Youde, 1982 — 46

2.7 The UMELCO Delegation with Prime Minister Thatcher at 10 Downing, 1982 — 54

2.8 The UMELCO and Prime Minister Thatcher during her visit, 1982 — 57

2.9 The first UMEXCO Mission to London at Lancaster House, 1983 — 68

2.10 Mr. Roger Lobo addressing the Legislative Council, 1982 79
2.11 The UMELCO and Foreign Secretary Sir Geoffrey Howe during his visit, 1984 82
2.12 The second UMELCO Delegation to London, 1984 89
2.13 The author meeting Chairman Deng Xiaoping in Beijing, 1984 99
2.14 The press briefing after the UMELCO Delegation to Beijing, 1984 103
2.15 The UMELCO Delegation to Beijing, in front of the Temple of Heaven, 1984 108
2.16 The Hong Kong Executive Council, 1984 115
2.17 The author with Dr. Allen Lee at the Summer Palace, Beijing, 1984 119
2.18 The Hong Kong Delegation attending the 35th National Day Celebration in Beijing, on the Great Wall of China, 1984 120
2.19 The third UMELCO Delegation with Prime Minister Thatcher in London, 1984 124
2.20 Governor Youde meeting the Japanese Prime Minister in Tokyo, 1984 126
2.21 The Sino-British Joint Declaration Signing Ceremony in Beijing, 1984 127
2.22 The Chinese leaders with the Hong Kong Delegation in Beijing, 1984 129
2.23 Prime Minister Thatcher addressing the Legislative Council, 1984 130
2.24 The Farewell Party to mark the end of the Exclusive Appointment System for the Legislative Council, 1985 134

Chapter 3

3.1 The UMELCO dinner for Director Xu Jiatun of the Xinhua News Agency, Hong Kong, 1985 140

3.2 The author speaking at the Dragon Boat Festival Dinner in London, 1986 143

3.3 The funeral procession of the late Governor Youde, 1986 147

3.4 The Hong Kong Polytechnic, 1986 150

3.5 The 15th Anniversary of the City University of Hong Kong, 1999 152

3.6 The Hong Kong University of Science & Technology, 1995 153

3.7 A bird's-eye view of the Hong Kong University of Science & Technology, 2000 156

3.8 The Swearing-in Ceremony for Governor Sir David Wilson, 1987 160

3.9 The Hong Kong Executive Council, 1987 165

3.10 A rally held in May 1989 at Statue Square in support of the student movement in Beijing 171

3.11 Visit of the Business and Professionals Federation of Hong Kong to Beijing, 1993 179

3.12 The Hong Kong International Airport, 1998 183

3.13 Celebration of the 4th Anniversary of the Liberal Party, 1998 190

3.14 Governor Patten's Open Forum for his political package, 1992 197

3.15 The author addressing the 2nd plenary session of the Preliminary Working Committee in Beijing, 1993 208

3.16 The author accepting the PWC Appointment Certificate from the NPC Chairman, 1993 216

3.17 The Budget Expert Subgroup of the Sino-British Joint Liaison Group, 1997 230

Chapter 4

4.1 The End-of-Term Dinner of the Provisional Legislative Council, 1998 241

4.2 The Chinese leaders and members of the Hong Kong SAR Preparatory Committee, 1996 252

4.3 Meeting of the Selection Committee Group of the Preparatory Committee in Beijing, 1996 256

4.4 The Convenors of all the Sub-Committees of the Preparatory Committee and members of the Secretariat, 1997 263

4.5 The new wing of the Convention and Exhibition Centre at night, 1997 270

4.6 The Sovereignty Return Ceremony on 1 July 1997 274

4.7 People gathering at Time Square for the sovereignty transfer count-down on 30 June 1997 277

4.8 People gathering in a community centre watching the sovereignty transfer on 1 July 1997 278

4.9 The Establishment Ceremony of the Hong Kong SAR on 1 July 1997 281

4.10 The Swearing-in Ceremony for members of the Hong Kong SAR Executive Council, 1997 283

4.11 The HKSAR Chief Executive, Mr. Tung Chee-hwa, shook hands with the author, the Executive Council Convenor, after the Swearing-in Ceremony on 1 July 1997 284

4.12 Chinese leaders and members of the executive, legislative and judicial branches of the HKSAR, 1 July 1997 286

4.13 The First Grand Bauhinia Medal Presentation Ceremony on 2 July 1997 290

4.14 The author and his friends at the Government House after receiving the GBM Award on 2 July 1997 292

4.15 President Jiang Zemin presented his calligraphy scroll "Hong Kong Faces a Better Future" to the HKSAR, received by the HKSAR Chief Executive, Mr. Tung Chee-hwa, 1997 295

4.16 The HKSAR Chief Executive, Mr. Tung Chee-hwa, addressing at his first press conference, 1997 304

4.17 The Hong Kong SAR Executive Council, 1997 306

4.18 The Unofficial Members of the Hong Kong SAR Executive Council at Tiananmen, 1999 308

4.19 Happy retirement card for the author from members of the mass media, 1999 310

4.20 The BPF Forum on Hong Kong SAR's Economic Future, 1999 312

Maps

The Hong Kong Special Administrative Region *Front endpaper*

Hong Kong in Its Regional Setting *Back endpaper*

Foreword

I am not one who indulges in nostalgia or needs to justify myself to the past, which anyway is for historians to assess and record. I therefore did not plan to write my memoirs at first, but my friends and associates goaded me into the travail. They stressed that I am probably the only native son of Hong Kong who has been closely and actively involved in the whole process of Hong Kong's returning to China. Furthermore, facts as far as they can be ascertained should be preserved, lest myths will substitute for truth, which is not uncommon in matters of state and politics.

I conceded to their entreaty and the story contained in my memoirs belongs to the whole community for which I served in what I gathered to be the public's best interests. I am privy to a lot of information from all the three parties concerned — Hong Kong, China and Britain.

Memory is very selective and porous. The mind is like a sieve, which as time goes by drains the fluid and leaves behind residues that are generally dramatic. For almost half a century I participated in the administration of Hong Kong, first when it was a British colony and then as a Special Administrative Region of China. Many decisions taken in which I had a part passed and the details about these, once so gripping, are mostly forgotten now. But there was one stretch, the twenty years between 1979 and 1999 when I finally retired from politics, which has remained vivid because the implications from that time — the Sino-British negotiations and then the transition from the British colonial rule to a high-degree of autonomy under China — continue to reverberate.

My testament centres mainly in those two decades of trials and tribulations through which China and Britain, and also Hong Kong between them, changed for the better. China has come out of isolation, persisted with its economic reforms, erased the shame of the Opium Wars, and shaken the world. Britain has finally shelved its imperial past, relinquished its role as an aloof island nation that has to be a beacon for other peoples it once ruled, and come to terms with its status as a member of the greater European Community. Hong Kong has also been evolving, even though the process is not complete, as it attempts to be at once Chinese and cosmopolitan, proud of its ancient heritage and confident of its future.

All along, others and myself who wanted to achieve a just and practical solution to the Hong Kong conundrum did so with one dominant objective — to cater for the dignity and sovereignty of China, the grace of the United Kingdom, and the aspirations of Hong Kong. Somehow, through the doubts and agonies, we have now accomplished more or less all our aims and we can face our own consciences and sleep well at night.

Others who endured similar experiences as I did may not see the happenings exactly as I do today. This is not because our conflicting reflections are faulty but rather because we inevitably tint our eyes with our own ideals. Two persons, lying side by side in the meadow and gazing at the floating clouds, may discern vastly different configurations. I never claim to be authoritative but I do assert my recollections are authentic. I shall say no more as I let my memory speak.

Sze-yuen CHUNG
Hong Kong, May 2001

Acknowledgements

The author wishes to thank both Dr. Steven K.L. Poon and particularly Dr. Allen P.F. Lee wholeheartedly for their information, advice and assistance throughout the whole process of drafting and production of the memoirs. Dr. Lee was a member of the Hong Kong Legislative Council uninterrupted for twenty years from 1978 to 1998 and its Senior Member from 1988 to 1992. He was also a member of the Executive Council from 1985 to 1992, and thus has been closely involved in the whole process of reunification.

Grateful thanks also go to Mr. Wong Yan-lung, a barrister, for reading and giving professional advice on the English and Chinese manuscripts, and to Mrs. Esther Wong for checking both the scripts.

The author is indebted to both Mr. Bernard Fong and Miss Siring Li for their able assistance in preparing respectively the English and Chinese drafts.

Some of the photographs were taken from the publications of the UMELCO Office, the Hong Kong Government and the Hong Kong SAR Government, and the author wishes to express his appreciation for their permission to do so.

Abbreviations

BDTC	British Dependent Territory Citizen
BLCC	Basic Law Consultative Committee
BLDC	Basic Law Drafting Committee
BN(O)	British National (Overseas)
BPF	Business and Professionals Federation of Hong Kong
CE	Chief Executive of the HKSAR
CPG	Central People's Government
CPPCC	Chinese People's Political Consultative Conference
EXCO	Executive Council
GDP	Gross domestic product
HKJBCC	Hong Kong/Japan Business Co-operation Committee
HKMAO	Hong Kong & Macao Affairs Office
HMG	Her Majesty's Government
JLG	Sino-British Joint Liaison Group
JP	Justice of the Peace
LEGCO	Legislative Council
MP	Member of Parliament
NPC	National People's Congress
PC	Preparatory Committee for the HKSAR
PLA	People's Liberation Army
PLC	Provisional Legislative Council
PRC	People's Republic of China
PWC	Preliminary Working Committee of the PC

RHKJC	Royal Hong Kong Jockey Club
SAR	Special Administrative Region
SC	Selection Committee for the First Government of the Hong Kong SAR
TDC	Trade Development Council
UMELCO	Unofficial Members of the Executive and Legislative Councils
UMEXCO	Unofficial Members of the Executive Council
UMLEGCO	Unofficial Members of the Legislative Council
UST	University of Science and Technology
XNA	Xinhua News Agency

Chapter 1

Early Reflections

My First 24 Years

Early Education

The Hong Kong of my youth was harsher yet more genteel than the one in which I live now. Back then when I first made sense of my surroundings, the city was a little known colonial outpost of subtropical languor. This is hard to conceive today in its incessant, modern bustle of world fame. What passed for the heart of the civilization was a mixture of market place and business centre, in which two races, the Chinese and the expatriate British, coexisted but did not too often commingle, except as an absolute necessity. One group played cricket, in bowler hats under the mid-day sun, a game lasting days totally incomprehensible to the Chinese. The other in turn enjoyed a distinctly different culture, especially the noisy Cantonese opera. They tolerated each other by not having much to do with each other — a mutually suitable arrangement.

I had grown up in such a world. The main story I am going to tell covers roughly the last twenty of my nearly fifty years of public service. But before doing that let me now start at the beginning of my life. I was born in November 1917 on the Hong Kong Island, then dubbed "Victoria". My father arrived in Hong Kong from his native Foshan County, Guangdong Province, in his young days. I am the eldest child of his third wife and the fifth of his eight sons. He was a metal merchant, mainly doing imports. I also had three sisters. Some of my siblings I have never seen.

I could not remember there was any kindergarten in those days. Like others, I attended a Chinese school for my six years primary education. This was followed by eight years (started from Class 8 moving up to Class 1) secondary education in Angle-Chinese schools using English as the medium of instruction. Many teachers were expatriates, mainly from Britain.

I was quite active in extra-curricular activities during my teens — a member of the St. John's Ambulance and a qualified lifesaver from the Royal Society for Life Saving. I played soccer, basketball, ping-pong (table tennis) and tennis, but volleyball was my favourite sport and I represented my school, St. Paul's College, to win inter-school championship. In those days there were nine players (not six as today) on each side making a formation of 3 by 3. The players were not required to rotate and shorter persons like myself normally were acting as defenders positioned at the last row of the formation. There will be more about this in a later section.

After matriculating from St. Paul's College in 1936, I went to study at St. John's University in Shanghai, with the intention of continuing my education in the U.S.A. after my first degree. A novel about an engineer who helped to develop the infrastructure of China and to raise the living standard of his people inspired me. So I longed to be an engineer and, for that reason, I enrolled in the engineering faculty. A year later, during my summer vacation in Hong Kong, the Japanese army invaded Shanghai and cut me off from St. John's. I then sought and obtained admission to the University of Hong Kong.

In those pre-war days, the University of Hong Kong was providing a 6-year course for medicine and 4-year courses in arts, science and engineering disciplines. It had a student population of about 400 with an enrolment of approximately 80 students in the engineering faculty.

Three of us in the third year of the University devised a unique way of gaining real-world experience by putting in a total capital of a few thousand Hong Kong dollars to establish and operate a small machine shop at High Street near the University. I took overall charge of this experimental operation.

In May 1941, at the age of 23, after winning all the academic awards and prizes available, I graduated in engineering with first class honours, the only one to have done so in the whole faculty for that year. A month after my graduation, Mr. E. Cock, the General Manager of the Kowloon Whampoa Shipyard in Hunghom, hired me as an assistant engineer working in the machine shops at a monthly salary of 200 Hong Kong dollars. At that time the expatriates from Britain dominated the engineering profession in Hong Kong and the whole enterprise of a few thousand people employed but two Chinese professionals. The other Chinese was working in the design office.

Dangerous Adventure

Back in those innocent times of 1941, in retrospect, not many of us knew how precarious Hong Kong's situation was. The insularity of the Colony blinded us to the urgency, to the storm looming. Ten years earlier Japan had seized Manchuria and four years earlier its Imperial Army had pushed south, sparking a full-scale invasion of an already strife-stricken and torn China proper. Hong Kong seemed safe to the many who deluded themselves that the Japanese would not challenge the British with their invincible Royal Navy. The

American President, Franklin Roosevelt, called 8 December 1941 (Western Pacific Time) "The Day that will live in Infamy" when the Japanese raided Pearl Harbour in Hawaii.

The aggressor had mastermind the blitz not just for those islands out in the middle Pacific Ocean, but also for the one on which I was living. Japanese Mitsubishi "Zero" airplanes on that Monday morning flew sorties against Hong Kong, whose defence was porous and perfunctory, even though the defenders — ethnic Chinese, Indians, Britons, Australians and Canadians — were brave. The garrison just could not cope with the bombing and the strafing by a force that had total air superiority and control of the sea-lanes. I remember seeing the streaks of tracer shells light up the sky and hearing the constant staccato of machine guns as well as the thud, thud, thud of ordnance being dropped and the rattle of explosion getting nearer and nearer. I had joined the Auxiliary Transport Services and was dispatched by the civil defence to the Wanchai Vocational School to take charge of its motor car repair section. We knew whatever we were doing could not stall the Japanese army. After 17 days of resistance the British eventually surrendered on Christmas Day 1941.

The Japanese, once they had settled in, marshalled the people to work to aid their war effort. The Authorities were drafting many workers back to the Kowloon Whampoa Shipyard to fix and refit Japanese warships. I did not want any part, however tiny and involuntary, in the Japanese design on the rest of Asia. So early in 1942, I slipped out of Hong Kong for "neutral" Macao. The then fascist Portuguese, like the Spaniards, did not join either the Axis or the Allies, ensuring that not only their territories were spared but also their overseas domains. Macao was the exit route for many from Hong Kong, some of whom would eventually trek up to free China's wartime capital Chongqing in Sichuan Province, in the formidable Yangtze gorges. The Japanese also had a policy of making the entry into Hong Kong impossible but the exit to Macao easy so as to ease their food supplies. Thus I left my hometown with little difficulty yet a lot of anxiety about relatives and friends trapped under occupation. In Macao, I billeted with the family of Cheung Yung-hing, a young lady of grace I had been dating in Hong Kong.

Yung-hing had been my confidante before the War. She had enrolled at Lingnan University, which had decamped from Guangzhou to the University of Hong Kong to escape the occupation. Yung-hing was not just my love, she was my solace and, in 1942, my opportunity for freedom; and it was in tranquil Macao, with the world in arms, that I proposed to her. We got engaged when all else seemed bleak or desperate and planned to flee to the Mainland, far to the north, to Jiangxi Province.

At the University of Hong Kong, Tsang Wah-shing was one of my engineering lecturers. As the Japanese headed south, he went north to offer his service to the provincial government, which put him in charge of a machine factory in the outskirts of Taihe, the wartime capital of Jiangxi Province. We were able to communicate and he urged me to join him in Jiangxi and contribute to the national defence. Honoured and elated, I wanted to go at once but suddenly realized that I had to take with me the books, manuals and papers related to the job of a chief machine designer. With China at war, it was not possible to obtain these invaluable volumes. Those I had abandoned in Hong Kong in my haste to get out would now have to be retrieved.

Now I was suddenly presented with a unique predicament of having to sneak back for the books and also for a visit with my relatives again for one last time — and perhaps really for the last time. Going back would be much harder for the Japanese were wary of agents and saboteurs who, when caught, would be, if in luck, summarily executed with a swish of the samurai sword and, if not, tortured for days before decapitation. With the bravado of youth, I was determined to return to Hong Kong and so hired a motorized junk in Macao for the trip — or folly. The boatman checked me over and told me I would stick out because I was too pale. He urged me to tan myself for a couple of weeks so that I could pose as a fisherman who had strayed into Hong Kong.

We set sail very early in the morning on a teen-foot vessel in choppy waters for the 35-mile voyage across the swelling South China Sea. The boat bobbed away from Macao in reasonably fine weather and for much of the day I leaned against the gunwale, my head at times no more than about seven inches from the waves, and periodically retched. Whilst my stomach turned, and my head too, I was fortunate since I did not encounter any marine patrol. The junk docked at Aberdeen, a fishing village on the southwest end of the Hong Kong Island, at about seven in the evening and in calmer waters that belied my inner anxiety. I clambered ashore, still seasick and jittery, and, after composing myself, boarded a bus for my home on Pok Fu Lam Road near my alma mater, the University of Hong Kong. I thought I was safe and dry but I was wrong, almost dead wrong.

Recuperated from my voyage, and staying in Hong Kong for several days, I sorted and packed the precious consignment into two trunks. These were to be delivered along with me to the Hong Kong and Macao Terminal for the ferry *Pakunyuan* for the return trip, which I reckoned should be a much easier excursion. A companion and I, lugging the contraband, took the route along Pok Fu Lam Road towards Queen's Road West in Sai Ying Pun district through a Japanese checkpoint, a routine inconvenience. These sentries made spot checks usually. This time, though, the Japanese soldiers stopped and ordered us to get into their sentry box. We cold-sweated, quivering all over, but yet had to hide our trepidation. We knew if the Japanese had searched the two trunks plus their contents, we would be in peril. After waiting and shivering in the sentry for about ten minutes, with our lives in the balance, we were told to leave. Having cheated death, and not flinching, we gladly left and boarded the vessel for Macao *en route* for Taihe in Jiangxi Province.

My Time Outside Hong Kong

Work in Free China

Not many people know that the Chinese Government of Chiang Kai-shek had entrusted me with managing an electric power plant cum water works that had been handed over by the Japanese after the War. The work I had performed at the plant from 1945 to 1946 and also in other earlier assignments in China from 1942 could have changed my life.

Shortly after arriving in Jiangxi in early 1942, I acquainted myself with the Taihe machine factory and discovered it desperately needed help. I contacted my former schoolmates at the University of Hong Kong as well as my fellow mechanics of Kowloon Whampoa Shipyard and implored them to come and continue their work away from the Japanese occupation and for national redemption. They responded promptly and positively, coming to Free China at grave risks to do what they could for their country.

Later in 1942, after joining the Taihe factory, I married my betrothed who had gone through so much with me. After the simple wedding, I was tasked with establishing another machine factory and becoming its general manager. At the same time, I also lectured as a part-time associate professor at the Chiang Kai-shek University (a varsity that subsequently transplanted to Taiwan during the later Civil War). One of the other important jobs I did was to design for the National Tea Corporation a factory in Hunan Province for making tea bricks for export to Russia. In 1944, in the last desperate push into Free China, the forces of Dai Nippon poured into Jiangxi as the

Plate 1.1 *The author and his wife at the Diplomatic Corps Ball, 1974.*

resistance retreated. I joined the exodus and, upon reaching a small town near Xingquo, worked at a newly opened machine factory making textile equipment.

Then in August 1945, nearly four years after the Japanese shattered my world in Hong Kong, the war in the Pacific ended and a new age dawned. The provincial government of Jiangxi took back from the Japanese the electric power plant cum water works in the city of Nanchang, the capital of Jiangxi, and nominated me as its plant manager. At that time the provincial governor was Xiong Shihui and his Minister for Works was Hu Chiazhao, whose son, Weimin, had been my favourite student at the Chiang Kai-shek University and we were very close. The connection could prove fortuitous because Governor Xiong and Minister Hu were destined for more important postings for the post-war reconstruction of China.

Near the end of 1946, Xiong at the order of Generalissimo Chiang assumed command of the three northeastern provinces of Heilongjiang, Jilin and Liaoning, which constitute Manchuria. The Government in Nanjing transferred Xiong, one of the most competent officials of the period, to govern Manchuria because it was the hub of China's heavy industries, most of which were developed by the Japanese during their occupation since 1931. Hu Weimin sought me out to say that his father would be transferred along with Xiong to the Northeast and asked me to join them there. His earnest request presented me with a dilemma. I could relocate to Manchuria out of patriotic duty and also an opportunity for promotion. I consulted my wife, the source of comport and the compass of my life. "Where should we head, to the north or the south?" She softly told me how homesick and weary she had become in her wanderings with me during the past five years. I had led her farther and farther away from her family. She would stand by her husband without demur, wherever he ventured for that was the fate of women in her time and because of her devotion to me. Nonetheless, she could not disguise her anguish and the thought of being so far from her fond Hong Kong and Macao. This was one reason, and a very compelling one, for my not going north.

I had done a myriad of jobs, all required by the exigency of war, and yet I was not highly qualified on paper in the more competitive civilian life. I had only one bachelor's degree before the Japanese invasion of Hong Kong. Though I had lived through a lot and seen scenes I had wanted to forget, I was still relatively young at 29 and ought to further my formal education. This I was resolved to do, to learn more and to get accustomed to the world beyond the Far East. I was just as determined to come back after my foreign sojourn to serve Hong Kong and the Chinese nation. So at the end of 1946, I resigned from my job in China and returned to Hong Kong. Later in life, when I looked back on my days in China, had I accepted the offer to Manchuria in 1946, I knew my whole life would have been vastly different from the course I had subsequently taken in my hometown.

English Sojourn

One of my university schoolmates, Lai King-sung, who had worked with me in Jiangxi came back to Hong Kong earlier than I did. His family was running the World Light Manufactory producing hurricane lanterns mainly for export to Africa. These lanterns are kerosene lamps resistant to rain and wind and ideal for outdoors. Business was booming and hence the Lai family wanted to expand production and employed me as the Chief Engineer on a monthly salary of a thousand Hong Kong dollars, a handsome sum for at that time a female worker's daily wage was about three dollars. For the next two years I worked at the factory while applying for a scholarship to study overseas. The British Council eventually agreed to endow me with a research fellowship and I would go to the United Kingdom in the late summer of 1948.

But before I sailed for Britain, I returned to the Chinese Mainland again, this time to Shanghai for a national volleyball tournament as the Vice-Captain of the Hong Kong team. My classmate of St. Paul's, Ip Yuk-lam, now the Permanent Honorary President of the Chinese Chamber of Commerce, was the Team Manager. In 1948, the Kuomintang Government, as one of its last acts on the Mainland, organized a National Sports Meet in Shanghai. At that time there were already commercial air passenger flights between Hong Kong and Shanghai. Our Hong Kong team won the national championship, and with the trophy in hand, rushed back to Hong Kong as the Communists closed in.

A few weeks later, I was pumped and primed for the voyage to England. The journey lasted exactly 28 days through the South China Sea, the Indian Ocean, the Suez Canal, the Mediterranean, and finally, the Atlantic on a grand sweep of the Empire. On board the ocean liner SS *Canton* heading for the English port of Tilbury near London, I looked forward to seeing the outside world. One of the most memorable parts of the odyssey took me down through the Strait of Malacca, past Malaya, Singapore, the Palk Strait separating then Ceylon (now named Sri Lanka) and India. The ship continued towards the Western Hemisphere, through the Suez Canal, the Mediterranean Sea, and onward sailing around Gibraltar into the Atlantic Ocean. Only then, as a seafarer, had I a glimpse of the British holdings and an inkling of the scale of the British domain, which included all the key ports in the maritime trade route. During those four weeks the slow boat conducted numerous port calls for passengers and provisions. I, like other pilgrims, made the most of the shore visits to explore the diverse realm.

Upon arrival I spent a week in Manchester to take a familiarization course run by the British Council and then moved to Sheffield, where I enrolled myself in Sheffield University's Engineering Faculty as a doctorate degree student, under the illustrious Professor H. W. Swift, an authority in cold working of metals. After settling down in my research work in about six months, I sent for my wife to join me in England. She gave birth in 1950 to my second daughter, Dora, in Sheffield, five years after Lily had been born in China.

After two years of intensive research work, I was awarded a Doctor of Philosophy degree in engineering and continued to work at the University as a Research Fellow. I published about six or seven

Plate 1.2 *The author with his family and relatives at the University of Sheffield, 1985.*

papers within a year, an output considered prolific. One of these papers — on “deep drawing of metals” — won the Whitworth Prize of the Institution of Mechanical Engineers in London in 1952 when I was already back in Hong Kong. A large British company, GKN, offered me a senior research officer post with an attractive annual salary of nearly a thousand British Pounds (HKD16,000), thus opening up a research career for me in the United Kingdom. Britain the country, after my three years there, was no longer as alien as it had been at first sight. Beyond Sheffield lay the much more inviting Manchester and London, where British culture was again flowering. I once more consulted my wife, Yung-hing, whose lodestar was fixed to Hong Kong and Macao. Also as a British Council Research Scholar I had moral commitments to Hong Kong. So, at the end of 1951, we, all three of us, packed our belongings and, like vagabonds, shipped off — this time homeward bound.

Post-war Era of Hong Kong

Industrial Revolution

The three years that I was away again from my native city were a period of upheaval. The Communists in 1949 had trounced the Kuomintang and pushed it across into Taiwan. Some feared that the Red Army would also drive the British to the sea, which would have been easy, but instead the situation stabilized with the Chinese not crossing the border, not even causing any nuisance.

I was in England when the Communists mopped up the last of the opposition on the Mainland, and in October 1949 proclaimed the People’s Republic in Tiananmen Square. The triumph of one force meant of course the defeat of another as hundreds of thousands of refugees entered Hong Kong, reversing the traffic of eight years ago when many from the city had gone north to escape occupation and privations. These asylum seekers would transform Hong Kong, even though at the time many dreaded that they would be a burden, not a boon.

Here I wish to digress and discuss briefly Hong Kong's past. The territory covering about 1,000 square kilometres, reclaimed land included, had for centuries survived as an obscure corner of China, so remote that it was only cursorily governed by out of favour officials sent from the capital. Subsequently pirates, fugitives and even a deposed Sung Dynasty emperor sought refuge in Hong Kong.

Prime Minister Lord Palmerson, who had ordered the taking of Hong Kong Island for Queen Victoria, dismissed the place as a barren rock with hardly a house on it, a rather apt description, which did not earn him the gratitude of Her Majesty. The Royal Navy in 1841 attacked China in the first of the two Opium Wars and, having defeated the completely antiquated enemy, imposed on the vanquished the Treaty of Nanking, in which the Hong Kong Island was ceded in perpetuity. The victor was not content with so modest a prize and chafed for more — and more meant a mainland appendage. This was accomplished in 1860 by the Second Opium War, a campaign that forced the Chinese to surrender the southern portion of the Kowloon Peninsula, also in perpetuity under the Convention of Peking. In 1898 the British further succeeded in wresting the rest of the Kowloon Peninsula and the New Territories (comprising 92 per cent of the total land area of the territory) from China under the Convention of 1898 for a 99-year lease from 1 July 1898 to provide lebensraum to the Island.

The Japanese from Christmas day 1941 until their unconditional surrender of 8 August 1945 controlled and ravaged Hong Kong. In September, more than a month after the Victory over Japan Day, the British retook the Colony and prepared for the return of the Governor, Sir Mark Young. By then China was too consumed in its own internecine war to bother with the detail of history that was Hong Kong. Four years later the Communists likewise did not think the timing was right to snatch Hong Kong back from the British for they were too busy consolidating their grip on the Mainland, menacing their rival on Taiwan, and watching warily the developments on the Korean peninsula. At that time the British Foreign and Colonial Office had advised in 1949 the Prime Minister not to fight for Hong Kong. The Government in London, assessing the volatile situation inside China, reasoned that it would be futile for the British to defend. The colonial forces were ready to give in if the battle-hardened Communists swooped down from Guangzhou.

For a century since the British took Hong Kong in 1841, the territory had survived as an entrepôt, a role rendered obsolete when the Japanese invaded. For three years and eight months of the occupation, Hong Kong turned into a city of insomnia with the economy stalled and the people eking out a most meagre subsistence. After the War the city stirred back to life like a beast from hibernation. Every year for the next five after liberation, the value of imports and exports expanded 40 per cent. In 1946 Hong Kong had a foreign trade worth HK$1.7 billion (then US$300 million) and in 1951 the tally was HK$9.3 billion. Back then the Hong Kong industries were insignificant and only from the mid-1950s onward did manufacturing start to develop.

China joined in the Korean War in 1950, causing the United Nations to impose sanctions against it. As a result Hong Kong's burgeoning foreign trade collapsed, losing one-third of the market within three years. As if the sudden recession was not depressing enough, the territory had to accommodate the exodus from the Mainland as the Government there started to nationalize industries, confiscate assets, and end the grace period for capitalists. In a bat of the eye, the population had increased from two to 2.6 million, just when the economy was shrinking and when social services were sparse. Suddenly shanties mushroomed on the hillsides and tens of thousands scrambled for odd jobs and alms.

Not all who streamed into Hong Kong were paupers. Some of the refugees had come from Shanghai, once the most urbane of places in Asia, and scores of them had brought along not just wealth but also the spirit of enterprise. Before they fled, some had redirected their most modern equipment, ordered from the West after the War, to Hong Kong for safekeeping. Once secure in the territory and certain there were no immediate possibility of their return to Shanghai, these exiled factory owners restarted their textile business in the adopted city. The textile industry concentrated in Tsuen Wan, in the southwestern New Territories. With their commercial acumen, modern equipment and cheap labour, they helped the export-oriented textile industry flourished. Not only did they change and charge the economy; they also set moral examples for other denizens of the city. The territory began to prosper.

Rumours spread that the British had in the early 1950s sent feelers to gauge the Chinese attitude towards Hong Kong. Sensing the Mainland Government was in no hurry to settle the issue, the British relayed the assurances to the businessmen who, with the impetus, invested even more in the territory and sustained the boom. Hong Kong's exports surged from the late 1950s through the 1960s and into the 1970s, altogether a very heady time. Hong Kong had gone through its industrial revolution and manufacturing became the economic mainstay. Industrialists diversified their productions, venturing into new products such as plastics, toys, enamelled wares, shoes, wigs, light consumer electronics, etc., catering to and adjusting for whatever the global market wanted. By 1975 Hong Kong had graduated into one of the main light industrial centres with labour-intensive manufacturing accounting for nearly a third of the gross domestic product (GDP) and employing more than half of the labour force. People were living better with the GDP per capita reaching HK$10,000 (USD1,600). The export-oriented manufacturing continued to prosper and Hong Kong's GDP per capita had greatly improved to HK$30,000 (USD6,000) in 1980 and HK$50,000 in 1985.

The bonanza did not only benefit the employers but also their employees, whose wages rose along with their productivity and skills. For every dollar Hong Kong earned 60 cents went into the pocket of the working man or woman. The rise in income was registered with the rise of living standards and expectations. Back in 1953, after the Boxing Day fire in Shek Kip Mei shantytown, the Government initiated the public housing programme for some of the tens of thousands of squatters. The emollient scheme took the hardest edge off Hong Kong life and gradually accommodated more and more people who no longer worried about not having a roof over their heads. However flimsy the first batch of public tenements was, a home was a sweet home. The Government also became more enlightened; sensing it had to provide other social services, such as universal healthcare, mandatory and free education and modest benefits for the elderly.

Some families no longer had to fret about the daily necessities, a very liberating feeling. These people, imbued with the work ethics plus the creed of self-reliance, could begin to save and invest. A middle class emerged to go with a very resilient working class. These were the forces that spurred on the property market and also innovation and adaptability — all told a winning combination for a place that had once been barren.

My Business Career

I came back to Hong Kong at the end of 1951 from England with a newly acquired doctorate degree in engineering and assumed my previous job with the World Light Manufactory as its Chief Engineer and later Deputy General Manager. But the African economy had deteriorated, diminishing the market for hurricane lanterns and causing the World Light to suspend operation. I then started my own engineering consulting business in 1953 to assist investors to start their own factories. I was on a roll and over the next three years helped launch four factories, one each for glass bottle making, for cold storage, for cotton baling and for flashlights. The last was for a rich and elderly refugee from Shanghai, Mr. V. K. Song, who put his name to the company, in which I had a modest share. The factory was located in To Kwa Wan, Hunghom, on the Kowloon Peninsula and employed a British patented process of mine. The place just hummed along with the modern, semi-automatic machinery.

Within a short period Song's flashlights, or what the British call "torches", became popular, particularly in the United States, whose buyers raved about their low cost, high style and reliability. The largest customer for Song was the world famous American Eveready, which in 1956 offered to invest in the company. The capital injection would allow Song to expand and to shine his light on many more consumers. But Song had his doubts, afraid the Americans would eventually take over his beloved enterprise. Eventually the pioneer relented and offered to sell out to the Americans who would only accept if I packed in my own consulting business and took charge of the company as its General Manager. I did after some initial hesitation and that proved a turning point for my business career. The year, 1956, also proved memorable for my wife and me as we eventually had ourselves a son, Gilbert, on our third attempt.

The Song subsidiary of Eveready continued to prosper, becoming the leading light of Hong Kong industry. Entering the 1960s the company underwent a major transformation by constructing a ten-storey factory cum office building on a 30,000 square feet site at San Po Kong, a new industrial town near the Kai Tak International

Plate 1.3 *The author's son, daughter-in-law and two grandsons, 1995.*

Airport. Song also acquired a new identity to go with the new address — Sonca Industries Limited. I became the Executive Chairman of the Board whilst a returned engineer trained in the U.S., Chan Tou-suen, succeeded me as the Managing Director. The company flourished ever more in the 1970s by erecting more and newer premises and expanding to become the world's largest flashlight manufacturer, employing nearly 5,000 workers and with products exporting to about one hundred countries.

My career's shift from engineering to management was not to be the final change. Sonca won industrial kudos and also the attention of the Colonial Government, which reckoned that it had to draw locals into its confidence if it were to administrate the territory well. Without my trying, the Administration tapped me for public service.

Plate 1.4 *The industrial complex of Sonca Industries Ltd., 1966.*

Beginning of Public Service

I had never engaged in textile business but it was that trade which led me into four decades of public service. When the transplanted industrialists from Shanghai moved to Hong Kong, some quickly set the looms spinning and the fabrics flowing to the global market. Our city's foray into the textile trade worried the British and the American workers. The British, under tremendous union pressure and under the sway of the Labour Government, led the way with restrictions on textile imports from Hong Kong, one of its "dependent overseas territories". The then Hong Kong Governor, Sir Alexander Grantham, went to London to lobby but failed to budge the then Foreign and Colonial Office. In those days governors were British overseas civil servants appointed by, and answerable to the Foreign and Colonial Office, and had no power to bargain with the British Government on behalf of a colony.

At that time the Hong Kong manufacturers were not organized and had no representative of their own to defend their interests. The glaring omission prompted Sir Alexander in 1957 in a speech to the manufacturers to urge them to establish a proper industrial association to argue their own case. Such a confederation, independent of the government, should not differentiate, nor discriminate against, various creeds and races, and should embrace all factories, large and small, of all trades and nationalities. It should be able to speak with one united voice for the whole industry. With leadership, the textile manufacturers could then forcefully negotiate with and cogently explain Hong Kong's situation to the British and American Authorities. The succeeding Governor, Sir Robert Black, in the following year deputized the Senior Chinese Member of the Executive Council, Sir Sik-nin Chau, to head a Working Party, of which I was also a member, to found the proposed "Federation". This mandate would involve me in public life for more than 40 years until my retirement in 1999.

Two years later, in 1960, the Federation of Hong Kong Industries was established by statute with Sir Sik-nin as its Chairman, Colonel Douglas Clague (later Sir) as Vice-Chairman, Mrs. Susan Yuen as Secretary General, and me as a member of the Governing Council. The Federation during its first few years implemented several key initiatives to further the development of industries, and one of these was the founding of the Hong Kong Trade Development Council in 1966. Governor Sir David Trench appointed Sir Sik-nin as the Council's first Chairman and I succeeded him as Chairman of the Federation. By then I had become a "Provisional" Legislative Councillor who was neither an official nor a mandarin and had also been drafted into a battery of government committees. The Governor inserted me, like a wedge, into the Hong Kong Government Trade and Industry Advisory Board, Hong Kong Telephone Advisory Committee, Hong Kong Aviation Advisory Board, Hong Kong Government Radiation Board, Working Committee on Productivity, Justice of the Peace, etc. Suddenly from relative obscurity I had achieved public prominence. On the roller coaster I had absolutely no idea that the ride would last four decades and span two generations.

"Perennial Temporary Legislator"

In the 1960s I had a nickname the "Perennial Temporary Legislator", a contradiction in term, an oxymoron, but it was apt when I first assumed the sobriquet.

After the War the British, with their empire dwindling, had to find postings for redundant overseas civil servants ousted from colonies that had achieved independence. Hong Kong became a catchment basin for these displaced officers. Many of them had been stationed in Africa and Malaysia and were far too young to retire. The then Financial Secretary (later Colonial, then renamed Chief Secretary) Sir Philip Haddon-Cave had served in East Africa. Sir David Akers-Jones, later the Chief Secretary and Acting Governor during the mid-1980s, was from Malaysia. What this meant was a breed of expatriate mandarins had arrived with scant knowledge of local customs and dialects. They need a lot more assistance from the natives.

For all these years, until 1985, Hong Kong had operated under a unique system of rule by consultation and consensus. Elections were limited to the Urban Council, which dealt with only sanitary and cultural affairs, and more recently District Boards, which are basically advisory bodies on local district affairs. For the administration of Hong Kong, the Governor appointed the Executive Council (EXCO), or the Cabinet, whose members advised him and were entrusted with certain political and public relations duties. EXCO members tended to be prominent members of the community and conglomerates. The Governor also appointed individuals to the Legislative Council (LEGCO) who debated and enacted the draft laws as well as vetted the budget and approved expenditure.

Since those Whitehall appointees, the Governor and his mandarins did not really know who were suitable for the sensitive office, they introduced a system for testing the candidates, a sort of probation. When a substantive member would be absent for a week or more, a temporary member would be appointed to fill the place. Whenever the Governor had a vacancy in the LEGCO or EXCO after a substantive member had completed his term and was not re-appointed for whatever reason, he would select a replacement from a list of temporaries to fill the vacancy.

In April 1965 I was surprised to receive a letter from Governor Sir David Trench inviting me to temporarily fill in a LEGCO vacancy for a few weeks. Subsequently I was called to sub in the LEGCO on and off for a stretch of over three years, prompting the then Financial Secretary, Sir John Cowperthwaite, to dub me the "perennial temporary legislator".

This breed of temporary legislators went extinct, like dinosaurs, in the mid-1970s and that of temporary Executive Councillors in the mid-1980s.

Chapter 2

Sino-British Negotiations

The Inception

Hong Kong's Future on the Agenda

Today, the Chinese flag flutters over Hong Kong where the Union Jack once did. The change, and all it entails, is the result of the Sino-British Joint Declaration which upholds this society's way of life and which epitomizes the best in co-operation between the once hostile nations. To this day many still argue whether the British or the Chinese had first raised the issue of Hong Kong's destiny. Most probably, though, the Hong Kong Chinese, myself among them, had considered the question of 1997 before anyone else.

The person most aware about the beginning of the process was the former Governor, Sir (later Lord) Murray MacLehose. I was, without my trying, the Chinese in the Colony most knowledgeable about what actually transpired from the beginning of the negotiations through the transition to the establishment of the Special Administrative Region (SAR). I must stump up the pieces in my possession to help readers assemble together the jigsaw.

Sir Sik-nin Chau was the undisputed leader of the ethnic Chinese community between 1950 and 1960. He was the Senior Chinese Member of the Executive Council, the governor's inner sanctum. In those days, all Chinese members of not only the

Plate 2.1 *Sir Sik-nin Chau leading the Hong Kong Trade Mission to the European Economic Community, in Italy, 1963.*

Executive but also the Legislative Council were billed as representatives of the Chinese people. This was quite obvious since Hong Kong was under British rule and all senior officials were hailed from the United Kingdom and not familiar with the subjects for whom they made policy decisions. His position was supreme in the Chinese community.

The Government adeptly chose the credible Sir Sik-nin in 1958 to head the Working Party of the aforementioned Federation of Hong Kong Industries, and to chair the organization when it was formally chartered two years later. In 1966 he became the top man of the embryonic Trade Development Council (TDC) and the Management Association. When TDC was finally hatched the Governor naturally passed the responsibility for it to the banker who, however, by TDC's convention, could not preside simultaneously over the Federation of Industries. Sir Sik-nin, thereby, graciously bequeathed to me his post at the Federation of Industries just as the political and economic climate was overheating.

The Red Guard zealots had run wild in 1967, inflaming passions not only on the Mainland but also across the border. The Cultural Revolution first spilled over into Macao and then spread to Hong Kong in May. The protests escalated into skirmishes between demonstrators and the police and the skirmishes flared into riots. The mayhem got so out of control that a mob thronged Upper Albert Road and besieged the governor's mansion called Government House, a building converted into a virtual fortress a quarter century earlier by the Japanese army. Governor Sir David Trench was confined in the residence during the worst of the unrest. About three weeks later the street action subsided, superseded by a terrorist bombing campaign which killed a few innocent children and alienated some of the leftists' sympathizers.

Some of the people, especially professionals and businessmen, started an exodus out of Hong Kong. The tidal wave of immigration continued for a while. What little trust they had in the Chinese Government evaporated and dissipated like the teargas that the police had fired at the rioters. The most nervous of them figured Hong Kong's future was dicey and would not risk it. This became a part of the familiar pattern of confidence falling and people quitting.

Sir Sik-nin assembled, through the Federation's Secretary-General Susan Yuen, a number of industrialists, such as Ann Tse-kai, James Wu, Chuang Chung-wen and myself to form a special group. We met about once every couple of months at the penthouse of Sir Sik-nin's Hong Kong Chinese Bank headquarters where we pondered the future of Hong Kong, if there was to be any. When the prescient six or seven of us began conducting our conclaves, we reckoned the crunch time was still three decades away in 1997. The seers among us consoled each other that, to China, the Taiwan question was much more pressing. The People's Republic would surely resolve that tangled issue before it tackled the less urgent matter of Hong Kong at leisure. So woes passed, worries too. Comforted by our own delusions we disbanded our talk shop in 1969 as both the economy and the confidence that underpinned it recovered. This conclusion was later proven wrong, dead wrong.

Over the next few years no one thought much about the Hong Kong conundrum. The state of denial continued until the middle of the 1970s. I was already then a legislator, having been confirmed by the then Governor, Sir David Trench, in 1968 and no longer "temporary". Four years later in 1972 the new Governor, Sir (later Lord) Murray MacLehose, additionally promoted me to the Executive Council and made me in 1974 the Senior Member of the Legislative Council.

As Hong Kong settled into peaceful development, China underwent dynastic changes. Premier Zhou Enlai, the moderate in the Government, died in January 1976 of cancer. The country went into mourning. Before the grief for Zhou had waned, Mao Zedong passed away in September. The heir apparent Hua Guofeng rose to power and fell from it two years later. Meanwhile the Government arrested "the Gang of Four" conspirators blamed for the Cultural Revolution's excesses and the Communist Party redeemed Deng Xiaoping for the second time. The National People's Congress (NPC) in February 1978 endorsed Deng's proposed economic reforms and opening up to the outside world.

Back in the Colony the property market boomed. Banks were beginning to be concerned about their mortgages, which typically had to be paid off between ten to twenty years, the majority being fifteen. The lords of the houses of usury calculated that if they were to ratify new loans from 1982 onward, these would be due by 1997. This was the apocalyptic year when parts of the "leased" Kowloon and all of the New Territories might have to be returned to China according to the Convention of 1898. Banks would be imprudent to lend and indeed companies, particularly the capital-intensive electric power stations, would be reluctant to invest until they could clear away the uncertainties.

When the Unofficial Members of the Executive and Legislative Councils (UMELCO) heard about the financial sector's disquiet, they discussed the concerned among themselves and reflected the anxieties to the Governor. Sir Yuet-keung Kan and I, as the Senior Member of the respective EXCO and LEGCO, worked closely and now with an edge to our common purpose. The immediacy of the Councillors' reaction to the spectre of 1997 was also not surprising, considering so many of these office holders came from the banking and business community.

Politics and economics affect each other and dissolve into each other much as salt and water do. Governor Sir Murray was keenly sensitive to that, which was why he in 1977 appointed the Financial Secretary, Sir Philip Haddon-Cave, to head an Advisory Committee on Diversification to explore Hong Kong's prospects. He was specifically interested in understanding the dynamics of China's reforms, the end of isolation, the advantages of its ample land and abundant labour, and how these factors might tempt local industries to migrate north. This Committee, a high-power think tank, comprised Hong Kong & Shanghai Banking Corporation's Chairman Michael Sandberg (later Lord), Jardines' taipan David Newbigging, *Far Eastern Economic Review*'s editor Derek Davies, prominent businessmen and industrialists Ann Tse-kai, Lee Quo-wei (later Sir),

Li Fook-wo, James Wu, Ngai Shiu-kit and others. All told the crew numbered 14. I also belonged to this brain trust, and few of us, particularly Derek Davies, mooted the 1997 issue with the Chairman Sir Philip.

The Governor planned to visit Beijing in March 1979, the first ever incumbent Governor to do this. He would bring along Sir Yuet-keung Kan as the Senior Member of the EXCO and political advisor, and the future governor, David Wilson (later Lord). They brought back from the Chinese capital assurances from Deng, most distinctly the emotive, if vague, appeal from the supreme leader to the people of Hong Kong "to put their hearts at ease". Not one informed source came up with a full account of what had been discussed in Beijing at the time. We, at the UMELCO, nagged Sir Yuet-keung about this for years but he would not break his vow of silence.

The press only pieced together a plausible story from rumours circulating among the community. Through these grapevines we learned how Sir Murray wished to propose to the Chinese a plan. The scheme involved both sides papering over the issue of 1997 and the Hong Kong Administration selling land in parts of the "leased" Kowloon and the New Territories in terms of 15-year lease as if the deadline did not exist. The British Government, however, objected to such a suggestion, which Sir Yuet-keung also opposed on the ground that China would rebuff the Governor and, thereby, panic investors. Sir Murray subsequently decided he would only broach the subject if he felt the meeting with Deng was cordial.

The atmosphere of the talk was genial enough for Sir Murray to introduce the subject. The Governor hinted to Deng that his Government and China should both evade the 1997 question to let land transactions carry on as usual. The Chinese leader was not psychologically prepared for such a blunt approach and answered that he would rather raze Hong Kong to the ground than delay taking back lost territory. Deng, however, was conciliatory, suggesting to Sir Murray to return to the territory and to tell the business people they "can rest their hearts at ease".

So it was a few words on which Hong Kong was supposed to rest its future. For a while that promise sufficed to prop up the market, both stock and real estate, but such a foundation was flimsy and many people continued to have doubts on the story.

All these years I too was puzzled by this story until one day in May 1983, when I was in London attending a New Fellows Dinner of the Royal Academy of Engineering and to receive an Honorary Fellowship from the Institution of Mechanical Engineers. I had lunch with Lord MacLehose alone on 4 May and one of the subjects touched upon was his visit to Beijing in March 1979. I asked him about who actually first raised the 1997 issue during his meeting with Deng. He replied that it was Deng who first raised it. He however added that prior to his trip he did relay to the Chinese Authorities that he would mention to Deng his proposal of selling land in the leased territories with 15-year lease as if there were no 1997 deadline. But before he had an opportunity to do that, Deng spelt out the Chinese position of taking back Hong Kong not later than 1997. When MacLehose asked Deng how he should say to the public on his return to the Colony, Deng then suggested that he tell the people "to put their hearts at ease".

Back in Hong Kong, Sir Philip and his think tank delved not only into the economic worries stemming from the issue of 1997 but also their political implications. However, the gurus felt the subject was far too sensitive and agreed to deal with the topic in a separate secret letter. The Advisory Committee wrote: "The effects of the lack of certainty about Hong Kong's longer term future continue to be felt within the economy. As the economy moves up market, and the capital element in the final cost of its output increases, industries will increasingly need recourse to longer-term finance. The uncertainty about Hong Kong's longer-term future could well mean that banks become less willing to undertake long-term loans and investors become less willing to invest in projects which offer only long term returns. Thus uncertainty will impede the diversification of the economy and inhibit its growth rate."

The Advisory Committee's assessment was that a single, vatic phrase "to put their hearts at ease" from Deng could not sustain confidence and the economic development that hinged on it. They further said in their secret letter: "In essence, therefore, we would wish to place on record our view that Hong Kong's future development, particularly in terms of economic growth, is bound to be seriously hampered, sooner or later, should there be continuing uncertainty as to its political future." They believed that there was a growing body of opinion that at that time it was an opportune moment for both Britain and China to begin preliminary negotiations on the subject of sovereignty, because the complicated issue could not be settled in haste. The longer the delay the more perplexed and vexed people would be.

The Advisory Committee on 18 January 1980 submitted to the Governor their 4-page secret letter, signed by the Chairman, the Financial Secretary, and all its 14 members, namely, Ann Tse-kai, Li Fook-wo, M. Sandberg, Lee Quo-wei, Ngai Shiu-kit, James Wu, D. Davies, D. Newbigging, Chen Shou-lum, Leslie Gordon, Keith Legg, myself, and the two senior government officials, the Secretary for Economic Services and the Secretary for Commerce and Industry.

Upon receiving the secret letter, Sir Murray on 30 January 1980 sent a curt reply of only two sentences: "I am obliged for your letter of 18th January signed by members of the Advisory Committee. I have noted its contents."

Leading the Executive Council

I passed the mandate as the Senior Member of the Legislative Council to Oswald Cheung (later Sir) in September 1978 to devote more time to my Executive Council posting. A year and a half later, in early 1980, Governor Sir Murray told me Sir Yuet-keung's term as the Senior Member of the Executive Council would not expire until August but he had insisted to advance his retirement to March. Sir Murray then asked me to take over from Sir Yuet-keung in August because Sir Sidney Gordon, then second in rank, would serve as the Senior Member during the intervening period before he too would retire in August.

Plate 2.2 *The author with Sir Y. K. Kan, 1978.*

I felt honoured, somewhat astonished, and hesitated about accepting this sudden appointment because Sir Yuet-keung's hasty departure had to be motivated by what he knew and I did not. Could his premature departure been caused by the convergence of two developments, the British Nationality Act and the future of Hong Kong? Were these two issues so disheartening to him? He did not let on but I could guess.

The United Kingdom was in the throe of debating the Nationality Act, the end result, and aim, of which was to rescind the birthright of British passport holders to live in that country. The people in the territory, already agitated by that motion, would be further worried as they contemplated the 1997 question, a double blow about which they were powerless.

I realized that were I to succeed Sir Yuet-keung I would be simultaneously confronted with those two volatile and related issues. Expatriate mandarins, with assistance from the Legislative and Executive Councils, ran the colony, despite the "localization" policy that had been launched nominally in the 1960s. Even the Senior Unofficial Member of the Executive Council was a non-Chinese until the 1970s. Some of these mandarins were thoroughly professional but their commitment to Hong Kong was suspected, perhaps tenuous, since the majority of them eventually retired to the United Kingdom or Australia. Many in the colony, with their lives and assets at stake, could not trust these civil servants to empathize with their plight or to defend their interests. The governor, as an outsider, was no exception. Those with no long-term plans for themselves in Hong Kong were charged with making long-term plans for others who had. This struck many as dubious, if not somewhat absurd.

I had been, in 1980, a full legislator for a dozen years and an Executive Councillor for eight. The duty for representing the local

Chinese to the highest echelon fell with a thud on my shoulders. I understood that it was my role to mediate between the governing and the governed, as well as to reconcile conflicting interests, which might, and did, arise. I had confidence that I could exercise the judgement to do right for both sides and for my own conscience. From the moment I accepted the challenge my life and the destiny of Hong Kong were fused.

UMELCO Debated the 1997 Question

The Unofficial Members of the Executive and Legislative Councils, together given the initials UMELCO, had played a distinct role throughout the time of the British and Chinese negotiations over Hong Kong. From very early on, we members had first the inclination, then an initiative, to inform and involve the people in the proceedings the best we could. This activist approach offended some vested and national interests, but that was the only course open to us if we were to win the public trust and execute our duties.

Ever since I became the Senior Member of the Executive Council in August 1980, many individuals and groups had expressed to me their concerns and asked me to convey these to Her Majesty's Government. The Hong Kong Observers, a cadre of liberal intellectuals, and the Reform Club, an embryonic political party, were among those that volunteered opinions. I compiled these submitted views and turned them into an issue for the UMELCO to consider.

The UMELCO back then functioned as two halves of one entity, a spirit of co-operation hard to imagine now in a more divided community. The chiefs of the assemblies, one called the Senior Member of the Executive Council and the other the Senior Member of the Legislative Council, exerted considerable influence. Others in the chambers heeded their views and together they helped the Government shape, argue and implement policies. Since the Governor appointed all legislators and Executive Councillors, he also relied on them to educate him about a society he hardly knew and connect him with a people he had only the most superficial contacts. The arrangement chimed along until the early 1990s when the consensus was broken, which is another story for a later chapter.

Earlier on the UMELCO recognized the two positive developments on the Mainland which had great relevance for the 1997 issue. First, we believed the Chinese economic reforms were irrevocable, marked by the opening up of society, a liberalizing economy, and the founding of the first Special Economic Zone of Shenzhen near Hong Kong and based, in part, on the Hong Kong model. What we were witnessing was, we thought, the beginning of a long, persistent process that would transform China and the reforms were the first step. These changes were largely internal, driven by the dynamics of a modernizing nation.

Second, China had been sending thousands of young scholars and engineers to the West for further training. We felt that these individuals would be exposed to the cultures of North America and Western Europe. They would return not only with engineering and scientific knowledge but also an appetite for political, social and cultural experiments. The impact of their home-coming, and the senior positions they would ultimately hold, should modify the characteristics of a community not yet broken totally free from its feudal bonds.

These two were our interpretation of events on the Mainland. We also figured someone as sage as Chairman Deng understood the consequences of his economic reforms which he was willing to risk, because he could not allow the country to lag any further behind during his watch. What he had set in motion was an evolution from which there was no turning back and Hong Kong would benefit from it.

Shortly after I became the Senior Member of the Executive Council, the British Foreign Secretary, Lord Carrington, visited Beijing. On his way back to London, he paused in Hong Kong in March 1981 to meet with the UMELCO. We got news that China had initiated the discussion of the 1997 question with the Foreign Secretary, and Carrington would seek our opinions to help prepare for the tough negotiations ahead.

Many pundits in the territory also looked for signs, for shifts of the vane to judge which way the wind was blowing. They, like ourselves, detected a telltale flutter from the gauge when on 30 September 1981, the Chairman of the Standing Committee of the National People's Congress, Ye Jianying, in an interview with Xinhua News Agency (XNA) revealed a plan for the peaceful reunification with Taiwan. Marshal Ye, revered as one of the revolution's "seven immortals", proposed a nine-point programme for the reunion. Among these points were two which we considered had relevance for Hong Kong:

(1) After the country is reunified, Taiwan can enjoy a high degree of autonomy as a special administrative region and it can retain its own armed forces. The Central Government will not interfere with local affairs on Taiwan.

(2) Taiwan's current socio-economic system will remain unchanged, so will its way of life and its economic and cultural relations with foreign countries. There will be no encroachment on the proprietary rights and lawful right of inheritance over private property, housing, land and enterprises, or on foreign investments.

Plate 2.3 *The UMELCO and Foreign Secretary Lord Carrington during his visit, 1981.*

Humphrey Atkins (later Sir), the British Lord Privy Seal, visited Beijing in January 1982 and on his return trip dropped in on the UMELCO. He disclosed that he had met Premier Zhao Ziyang and Vice Premier Ji Pengfei, and discussed the Hong Kong issue. He emphasized at the outset that it was the Chinese who had raised the issue of 1997, not he. He nonetheless figured that the Chinese Government had yet to reveal any clear direction or set of criteria to the talks. He also believed that the Chinese had not yet decided how they should proceed. The Chinese had also told him that they would in due course talk to various circles in Hong Kong and would preserve the interests of investors in Hong Kong.

Our English guest and we concluded our meeting with the shared impression that China wanted to settle the issue with the British and was waiting for the right occasion.

The Chinese Invitation

Very few people would ever associate my name with the Chinese People's Political Consultative Conference (CPPCC) of the People's Republic of China. I now wish to reveal the connection. Early in 1982, I received a letter from Xinhua News Agency inviting me to join the Consultative Conference, an advisory entity comprising private citizens. Before July 1997, Xinhua was the *de facto* Chinese embassy in Hong Kong. The honour that China had wished to bestow on me was considerable, but it also presented a dilemma for me since I was already the Senior Member of the colonial Executive Council and had access to the top secrets on the diplomatic sparring sessions between the two countries. Even though, so far, the British and the Chinese contacts had been as cursory as these had been

Plate 2.4 *The UMELCO and Lord Privy Seal Humphrey Atkins during his visit, 1982.*

cordial, the two parties to the parley were technically adversaries, and it would be unwise of me to accept a rather awkward appointment.

In those days the Senior Member of the Executive Council was generally regarded as the "leader of the Hong Kong Chinese community". Preceding me in that capacity were Sir Sik-nin Chau, Sir Cho-yiu Kwan, and Sir Yuet-keung Kan. They likewise acted as emissaries between the Chinese public and the British Administration, who in their own styles strove to serve the community. The negotiations not only pitted China and Britain of today against each other but also raised the spectre of antipathy long ago, about which emotions remained heated. I could not in clear conscience be both trusted by the British and relied on by the Chinese, who would both eventually doubt my loyalty.

At that time I also served on other public bodies. One of these was the Hong Kong-Japan Business Co-operation Committee (HKJBCC) which was sponsored by the Trade Development Council to promote trade with Japan. Sir Yuet-keung Kan who chaired the TDC also chaired the HKJBCC. Both Ann Tse-kai and I were members of this Committee. Ann chaired the Communications Sub-Committee and I headed the Industrial Sub-Committee. The HKJBCC and its Japanese counterpart, the Japan-Hong Kong Business Co-operation Committee, took turns to host annual joint meetings in Hong Kong and Tokyo.

In February 1982, we all gathered at Tokyo for the annual event and I arranged a meeting among the three of us in the hotel room. I told my colleagues that Xinhua had extended an invitation to me to join the CPPCC. Both Sir Yuet-keung and Ann said they too had received similar invitations. I then expounded my earlier thoughts and said that if I were to accept the Chinese offer I would betray British confidence and they would not trust me any more

Plate 2.5 *The author with Sir Y. K. Kan, Mr. T. K. Ann and others in Japan, 1978.*

since conflicts of roles and interest were not just probable but inevitable. Equally the Chinese would not trust me. I then concluded that I would decline the invitation. Sir Yuet-keung confessed that since he had retired from the Executive Council in 1980, he had disavowed any interest in politics and would not meddle in the question of Hong Kong's future. He would not assist the Chinese and would, therefore, turn down the offer. This was to Sir Yuet-keung the decent exit.

We then provided Ann with an analysis of his position. The industrialist and Chinese scholar had already retired from the Legislative and Executive Councils, and later also from the chairmanship of the TDC. He was, however, still engaged in public affairs and was very knowledgeable about the operations of the Hong Kong Government. He could, and would, contribute his insights to the Chinese cause. Ann agreed and accepted the appointment, and later became the Vice-Chairman of the CPPCC, a post graded in the Chinese protocol as one of the leaders of the Government. During all these years he had contributed much to the successful transition.

A year later, Qi Feng, the Xinhua Deputy Director, and Lai King-sung, my university cohort who began working for the agency when his membership in the Communist Party was exposed, invited me to lunch at the Furama Hotel on 23 March 1983. They maundered on a range of subjects but what they were eager to know was whether I would be willing to join the CPPCC. They related a message from Liao Chengzhi, Head of the Hong Kong and Macao Affairs Office (HKMAO) of the State Council, that Liao appreciated the work I was doing for Hong Kong and in particular my authoritative reflection of the views and wishes of the Hong Kong people. The pair also said Liao was fully aware of my position at the time that might preclude me from accepting the invitation.

Qi and Lai apparently knew I had declined the offer a year ago but stressed the invitation would remain open to me indefinitely, for which I was very touched. This entreaty, I believe, meant the Chinese Government did not hold any grudge against me or had ever doubted my commitment to Hong Kong, and thus to my country too.

Arrival of Edward Youde

The year 1982 marked a shift in British attitude that was even tangible to us eight time zones away from London. The Argentina military invaded the Falklands and hoisted a flag that had not been flown for 150 years over that South Atlantic island, populated by several thousand shepherds. The British had up to then resigned themselves to a seat at the table of Europe, the Empire a distant memory. But the Argentine attack galvanized the whole nation. Thatcher, whose popularity was sinking, seized the chance for glory. The whole country rallied around the Union Jack. The swift, decisive retaking of Port Stanley suddenly swung the United Kingdom from acceptance of its decline to a new surge of confidence. Thatcher, the first woman Prime Minister of Britain, was now getting into stride. The "Iron Lady" began to wonder why she had to accept the advice of the Foreign Office Sinologists and diplomats who so far had cautioned against riling up the Chinese over Hong Kong. The "Iron Lady" had by then forged a "special relationship" or "partnership" with the American President, Ronald Reagan, who shared her doctrinaire loathing for Communist rule. All this background was an important backdrop to the British and Chinese negotiations.

Britain retired Sir Murray as Lord MacLehose to Scotland. His replacement was the Welshman Sir Edward Youde who, like Lord MacLehose, spoke fluent Putonghua and admired Chinese culture as well as loved peppery Sichuan cuisine. He and Lady Pamela were models of propriety and their humility moved us in the colony. The career China specialist had had four stints on the Mainland, the last term of duty was between 1974 and 1978 when he was the British Ambassador in Beijing. Whilst posted in the capital he made a few trips to Hong Kong and had met members of both the Executive and Legislative Councils. He was no stranger to us but yet we did not really know him until he was sent here to govern — and not just to govern but to do it after the exit of a very popular Lord MacLehose, the reformer.

The Youdes' affection for China was as genuine as it was infectious. They had travelled extensively throughout the Mainland to get acquainted not only with the landscape, but also the diverse people of the country with a quarter of humanity and also that share of global problems. He also read Chinese avidly, not only literature but also the newspapers so that he would understand the thoughts and feelings of the populace on the verge of change. He had served in New York and Washington too but his more influential posting had definitely been in China. Before coming to Hong Kong as the Governor, Sir Edward had been the Foreign Office's Chief Clerk. This meant he had access to all the sensitive documents, including those pertaining to Hong Kong.

Long before Sir Edward's arrival the Unofficial Members of the Executive and Legislative Councils had conducted a series of meetings on the 1997 issue. We welcomed him to the Colony and to the debate of the issue, hoping he would add his expertise, insight and special knowledge to the deliberations. Prior to his arrival I had sent to him in London a copy of my welcoming speech for his inaugural ceremony, in which the 1997 issue was raised. The purpose was to prepare him for a substantive reply at the ceremony. He did not respond and I interpreted that he had no objection to what I was going to say.

The Chief Secretary, Sir Philip Haddon-cave, and I led the inaugural ceremony for Sir Edward on 20 May 1982. As planned I took the occasion to address the issue of Hong Kong's destiny and said, *inter alia*,

> "Your excellency will have many preoccupations in the administration of Hong Kong but I hope you, Sir, will agree with me that the first priority must be the question of the future of Hong Kong, which is of such concern to us all. Our continued economic prosperity and social stability are very much dependent on the confidence we the people of Hong Kong and our overseas trading partners have in the long-term future of Hong Kong. To maintain that confidence, it is necessary that the future of Hong

> Kong be satisfactorily resolved as soon as possible. It is inevitable that you, Sir, as the Governor of Hong Kong, will play an important role in such a resolution. In your endeavours in this regard Your Excellence can be assured of our wholehearted support."

The Governor, just sworn in, replied in a prepared speech which in part read:

> "For this [resolution] to be achieved Hong Kong will need confidence in its future. It is not surprising, given the circumstances of the lease that this issue should now be raised. I believe that there are sound grounds for confidence and that

Plate 2.6 *The Swearing-in Ceremony for Governor Sir Edward Youde, 1982.*

the omens are good. The commitment of Her Majesty's Government to Hong Kong and the interests of its people remains firm. The relationship with the People's Republic of China on which so much depends has never been more cordial. If there is an issue to be addressed, there is also in addressing it, a common recognition of the vital importance of the continued prosperity and stability of this Territory and a common wish to preserve them. In consequence I see good reason why confidence should remain high."

His public answer to our query firmly put the issue of Hong Kong's future on the top of his agenda. A month and a half after that ceremony, 9 July to be exact, Sir Edward called the UMELCO to a special meeting to discuss about the Prime Minister's visit to China in September on the issue of sovereignty. We expressed our view that it was not viable for the island and the southern peninsula to stand alone as a colony if the northern peninsula and the New Territories were to be returned to China in accordance with the Convention of 1898. Unless the United Kingdom could get an extension on the lease of the land, which constituted more than 90 per cent of the colony's total landmass, it would have to hand the whole region back to China.

The UMELCO referred to the debate of the House of Commons on 15 June of that year in which the Parliament insisted that the Island had been ceded to Britain forever and the Colony should continue on its own minus its hinterland. This conclusion was to us clearly fanciful. At that time there were rumours which reckoned, provocatively we thought, how Britain should insist that the treaties, whether unequal or not, were valid and China should be held to them. Thus the views of the Commons and Hong Kong differed and the UMELCO entrusted their opinions to Sir Edward to be conveyed to the British capital.

A week after the session, Sir Edward again convened another UMELCO meeting on 16 July, saying he had already conveyed their thoughts to London, and that eight days later, on 22 July, he would travel there himself to relay and reaffirm the message in person. We emphasized once again that the territory as a whole was not economically divisible. What we should reasonably seek was some sort of arrangement in which China would allow the British to continue governing Hong Kong as a caretaker administration whilst recognizing that its ownership belonged to the People's Republic. This should be the deal that the British could put on the diplomatic table once negotiations with China began. The UMELCO felt that such a stance was the best way for preserving confidence, prosperity and stability as well as meeting the views and wishes of the great majority of Hong Kong people at that time.

In fact, the realists in Hong Kong had long understood that there was no possibility of Hong Kong becoming independent, which was the usual course of "de-colonization". Back in 1972 when the People's Republic of China took its seat in the United Nations, one of its first acts was to delete the names of Hong Kong and Macao from the UN's list of colonies. China, while not wishing to harp on the wrongs of the past done to the nation, was practical and deferred the taking back of Hong Kong and Macao. The People's Republic would be patient in dealing with those two lost territories but it would never countenance independence. At that time the British Conservative Government of Edward Heath did not object and, consequently, continued sending the colonial officers to run the territory and to discourage any move towards independence.

Sir Edward went to and returned from London, bearing the message. He assembled the UMELCO on 6 August to brief us on what had transpired during his trip. He said he had, as reported, met the Prime Minister who was ebullient about visiting Beijing in September to discuss Hong Kong's future. He also suggested that a small UMELCO delegation should go to London to discuss with the Prime Minister her strategy for the China visit.

During the meeting, the UMELCO unanimously proposed that the Governor should be a member of the British Delegation for the negotiation with China and that he should also accompany the Prime Minister to Beijing and participate in the talks on Hong Kong's future.

The Open Forum

The Unofficial Members of the Executive and Legislative Councils initially wanted to form a small and specialized group to monitor opinions and formulate a strategy to deal with the 1997 issue, by then a public obsession. But, alas, the group could not be kept small since every Councillor wanted to join, and a group so big could not be called small, so everybody settled for regular meetings among us and also with the Governor. At that time, no one was elected and we therefore could not claim to "represent" but merely "reflect" the public views, even though more often than not we got the society's pulse just about right.

From the moment of Sir Edward's inauguration in May 1982, many more groups — besides the UMELCO one — clamoured to get into the act. The welter of opinions could be lumped roughly into five broad categories, ranging from the practicable to the wishful, if not daft. These were, as contained in an UMELCO paper compiled by the Assistant Secretary General, Joseph Wong (now Secretary for Civil Service), in August 1982:

(1) The *status quo* as British continues to rule Hong Kong (proponents: the economist Edward Chen and law lecturer

Peter Wesley-Smith of the University of Hong Kong, and the Hong Kong Prospect Institute).

(2) Britain continues to rule Hong Kong but recognizes Chinese sovereignty (proponents: the Hong Kong Reform Club; Clare Hollingworth and Dr. John Young of the University of Hong Kong).

(3) Joint Chinese and British administration (proponents: Dick Lee, a friend of the Chinese Government, and Dr. Y. S. Cheng of the Chinese University of Hong Kong).

(4) China extends to Hong Kong the status of a Special Administrative Region under Article 31 which is being enshrined into the Chinese Constitution (proponents: Andrew Wong of the Chinese University of Hong Kong. At that time, people generally thought the provision was actually designed for Taiwan. President Jiang Zemin confirmed the suspicion at a ceremony commemorating the first anniversary of the Macao SAR in December 2000).

(5) China and Britain sign a treaty of friendship that extends the Hong Kong lease by 30 years (proponents: some individuals made publicly on 16 August).

The UMELCO analysed these five general viewpoints and believed the majority favoured the first one, the *status quo*.

At the same time, three comprehensive opinion surveys were conducted, one by the Reform Club, one by the Baptist College (later University), and one by the Hong Kong Observers. Their findings were:

(1) The Reform Club commissioned Survey Research Hong Kong Ltd. to conduct during March 1982 by telephone a poll of 1,000 respondents aged 20 years and over. Some

93 per cent of the interviewed subjects sought the *status quo* of continual British administration;

(2) The Baptist College conducted its own postal opinion survey in May 1982. This one polled 545 organizations employing more than 100,000 people. It was found that 85 per cent of the organizations wished for the British administration *status quo* for 30 to 50 years, even if the sovereignty were to return to China;

(3) The Hong Kong Observers commissioned also Survey Research Hong Kong Ltd. to conduct during May and June 1982 by the face-to-face method a poll of 1,000 persons, aged 15–60 years. The result was that 87 per cent of the respondents favoured the *status quo* of continual British administration.

But not just one side waged the public opinion war. The Chinese Government also started to exercise its "united front" strategy by inviting groups and individuals in Hong Kong to travel to Beijing to meet with the national leaders and discuss the future of Hong Kong.

Advising Thatcher

Early in September 1982, the Unofficial Members of the Executive and Legislative Councils decided to have five delegates to accompany Sir Edward to London to convey public opinions to and discuss the strategy with the Prime Minister. I was one of them. The others were Legislative Council Senior Member Roger Lobo (later Sir) who took over from Oswald Cheung in September 1981, Bank of East Asia Chairman Li Fook-wo, Swire executive Lydia Dunn (later Baroness), and Hong Kong Telephone union leader Chan Kam-chuen.

It was Sir Edward who suggested the names and our colleagues unanimously endorsed the list.

The Governor and the five of us on 8 September went to the Prime Minister's residence at 10 Downing Street for a working lunch that lasted for more than two hours. Thatcher was then at the apex of her power, flushed with confidence from the Falklands victory and her public popularity. Accompanying her were the Foreign Secretary Francis Pym (later Sir), his deputy Alan Donald (later Sir and Ambassador to Beijing in 1988), and two private secretaries.

We gave Thatcher a comprehensive account of the majority's views and aspirations. I, as the leader of the UMELCO delegation, specifically said since many residents of the territory had been refugees or their children, they were averse to Communist rule. Hong Kong was essentially a land of two separate statuses, one on the island and the southern peninsula was granted to Britain forever and the other was leased. We also recognized that the whole of Hong Kong was economically indivisible. I said our community had undertaken three major independent opinion surveys in which 85 to 90 per cent of the respondents (both individuals and organizations) wished for as little change as possible beyond 1997 under the British administration, but would accept Chinese sovereignty if that was necessary.

We felt that a generation of pragmatic leaders had emerged in China whose priority was the economic development of their country. Over the past few years China had opened up to the world. The country needed Hong Kong as its conduit to foreign technology and capital. Since the British and Chinese were on friendly terms, it was opportune to have Sino-British talks on the future of Hong Kong. We believed China was keen to preserve the vitality of the territory beyond 1997 but might not at the moment know how best to do it. The ultimate solution must be acceptable politically both within and outside China as well as be able to sustain confidence in and prosperity and stability of Hong Kong. It would take time and the British should be patient and prudent for itself and for Hong Kong.

In conclusion, we expressed the hope that during her visit to Beijing later in the month, the Prime Minister could reach agreement with the Chinese Government to commence official talks on Hong Kong's future. We also made the point that it would be essential to demonstrate, whilst the talks were going on, that progress was being made in order to maintain confidence in Hong Kong.

Our impression was that the Prime Minister grasped the issue fully. She assured us that she would fully relay our views and uphold our interests. She understood the importance of our confidence as well as the early need for a solution. She however realized the sensitivity of the matter for the Chinese as well as the ideological differences between her Government and theirs. She then avowed her moral obligation for the people of Hong Kong.

We in the delegation at the time were not naïve nor in denial. We know China would eventually recover Hong Kong but we were also playing for time — say 20 or 30 years — when the country had progressed enough economically to make the reunion more acceptable. That, in gist, was the UMELCO's basic position, whether or not it was Britain's.

A Lady's Place

Our first visit to London in September 1982 followed the usual protocol, which is what the British are especially good at, investing so much in their ritual of state. We, five Unofficial Members of the Executive and Legislative Councils, descended on the British capital and were led by the Governor Sir Edward Youde. Before the session with the Prime Minister on 8 September at 10 Downing Street, we visited various Parliamentary Ministers and Whitehall officials who had dealings with Hong Kong to show our appreciation. We also thought we were quite egalitarian and gallant as we insisted that Sir Edward walked ahead and then ushered Lydia Dunn, the only lady in the delegation, to be second in line rather to proceed according to seniority. "Lady first" was our motto. Dunn, however, thought we men were courteous to a fault and suddenly wanted us to keep serial ranks. All this reshuffling occurred within a minute or two whilst we were walking towards 10 Downing.

Plate 2.7 *The UMELCO Delegation with Prime Minister Thatcher at 10 Downing, 1982.*

Our group followed Sir Edward into the Prime Minister's Georgian residence. We, lining up strictly according to the protocol, went up the stairs for the Cabinet Meeting Room. The official photographer then arranged us for a historic picture, one of those stilted shot that would proudly adorn many mantles. Jostling for a shot also was a legion of television camera crews. In the ensuing media melee, we all got into a jumble, standing this direction and that for the photo call. By the time every one settled into place, the Prime Minister was in the middle according to design, with the Governor to her right and myself to her left. Roger Lobo, whose name in Portuguese means "wolf", had by then sidled along with Chan Kam-chuen further to the right of Sir Edward, while Li Fook-wo and Dunn had planted themselves to my left, almost fading out of the picture frame.

Thatcher, ever the perfectionist, suddenly bolted from the formation and went to her left end of the ensemble. To Li, she said, "You should respect the lady and not let her (nodding at Dunn) stand at the end". Thatcher then abruptly, without giving a chance for Li to react and with a swish of her hand, guided Dunn by the elbow to the spot between Li and myself. Li blushed naturally and was staggered, not knowing how to react to the rebuke.

Whilst the Prime Minister was chiding Li for his manners, the television klieg lights were beaming and the press photographers were buzzing and jostling for angles. The din and the commotion just muffled what the Prime Minister said to the confused Executive Councillor. Li's friends, watching the television in Hong Kong, subsequently asked him about his encounter with the "Iron Lady", of whom his impression was vivid, if not also livid. The British have a knack for putting people either at ease or in their place. Li Fook-wo learned that first hand.

The Stalemate

The First Encounter

The British Prime Minister called on Beijing in late September 1982. She brought along a full retinue of Foreign Ministry Officials, Francis Pym, Sir Edward, Sir Percy Cradock, Alan Donald and a host of others. Everybody at the time properly identified Zhao Ziyang as the Premier of China, someone of equal standing to Thatcher. Everyone also erroneously referred to Deng Xiaoping as the "Chairman", a title that more or less died with Mao Zedong.

So on a crisp, hazy afternoon the Right Honourable Visitor left the colossal Great Hall of the People after the historic talk with Deng. She tripped on her way down the steps and would have toppled over if not for an alert officer's steady hand. Her stumble screened in all Hong Kong televisions, rattled some people, including myself, who feared her slippage suggested the meeting with Deng did not go well.

On 24 September before leaving Beijing the British and Chinese issued a joint statement that read:

> "Today the two leaders of the two countries held far-reaching talks in a friendly atmosphere on the future of Hong Kong. Both leaders made clear their respective positions on this subject. They agreed to enter into talks through diplomatic channels following the visit with the common aim of maintaining the stability and prosperity of Hong Kong."

Having arrived in Hong Kong, Thatcher on 27 September attended a meeting with the UMELCO to brief us on her visit to Beijing. The Prime Minister claimed she had spelt out, and achieved,

Plate 2.8 *The UMELCO and Prime Minister Thatcher during her visit, 1982.*

two objectives in her exploratory discussions with the Chinese Government. The first was to have both countries agreed on maintaining the prosperity and stability of Hong Kong. The second was that both Governments would commence diplomatic talks to resolve difficult issues.

The Prime Minister opined that the Chinese leaders did not fully appreciate the importance of the rule of law and a free society to the stability and prosperity of Hong Kong. She urged us, therefore, to enlighten the Chinese leaders on these attributes through our own channels.

At the end of our session with the Prime Minister we laid down two proposals. The first was that Sir Edward Youde would be a major figure on the British team who, as our Governor, had access to the views of the community and enjoyed public trust. The second was that the British Government should report publicly on the progress in the negotiations to calm the people's nerves and avoid rumours flying around.

We then bade her farewell, not aware that she had purposely omitted to tell us crucial matters in her talks with Deng.

Truth Unveiled

Two weeks after Thatcher's visit to Beijing the *Sunday Observer* of London on 10 October 1982 published a startling expose under the by-line of Arthur Gavshon. The journalist in the article of the heading "Blueprint for Hong Kong Rule", quoting Chinese diplomatic sources, disclosed that the Chinese Government had laid down five broad principles as the core of Beijing's position in negotiations with Britain over Hong Kong. These were, as published:

"(1) A reassertion of Chinese sovereignty over all the territories comprising the colony's 410 square miles;

(2) Establishment of the colony as a fully autonomous district under a regime chosen by the Hong Kong people, possessing its own internal security forces and with rights to develop direct commercial links with the outside world. Foreign affairs would be subject to Peking's control;

(3) Replacement of the British Governor by a Chinese national who would be elected with powers to build up an administration that could incorporate British as well as local personnel settled in Hong Kong;

(4) Establishment of an international free trade area by Hong Kong port and its present British-run environs on the mainland. Within that area foreigners and Chinese alike would be free to invest in safety, with proper rights guaranteed under Chinese law;

(5) Preservation by China of the rights to intervene, as the sovereign power, if a situation of extreme abnormality were to develop. 'Abnormality' would include any attempts by people in Hong Kong to secede from Peking's authority or any foreign military intrusion."

The journalist also wrote that two weeks ago, Deng Xiaoping and his fellow leaders had presented this set of principles to Thatcher during her visit to Beijing. The report claimed: "Publicly — as well as privately — Mrs. Thatcher has displayed little enthusiasm for Peking's proposals. She has had, however, no option but to agree to discuss them."

At that time, I was in London representing the territory for the opening ceremony of the Hong Kong Hall in the British Commonwealth Exhibition, and saw the newspaper article. I immediately went to see the Assistant Under-Secretary of State, Alan Donald, at the Foreign Office. He had been an attache to Beijing and two weeks earlier had accompanied Thatcher to the meeting with Deng. Donald and I were old acquaintances, but when I asked him about the truth of the *Observer* story he was evasive.

I returned to Hong Kong rather in anger and contacted the Governor who had also been on the mission to Beijing with the Prime Minister. Sir Edward did not reply to my query for he had his own orders from Thatcher to stay mum. Later I assumed that Sir Edward had then written to London to convey the UMELCO's grievance.

Naturally I reported the situation to my unofficial colleagues in both the Executive and Legislative Councils. We all felt angry about it and decided to follow up the matter with the Governor until the truth was known. We were wondering how we could go on co-operating with London when so early in the negotiations over Hong Kong it had kept us in the dark or, as in the Chinese slang, "inside a drum". If Britain could not trust us and would not show us its hand, it could not expect us, the UMELCO, to go along in blind faith.

A Place at the Table

The Unofficial Members of the Executive and Legislative Councils pressed Sir Edward to clarify or confirm the press report but in vain. The British Minister of State, Lord Belstead, himself not a career civil servant but a political appointee, visited Hong Kong and on 7 December 1982 met with the members of the Executive Council. Belstead at the meeting told us that the Prime Minister had heard three broad propositions from the Chinese side during her last visit to Beijing:

(1) China would regain both sovereignty and administration over Hong Kong in 1997 or earlier.
(2) China would establish a special administrative region in Hong Kong to be run by the people of the territory.
(3) China would not accept another government running Hong Kong.

The Unofficial Members of the Executive Council were very upset, criticizing the British Government for keeping the truth from us and noting that had it not been for the *Observer's* report we might have never known the full story. We felt that if the British treated us with such apparent disdain, then there was no way for us to help the United Kingdom form any negotiating strategy.

We stressed that the 1997 issue was a life or death one for the people of Hong Kong and we should accompany the British delegation to Beijing for consultation during the talks concerning our fate. The meeting with Belstead was tense, as members pointed to the precedent in which the members of the Hong Kong Textile Advisory Board had accompanied the Hong Kong Government delegation during negotiations of textile agreements with other governments. Belstead soothed us somewhat by promising to refer our request to the Prime Minister and to bring back her answer soon. I mentioned to the Minister that I would be in London between 17 and 28 December and would like to meet him there, if required.

Whilst in London, I received a message inviting me to meet Thatcher on 20 December at 10 Downing Street. During the audience with the Prime Minister alone, I expressed the profound dismay of my colleagues at not being taken into her confidence more than two months after her trip to Beijing. In my peeve I said to the Prime Minister that if the British Government did not trust the Unofficial

Members of the Executive Council, then we could not assist the United Kingdom in forging a strategy for the negotiations and we would forfeit our role. Thatcher admitted that she had not divulged the whole content of her talks with the Chinese because the disclosure might have panicked the people of Hong Kong.

I retorted that all eight of us in the Executive Council had been appointed by the Governor in part for our willingness to keep secret. I reiterated that the 1997 issue was vital to the people of Hong Kong whose views we could reflect to the British. If her government still could not trust, consult and inform us, some, including myself, might have to resign. I said what I said was with the blessing of my unofficial colleagues of the Executive Council. In fact, our tactic of absolute candour was half out of peeve and half out of the desire to sway Thatcher.

Seeing the Prime Minister was composed, I asked her to let some of us go with the British team to Beijing for the negotiations, yes, much as the textile advisors had accompanied the Hong Kong Government delegation in the textile quota talks. I also emphasized that not one official member (that is, civil servant) of the Executive Council was Chinese who could understand the needs and sensitivities of the local population even if he had a reading comprehension of the language.

Back in Hong Kong, I received a letter from Lord Belstead dated 13 January 1983, revealing that the Prime Minister had agreed to our demands for co-operation between her Government and the Executive Council for input into a strategy for the talks and for full disclosure. But according to Belstead, the British Government had reservations about our direct involvement with the negotiating team, hinting that China might object.

Later the British misgiving was proven right. The Chinese

resolutely refused a visa for the Director of the Hong Kong Government Information Services, Peter Tsao, to escort the Governor to the Beijing negotiations. We know, from the Tsao episode, our chance of taking any direct part in the talks was slim to nil as we let the matter drop.

Battle for Hearts and Minds

After the Thatcher visit in September 1982 China began waging a "united front" campaign for the hearts and minds of the Hong Kong people. The Chinese hoped to win us over with their sincerity and hospitality. This explained the extraordinary publicity they generated for their invitations to Beijing of delegations from the Trade Development Council and the Hong Kong Manufacturers Association.

Some of us were surprised that China had targeted in November 1982 the relatively obscure Hong Kong Manufacturers Association rather than the better known, to us, Hong Kong Chinese Manufacturers Association. The shrewd among us figured the Chinese side had confused the two organizations because their names were so similar.

The then Hong Kong and Macao Affairs Office Director, Liao Chengzhi, greeted the Association delegation comprising 30 representatives from a dozen trades, and led by their Chairman, Wong Kam, on 20 November 1982 at the Great Hall of the People. Liao, speaking in Cantonese, reiterated the four broad principles for reunification which, to repeat, were:

(1) China would recover Hong Kong in 1997;
(2) China would enshrine into its Constitution the prerogative of Hong Kong to form a Special Administrative Region (SAR) in which the people of Hong Kong would run their own territory in their own way;

(3) China would respect Hong Kong's existing way of life, personal freedom, and status as a free port and an international financial centre;

(4) China would allow Hong Kong to preserve its current laws, even though the territory's litigants could not appeal to the Privy Council in London, and the decision of its high court would be final.

After the Association came the Trade Development Council, led by Sir Yuet-keung Kan, whose delegates went to Beijing and Shanghai, ostensibly to discuss trade and commerce between the Mainland and Hong Kong. The group met the Chinese Communist Party General Secretary, Xi Zhongxun, who repeated more or less what Liao had said to the Manufacturers Association.

Those sessions set a pattern. Xinhua News Agency in early 1983 invited the legislator, Allen Lee, to pick and lead a group of young professionals to Beijing. Lee was born in Shandong Province and fled to Hong Kong in his teens. He went for his university education in the United States, studying engineering at the University of Michigan in Ann Arbor, and then returned to the territory to become the manager of a large American electronic factory. He was, in 1983, only 42, a young industrialist who, five years earlier, had filled a vacancy in the Legislative Council from which I had bowed out as the Senior Member. Because our backgrounds were similar to some extent, the media quipped that he was my chosen heir.

The delegation of young professionals led by Lee comprised some present and future important personages. They included the legislators, Stephen Cheong and Selina Chow, both, along with Lee, were to found the Co-operative Resource Centre in 1992. The Centre was developed to become the Liberal Party in 1994. Others were barristers, Martin Lee (later the first and only Chairman of the Democratic Party), and Andrew Li (the first Chief Justice of the SAR in 1997). They were joined by an architect, Edward Ho (later a legislator), a Medical Council member, Dr. Natalus Yuen, the *Far Eastern Economic Review* journalist, Mary Lee, Wing On Bank's Dr. Philip Kwok and Albert Kwok, plus financier Leung Kwok-kwong and merchant Christopher Leong.

Before leaving for Beijing, they spent months compiling a compendium of commentaries and essays, which was more or less a sort of position paper to be submitted to the Chinese leaders. The purpose was to impress on the Chinese leaders the gravity of the confidence crisis in Hong Kong and to explain their proposal of a "buffer" solution. What did they mean by "buffer"? On the last page of their paper, it stated:

> "The two systems (between the Mainland and Hong Kong) at present are vastly different in many areas. We believe there is a need to narrow these differences. We hope that through cordial British and Chinese relations, we may continue develop Hong Kong's economy and society and, at the same time, find a solution acceptable to both sides. The best method towards achieving that aim is to extend the current 14-year transition period so that we may clear away the shadow of 1997."

What the young professionals sought was a "buffer" by extending the 14-year transition period (1983 to 1997) of continual British administration to give time for the Mainland and Hong Kong economies and societies to become closer in their developments before reunification took place.

Lee in May 1983 led the delegates to Beijing where they met the Communist Party General Secretary, Xi Zhongxun, in a session that last longer than three hours and in which much of the time was devoted to explaining the position paper. The talk was cordial but the Chinese side refused to believe that there was a confidence crisis in Hong Kong and insisted that it was another British plot to prolong their hold on the colony. The Chinese side also rejected the "buffer" proposal. Not much was accomplished despite the earnestness of everyone involved.

On the last night before the delegation was to return to the territory the Deputy Director of the Hong Kong and Macao Affairs Office, Li Hou, and the Secretary General, Lu Ping, went to the hotel where the delegates were staying. They asked Lee and his deputy Stephen Cheong privately to delete the last of the 14 pages of the position paper dealing with the "buffer" proposal prior to publication. After some haggling Lee and Cheong eventually agreed.

The Chinese Government did not target the ethnic Chinese of Hong Kong only in its campaign for hearts and minds. The Mainland officials also trained their charm offensive on the top executives and owners of British conglomerates in the colony, such as the Swire brothers John and Adrian as well as Henry Keswick of Jardine and Matheson. Ambassador Ke Hua on 18 January 1983 invited British businessmen to lunch in the Chinese Embassy in London to brief them on the Chinese position in the talks on Hong Kong. The message was similar to what had been told to the Trade Development Council and the Hong Kong Manufacturers Association.

The Chinese Government was by then on the propaganda blitz. Xinhua Deputy Director, Qi Feng, and his colleague Lai King-sung (a fellow university alumnus as aforesaid) invited me to lunch at the Furama Hotel on 23 March 1983. They said China would enshrine into its Constitution Hong Kong's unique governance after 1997, specifically with the proviso that the laws would remain unchanged and there would be "Hong Kong people running Hong Kong". Since at the time most civil servants were already ethnic Chinese residents of Hong Kong who were running the territory, a more apt description should be "running Hong Kong the Hong Kong way" after 1997.

I told Qi and Lai how the people in Hong Kong were vexed and perplexed by the Chinese Government's fickle policies and attitudes over the years. Just putting Hong Kong's current systems into the Chinese Constitution was not sufficient to gain the confidence and trust of the Hong Kong people. I requested them to convey the public's profound worries to the Chinese leaders.

No Time Table for Talks

The British and Chinese Governments had issued a statement on Hong Kong in September 1982, agreeing to negotiate. But by now half a year had elapsed without any talk starting at all. In the meantime "microphone diplomacy" had blared away with both sides presenting their cases through their favoured media. The Chinese wanted to resolve the questions of sovereignty and administration at once before they were willing to discuss the future after 1997. The British's stance was just the opposite.

The UMELCO reckoned the most important concern was achieving guarantees for prosperity, stability, and liberty The people of Hong Kong were in no position to bargain with the Chinese Authorities and had to rely on the British Government to bid their case. If the United Kingdom were to surrender Hong Kong unconditionally, that country would have no other chips to play in the game of diplomatic poker. We, therefore, supported the British strategy to secure an arrangement that could truly put people's hearts at ease prior to conceding sovereignty.

Most Hong Kong residents were realistic. What they wanted

Plate 2.9 *The first UMEXCO Mission to London at Lancaster House, 1983.*

and expected from the United Kingdom was not much more than a treaty with China, that would buy enough time for the politics on the Mainland to stabilize and the economy to improve to make inevitable reunification not only desirable but also feasible.

The British were preparing for their summer national elections during the spring of 1983 and, even though the Tories were leading in the opinion polls, the outcome was not certain. The Chinese Government, we believed, felt it was not appropriate to talk about Hong Kong with the British until the other side's political situation was crystal clear.

The Prime Minister in March 1983 nonetheless wrote to Premier Zhao Ziyang, suggesting that if Britain and China could reach an understanding on securing the prosperity, stability and liberty of Hong Kong, then her Government would recommend to Parliament to endorse returning the territory to China. The letter implied that now there was a way to end the impasse and resolve the Hong Kong issue to mutual satisfaction.

The Breakthrough and Breakdown

The Conservative Party won the 1983 summer election by a landslide and the British once again was firmly under the helm of Margaret Thatcher. Having received her letter in March to Premier Zhao, the Chinese felt that negotiations with Britain could commence for how to maintain the stability, prosperity and liberty of Hong Kong after 1997.

The Hong Kong Governor, Sir Edward Youde, joined the British team as a senior member, but the Prime Minister rebuffed the attempt of the UMELCO for the UMEXCO to accompany Sir Edward and the rest of the contingent to Beijing, much to our disappointment.

The negotiators of the two Governments began the first round of negotiations in Beijing from 12 to 13 July and at the conclusion they issued a joint statement proclaiming the talks "useful and constructive".

But the climate for the talks deteriorated thereafter. At the end of the second round, held on 25 and 26 July, they could only portray their session as having been "useful", which sounded ominous. The contingents met twice again — on 2 to 3 August and 22 to 23 September — and avoided using any adjective, which signalled impending failure.

The negotiations obviously hit a snag. China intensified its propaganda war. Hong Kong's confidence melted and the free-floating currency continued to sink. The local dollar was worth $7.9 to the Greenback on 16 September and depreciated to $9.5 to the American unit a little over a week later, a fall of 20 per cent.

Another barometer of the public mood, the Hang Seng Index of stock prices, likewise plummeted by 150 points, bottoming out at 780 points, the nadir in 1983. On "Black Saturday", 24 September, consumers began panic buying and hoarding, emptying supermarket shelves of staples. The pandemonium marked one of the grimmest periods in the territory.

Relief, or at least reprieve, came from the Hong Kong Government which decided to peg the Hong Kong dollar at $7.8 to the U.S. currency on 17 October 1983, but these measures were palliatives because the only cure remained the satisfactory deal between Britain and China on Hong Kong.

The Councillors' Rage

Just when people were distressed by the lack of any concord on their future, Edward Heath visited Deng Xiaoping in Beijing. The former British Prime Minister, and arch nemesis of Thatcher who had ousted him in a Conservative Party coup, then dropped in on Hong Kong and the UMELCO hosted a working dinner for him at the Swire House headquarters at 7 p.m. on 12 September 1983. The arrangement was to have a sit-down discussion prior to the banquet.

Heath started the discussion by advising the UMELCO strongly to accept the Chinese proposition of the Hong Kong people ruling Hong Kong. He then told us that Deng had wished to resolve the Hong Kong question by no later than September 1984, two years after he and Thatcher had broached the issue. This, if I remember correctly, was the first time we heard of a deadline and we were flustered and concerned. Heath added that the Chinese would take unilateral action to regain Hong Kong in 1997 unless the British agreed to a settlement.

The members were shocked at the ultimatum and told the guest that many people in Hong Kong had had bad experiences with the Communist Party they now fervently distrusted. Heath responded by saying nobody could guarantee the future and no one could ensure China would honour any agreement on Hong Kong. He advised the Hong Kong people to be realistic.

Someone then asked Heath what might happen if Deng died. The veteran British Tory replied nonchalantly that every country had to cope with the problem of succession and so would Hong Kong, which, after all, had already learned to live with communism as a neighbour.

Before the party for Heath, we had earlier met to anticipate what the former Prime Minister might say. We had figured that he would behave in character and speak fondly of, if not also for, the Chinese Government, with which he had rapport. I was worried that some of my more obstreperous colleagues, particularly fiery Selina Chow, would bicker with an equally feisty Heath. Selina did, and Heath was rather annoyed.

At the end of the discussion I, as the host, in a summing up speech, said what the former Prime Minister had told us had convinced us of the persuasive power of the Chinese leader who had obviously impressed him. Once I uttered that Heath blew up, thinking I had snidely questioned his integrity, and demanded that I apologize. I did and tried to soothe him but he was implacable. In a huff he said he would not stay for dinner and would not change his mind despite my plea.

Heath, his face beet-red, then flounced out with his two aides in tow. We had asked him to wait for us to arrange for an official limousine to whisk him back to the Government House, but he declined even that bit of courtesy and, instead, hailed a taxi. I then immediately phoned and reported the incident to the Governor, Sir Edward, who was inexpressive. The next day the newspapers played up the joust and ever since then the breach between Heath and us could not be healed.

The First Concession

Britain and China had gone through four weary rounds of negotiations without any tangible progress. The stalemate triggered a confidence crisis in September 1983. The overwhelming sense of despair prompted the Prime Minister to invite all the Unofficial Members of the Executive Council (UMEXCO) to London for the second time. The UMEXCO were scheduled to meet on 6 October the Foreign Secretary, Sir Geoffrey Howe, a Welsh country lawyer, and Thatcher the following day.

As the Senior Member, I first spoke at the meeting reviewing the four rounds of talks with the Chinese, analysing the cause and effect of the "Black Saturday" debacle, and reporting the furious Chinese propaganda blitz. After extensive discussions, the UMEXCO agreed with the British to change its stance about first resolving the matter of British administration after 1997.

The British and Chinese resumed their talks in the fifth round on 19 and 20 October. The atmosphere seemed to have ameliorated dramatically and both actually issued a joint statement using once more the catchy words, "useful and constructive". This signalled to us a shift on the British side that enabled the negotiators to sound more sanguine.

The Chinese team's top representative, Yao Guang, during the fifth round revealed to the British the four broad principles for securing the future of Hong Kong. These were:

(1) According to Article 31 of the Chinese Constitution, Hong Kong would become a Special Administrative Region (SAR) of China;

(2) The people of Hong Kong would form the SAR Government with a high degree of autonomy on both administration and legislation;

(3) The Hong Kong SAR would continue with its way of life, liberty, rule of law, economic system, finance structure and capitalism;

(4) The Central Government would permit the above system remain unchanged for 50 years.

Back in the Colony the Executive Council on 26 October deliberated on the 1997 question, specifically those four principles put to the British by the Chinese. I said that what Yao had tabled in the negotiations was not new and, rather, was a rehash of what the Chinese side had been saying to the Hong Kong public it had been cultivating. What was new and significant, however, was that the Chinese plan was put before the British during the diplomatic talks. I further said the Chinese plan and their assurance of 50 years no change beyond 1997 appeared to be an acceptable arrangement but then, I asked, why the Hong Kong people were still not satisfied? Were the people too selfish or too greedy?

The answer to this question, I said, was given in the *Ming Pao* editorial of the same day, 26 October. It surmised that the Hong Kong people distrusted the Chinese Government because of its whims and wrath of the last three decades. If the past 30 years were any indication then no one could be hopeful about the promise for the next 50.

Target: Allen Lee

Ever since the gregarious legislator Allen Lee in May 1983 led a group of young professionals to Beijing, where they were greeted by the Communist Party General Secretary, Xi Zhongxun, he had become a favourite person for the Chinese to woo. Lee, at the Chinese request, returned to the capital in October of the same year, this time alone, and was met by the National Security Bureau Director, Zhuang Xin, and the former Foreign Trade Minister, Li Qiang.

The guest and his two hosts met separately on 6 October to discuss the future of Hong Kong. The hosts first made the following remarks to Lee:

(1) The Chinese side disagreed entirely with the position paper of the young professionals that had been submitted half a year ago;

(2) If the Chinese side were to extend the British rule by 15 or 30 years as the professionals had sought, then they would be as shameless as the traitor Li Hungqiang, who had signed away a swathe of Chinese territories to foreigners during the Qing Dynasty;

(3) The Chinese officials informed Lee that the eventual court of final appeal would be in Beijing rather than London where the Privy Council resided;

(4) Finally they indicated that if the British would not co-operate causing Hong Kong in chaos, the Chinese Government would be compelled to recover Hong Kong immediately.

Lee said to me afterwards that, prior to his trip to Beijing, he had mulled over the situation, realizing he was now China's target and feeling the heat. However, he felt he should try his best to persuade the Chinese leaders on how to resolve the future of Hong Kong. He had repeatedly explained to Zhuang and Li separately the young professionals' position paper but unfortunately the Mainland Authorities did not understand and could not accept. He said he had tried his hardest to explain the plight of Hong Kong and the position of the British, but instead of reaching some comprehension, the Chinese held even deeper and deeper suspicions of the British.

Britain Caved-in

The two pivoted rounds for the negotiations were those of the fifth (19 to 20 October) and the sixth (14 to 15 November 1983), after which the British reassessed their delicate position. The United Kingdom then realized that it could no longer demand continual administration or even authoritative influence in Hong Kong beyond 1997. Were the impasse to continue, the damage to Hong Kong and British interests would be severe. What was left for Britain to do was to secure an agreement that would be acceptable to the people of Hong Kong as far as that could be ascertained. Thus the fateful decision was reached with the Executive Council sat in Hong Kong in early December 1983 to make the final effort for a draft treaty that would restore Hong Kong to China.

The Governor, Sir Edward Youde, on 16 December called together the Unofficial Members of both his Executive and Legislative Councils. The purpose of this special meeting was for the Governor to inform the Unofficial Members of the Legislative Council the inevitable British departure from Hong Kong in 1997 and, with it, the end not only of the colonial governance but future authoritative influence. He told the UMLEGCO to keep the news secret until Britain could make the announcement at a suitable time.

As the Governor spoke about the British leaving the territory, the sounds of sobbing were heard particularly during the moment's otherwise sombre silence. Two Councillors in particular wept. They were Stephen Cheong, who went on to found the Co-operative Resource Centre, and Rita Fan, later an advisor to China and the President of the Special Administrative Region Legislative Council.

In the consuming gloom, the UMELCO decided to hold a series of meetings to map out their new strategy with a view to acquiring better terms for the reunification under the changed circumstances.

The Haggle

UMELCO's New Strategy

The negotiations could be divided into three distinct phases. The first lasted from the first to the fourth round, from early July to the end of September 1983. During this period the British contended that the vast majority in Hong Kong wanted the *status quo* of continual colonial administration, even if the sovereignty might have to be returned to China.

From early October 1983, in rounds five to seven, the British conceded that it was no longer possible for them to maintain their administration, though they asked for special influence over Hong Kong beyond 1997. The best they could get were the Chinese assurances of non-interference and the preservation of the present institutions plus the way of life.

The third, and climaxing, phase became evident in December 1983. The British acknowledged that they could no longer get China to extend their administration or special influence over Hong Kong after 1997. They then focussed on persuading China to conjure up a blueprint that would be amenable to them.

Before the final phase of negotiations the British and the Chinese Governments agreed to shuffle their respective negotiating teams. The Chinese replaced Yao Guang with the Deputy Foreign Minister, Zhou Nan, as the chief negotiator (Zhou in 1990 became the Director of Xinhua News Agency in Hong Kong succeeding Xu Jiatun who later fled to the U.S.A.). The British substituted Sir Richard Evans for Sir Percy Cradock as the Ambassador and chief negotiator. Sir Percy then became the special political advisor to the Prime Minister. Zhou and Evens entered the eighth and decisive round of talks from 25 to 26 January 1984.

From early 1982 UMELCO had monitored a series of opinion polls and concluded that the majority of the people wanted continual British governance but would accept a return to Chinese rule after a certain interval to allow the Mainland Government to reform. That phobia, at the time, was perfectly understandable since many of them were refugees or children of refugees who had fled China. Many still had on the Mainland relatives who were being persecuted.

The UMELCO reflected these views in the clearest terms to the British Government but we also made plain that we regarded ourselves as Chinese, Chinese who preferred capitalism to communism. Many of the refugees who got to Hong Kong did so through ordeals they could not forget. All these were prepared to tell and tell again to the British Prime Minister and the Foreign Secretary, even though to some in the United Kingdom we were "running dogs" and "collaborators", and to the Chinese we were "quislings" and "traitors". During 1982 and 1983, with the Chinese in their united front propaganda blitz, we found it very hard to challenge openly the Government on the Mainland and speak up for the people.

From December 1983 onward the circumstances changed. Britain tacitly accepted the return of both administration and sovereignty over Hong Kong to China. We, the UMELCO, could then openly bargain with the Chinese Government to get better terms for reunification. We therefore held frequent meetings to map out a new strategy for the UMELCO to bid openly for an agreement that was specific, detailed, substantive and enforceable for the sake of Hong Kong's future.

The Lobo Motion

The Unofficial Members of the Executive and Legislative Councils contemplated a strategy and came up with a two-prong approach:

(1) Mobilize public opinion on the terms of the Sino-British Agreement.

(2) Make known Hong Kong's views to both the British and Chinese Governments.

As an overture we then decided to hold a debate in the Legislative Council about the draft British and Chinese agreement. The UMELCO at a 24 February meeting agreed unanimously that the Senior Member of the Legislative Council, Roger Lobo, should move the motion, which stated simply and innocuously: "We deem it essential that any proposal for the future of Hong Kong should be debated in this Council before any final agreement is reached."

We had wanted to schedule the debate at the next LEGCO sitting on 29 February which, however, clashed with the date set for the annual budget. We then slotted the debate for the next earliest date, 14 March, and would announce this through the Government Information Services in the afternoon.

Plate 2.10 *Mr. Roger Lobo addressing the Legislative Council, 1982.*

The night that the news of the debate was released, Xinhua Director, Xu Jiatun, hosted a dinner for the UMELCO. He and I sat next to each other and naturally we talked about the motion. I said it was now fact that Britain had agreed to return the sovereignty and administration over Hong Kong to China in 1997. The debate would be about how to perpetuate capitalism in the future Special Administrative Region, protect the way of life, preserve the law, and maintain prosperity and stability. I stressed that such a Hong Kong, secured with a sound agreement, would benefit China immensely in its economic reform by earning foreign exchange and linking the country to the outside world.

I thought I had soothed Xu but the very next morning the two leftist newspapers *Wen Wei Pao* and *Ta Kung Pao* lambasted the UMELCO in their editorials. Such a response did not faze or frazzle us because we had expected this all along. The thinking of the Chinese Government was quite different from that of ours. The Mainland officials suspected that the British were using the Unofficial Members of the LEGCO to strengthen their bargaining position while posing as the executioner of the people's will.

Whatever China's umbrage, the debate was launched according to schedule. Lobo introduced his motion, saying, "The purpose of this motion is very simple. It means what it says — no more — and one might think that it could not easily be misunderstood or misrepresented. It is, as a newspaper has said, a debate about having a debate."

Besides Lobo himself and the Chief Secretary, Sir Philip Haddon-Cave, 20 other legislators expressed their opinions. They were, for the record and in the order of speaking, Harry Fang, Lo Tak-shing, Francis Tien, Alex Wu, Peter C. Wong, Wong Lam, Ho Kam-fei, Allen Lee, Andrew So, Hu Fa-kuang, Wong Po-yan, William

Brown, Stephen Cheong, Cheung Yan-lung, Selina Chow, Maria Tam, Chan Ying-lun, Rita Fan, Pauline Ng and Yeung Po-kwan.

Securing the full support for a debate about having a debate, Lobo concluded thus:

> "The acceptability of any proposed settlement lies in whether people believe that its terms will be respected and will endure:
>
> Faith cannot be created by orders;
>
> Trust cannot be induced by the exercise of power;
>
> And no settlement which fails to engender trust can possibly preserve our stability and prosperity.
>
> Finally, for those who questioned the wisdom of this debate, I believe it has amply justified itself."

Proclamation of British Exit

The Foreign Secretary, Sir Geoffrey Howe, visited Beijing for four days starting 15 April 1984. In the capital he spoke with his Chinese counterpart Wu Xueqian, Director of the Hong Kong and Macao Affairs Office Ji Pengfei, Premier Zhao Ziyang, and the ultimate authority himself, Deng Xiaoping. The trip was the most momentous since the negotiations began, as he confirmed to the Chinese Government that Britain would return the whole of Hong Kong's sovereignty and jurisdiction to it in 1997.

During his call, the British and Chinese had also discussed the Chinese proposal of creating a Sino-British Joint Liaison Group through the transitional period. The purpose of the Joint Liaison Group was to liaise, consult and exchange information during the transition and to ensure a smooth transfer of power in 1997.

Sir Geoffrey left Beijing for Hong Kong on 18 April and the next day met with the Executive Council and attended a banquet

Plate 2.11 *The UMELCO and Foreign Secretary Sir Geoffrey Howe during his visit, 1984.*

with the UMELCO. The Foreign Secretary on 20 April gave a press conference to announce that it would not be realistic to expect the continuation of British administration in Hong Kong beyond 1997.

By then that Britain would exit Hong Kong on 1 July 1997 was certain. The UMELCO felt that it was then their responsibility to ensure that:

(1) Any agreement would be one that the majority of Hong Kong people could accept;
(2) The systems in Hong Kong would remain basically unchanged for 50 years beyond 1997;
(3) China would not meddle in the domestic affairs of the territory.

When all those conditions were met, then the treaty that sanctified these requirements would be one that UMELCO could recommend to the people of Hong Kong.

British Sensitivity

The UMELCO learned at the end of April 1984 that the British House of Commons and House of Lords were to debate in the middle of May on the Sino-British negotiations over the future of Hong Kong. We wanted to sway opinion in the Parliament by rushing forth a delegation to London. We composed a litany or position paper of six concerns, two questions and four requests.

Our six concerns were:

(1) Will the essential elements of the Basic Law be enshrined in the Sino-British Agreement?
(2) If the Agreement was signed before the Basic Law could be promulgated, should the Parliament withhold ratification?

(3) Should Britain not insist on some mechanism to ensure Chinese compliance with its treaty obligations?
(4) Should Britain not insist on retaining some residue status in Hong Kong beyond 1997?
(5) How could Britain retain effective control so as to maintain confidence, stability and prosperity over the period of transition?
(6) What will be the fate of the British Dependent Territory Citizens? How will their rights and status be preserved? Will they have a right to settle in the United Kingdom and should the British Government negotiate settlement places for them?

Our two questions were:

(1) How is it proposed that acceptability be put to the test?
(2) What will HMG do if the Hong Kong people do not accept the Agreement or parts of it?

Our four requests were:
The Agreement should:

(1) Contain full details on the proposed administrative, legal, social and economic systems applicable after 1997;
(2) Provide adequate and workable assurances that the Agreement will be honoured;
(3) State that the Basic Law will incorporate the provisions of the Agreement;
(4) Guarantee the rights of the British nationals.

I then led a delegation of 12 members of the UMELCO for the mission to London on the evening of 9 May and was sent off by more than 20 of our colleagues. We were few in number but strong in conviction. The delegates were, for the record, Roger Lobo, Oswald Cheung, Mike Sandberg, Lo Tak-shing, Maria Tam, William Brown, Cheung Yan-lung, Allen Lee, Selina Chow, Stephen Cheong and Chan Ying-lun. The UMELCO's Secretary General Maurice Sargant, Administrative Officer Wilfred Tsui and a number of supporting staff also accompanied us.

When we arrived at the Heathrow Airport, we were thronged by a swarm of British pressmen and women. They had apparently already known at least part of the contents of our position paper, which could be regarded as our "petition", and asked whether our position was that if Britain was to give up Hong Kong, it should allow the people to live in the United Kingdom. We were surprised how quickly these reporters had known part of our position paper entitled "The Future of Hong Kong" which was released in Hong Kong only about 12 hours ago and, in particular, why they were only concerned with the issue of immigration. Later on we were able to know why.

Two days before our expedition to London, on 7 May, I personally handed a copy of our position paper to the Governor, Sir Edward Youde. He glanced through the petition without expression or comment. He knew and supported our mission to London and had arranged for the delegation to meet with the British Prime Minister, the Foreign Secretary and other senior officials in London. Although he did not say it, I assume he would relate the contents of our position paper to London. We have no objection as they would know it sooner or later.

A day later, on 8 May, the Executive Council held its usual Tuesday morning meeting. Just before the session was to begin, Sir Edward related to me a message from the Foreign Office expressing misgivings about our position paper and urging us not to distribute it. I replied that I could not decide on this by myself but I would relay the Foreign Office's objection at the UMELCO meeting scheduled to be held in the afternoon. I promised to report to the Chief Secretary, Sir Philip Haddon-Cave, about our decision in his absence since he was to leave Hong Kong later that day for the 14th round of talks in Beijing.

Whilst we were priming for the London visit, the British Foreign Office, wanting to thwart or discredit our mission, briefed the British press. They began frantically to put their spin on our delegation's purpose by frightening the British people about us, purposely coming to London to lobby for the immigration of a few million British colonial subjects in Hong Kong to their crowded country. The xenophobia would then work its crude magic. The misinformed British press thus discredited and maligned us and the Parliamentarians distanced themselves from us. At that time the British public still remembered the trouble of mass influx into Britain from their former African colonies and did not want another stampede from Hong Kong.

Hostile British Reception

In London the UMELCO delegation checked into Portman Intercontinental Hotel at Portman Square because it was centrally located. After separately meeting some Members of Parliament (MPs) in the afternoon, the delegation attended a joint meeting in the Parliament Building with the Anglo-Hong Kong and Anglo-China All Party Parliamentary Committees in the early evening. Many members of these two Parliamentary Committees, particularly those in the Anglo-Hong Kong Committee, were friends of Hong Kong or had close connections with Hong Kong. There were about 30 MPs attending the meeting including both the former Governor, Lord MacLehose, and Chairman of China Light & Power, Lord Kadoorie. They were, unexpectedly, rather frosty even prior to the meeting.

At the outset of the meeting, the MPs immediately needled us on the immigration questions, which totally distorted and distracted others from our mission's aim. They said we should have stayed in Hong Kong to counteract the propaganda of the Chinese Government. We stressed in the most emphatic way we could that the vast majority of the people of Hong Kong did not wish to leave but to stay, contrary to the misinformation spread about us. The person who disappointed us the most was the one we had counted on the most, Lord MacLehose, who deplored the timing of our visit and upbraided us for doubting the integrity of Her Majesty's Government. Other Members of Parliament who had heard the former Governor's rebuke of us jumped on the bandwagon. The meeting ended sourly for everyone and it did not bode well for the rest of the trip.

We returned wearily to our hotel and immediately held a meeting to assess our experiences for the day and re-examine our tactics. We were annoyed and some were utterly confused. We decided our consciences were clear, regardless of the reaction to our coming to London. We came to the British capital, to the Parliament, to espouse the thoughts and fight for the interests of the people of Hong Kong, not for our own selves. We believed our message was compelling and our cause just and it was either doing this or all of us giving up. At that moment my thought of resigning from politics came up once again. However when I realized the courage displayed by some of my colleagues, I did not think about it any more.

On the following afternoon, 11 May, the delegation met with the Foreign Secretary at the Parliament Building. Sir Geoffrey chided us for trooping to London and said that, as we were not elected by the people, it would be difficult to persuade the Members of Parliament and the British public that our views were those of the people. The guests, however, reminded the host that the UMELCO comprised individuals from all walks of life in the territory and understood the anxieties and wishes of their people. Although we were not elected, nonetheless, we did faithfully and accurately reflect the people's views. We stressed that we were not in London to discuss emigration to Britain but reasons for staying in Hong Kong. Anyway the Foreign Secretary gave us the impression that he was very much sensitive to the immigration issue and did not bother much about the other subjects raised in our position paper.

Furious at Sir Geoffrey Howe

Prior to our departure for London we had arranged for some of our colleagues to form a small task force led by Lydia Dunn to liaise with and provide support to the delegation.

After having been scoffed at by the Foreign Secretary at the meeting in the Parliament Building, I knew I had to get our views across to the rest of the world in some other way. We had to rally the public, our only recourse. So when we came out from the Parliament Building we saw a large number of Hong Kong reporters and TV interviewers waiting and were anxious for interview. I thought it would be an excellent opportunity to ask for support from the Hong Kong people. I then appealed solemnly to the Hong Kong people in front of the media's microphones and cameras:

> "Hong Kong has reached a crisis point and if you agree with the sentiments of the UMELCO position paper, please take this opportunity to make known your views. If you don't speak up now, you may not have another chance to do so."

This appeal was repeatedly broadcast on the radio and shown on the television as well as appeared on the newspapers in Hong Kong. We were told that it had aroused tremendous reaction from the population.

At the same time we relayed to Lydia Dunn, and through her to the mass media, how Lord MacLehose had chastised the delegation and how we had been misunderstood. We requested her to conduct

Plate 2.12 *The second UMELCO Delegation to London, 1984.*

a campaign in Hong Kong for public support. The exercise turned into a clarion call, more so than we had ever expected. The telegram and telex messages of support began to arrive, then avalanche.

Three days later, on 15 May, Sir Geoffrey hosted a working dinner for the UMELCO team. Before going we discussed our strategy and decided the best course was not for us to talk but to read out aloud to the Foreign Secretary and his colleagues at the Foreign Office telexes and telegrams of support from the Hong Kong public. Thus the British officials could hear the thoughts of people who were deprived a say in their future. Our plan was for each member of the delegation to select ten telegrams or telexes to be ready, and when I called at the outset of the meeting each one in succession would read out aloud the contents.

As we were enunciating every word in these emotive missives, we noticed Sir Geoffrey twitching and his face glowing redder with every syllable. When the third person, I remember it was Oswald Cheung, had been half way through his reading, Sir Geoffrey suddenly conceded. He uttered, "Enough! Enough! You don't have to go on. You do reflect the true views of the Hong Kong people."

Public Support for the UMELCO

The delegation returned to a rapturous welcome at the airport. The UMELCO Office had been inundated with post and telegrams. We received some 8,427 items of mail and telegrams from individuals, of which 8,400 fully endorsed, 10 partly supported and only 17 were explicitly against. We also got from organizations 1,509 submissions, of which 1,504 were unconditionally for, four gave partial support, and only one opposed. At that time we did not have fax and e-mail facilities, otherwise the number of messages of support would have been even much more. We also counted backings from 14 of the 18 District Boards in Hong Kong at that time, one was equivocal, and three had no expressed opinion.

The *South China Morning Post* sponsored Survey Research Hong Kong Limited to conduct by telephone a random opinion poll of 605 Hong Kong residents between 18 and 20 May. Of these 336 were men and 269 women, all aged 19 and above. White-collar workers accounted for 135, blue-collar workers 281, and the rest were either retired, housewives, students or unemployed. The results corroborated the mood we had long gauged from intuition and perception. The details of the survey result on the support of the Position Paper were:

Full approval	41%
Approve in part	41%
Disapprove of it	3%
No opinion	15%

What was more, the *South China Morning Post* in its publication on 25 May wrote:

> "The statement (position paper) has sparked a major controversy in both London and Peking, with members of parliament as well as Chinese leaders condemning it as unrepresentative of the views of Hong Kong people. The survey, however, paints a totally different picture and appears to be a clear vindication of the UMELCO line.
>
> "And as a further vote of confidence in UMELCO, the survey found that four out of ten people interviewed believed the statement would have a positive effect and that it would result in a more favourable agreement for Hong Kong after 1997.
>
> "The high degree of support for the UMELCO statement is

> significant, particularly in the light of attacks from British Members of Parliament — notably Mr. Edward Heath — who claim that UMELCO does not represent the views of Hong Kong people.
>
> "And the results are clearly at variance with the belief of some MPs that UMELCO represents the views of only a minority of people here."

Prior to the publication of this survey result on 25 May the *South China Morning Post* interviewed me by telephone on the previous evening and I said:

> "There has never been any question in my mind that we were accurately reflecting the views and wishes, fears and feelings of the people of Hong Kong, but while I was confident that we had it right there was no way we could prove it.
>
> "I am very pleased as now we have an independent survey to prove it. The survey was carried out in confidence and UMELCO were not told about it until the results were received."

Sir Geoffrey Howe's smiting us, or should I say spiting us, had accomplished the very opposite goal of galvanizing public opinion for a treaty that could satisfy people's yearnings for a future secured with freedom, liberty and the pursuit of happiness.

Discriminatory Nationality Act

My experience with the British, including those gleaned from the May 1984 visit, were that they are very sensitive and repulsive to coloured immigrants in recent decades. Prior to the administration of Edward Heath in the early 1970s, the Hong Kong British Government still issued British Citizen passports on behalf of the Foreign Office in London that qualified their holders to live in the United Kingdom.

I remember how in 1948, before my British sojourn, I applied for and obtained in Hong Kong a British passport to study in Britain. About a year later my wife, who was from Macao, could only obtain a one-off identification paper to join me in Britain. To facilitate our visits to continental Europe, I sent my Hong Kong-issued British passport together with my wife's identification paper to the Foreign Office in London for adding her name on to my passport. To my surprise, the British Government gave me a new British passport issued in London with the name of my wife in it.

Ten years later in 1959, I was doing a lot of business travel overseas. I did not have time to send my passport to London for a new one, as it would have taken about three months to process. I, therefore, again acquired a new British passport issued in Hong Kong, assuming that there would be no fundamental difference between securing the document in the Colony or in Britain. I was wrong. During 1960s through a series of immigration acts, Britain had rescinded the right of Hong Kong passport holders to live in the United Kingdom. At that time we were not aware of this insidious erosion of our right and did not raise any objection.

When the UMELCO delegation was in London in May 1984, Oswald Cheung, Lo Tak-shing, Maria Tam, Selina Chow and myself went to the Commons on 14 May to meet with Edward Heath. At his own initiative he disclosed to us how and why the British decided during his years as Prime Minister to abandon their obligation to receive their colonial subjects from Hong Kong. Heath said the policy was mooted in 1972 when the People's Republic of China gained the seat in the United Nations once occupied by the Republic of China. The new entrant to the UN demanded and the world body agreed to delete both Hong Kong and Macao from the UN list of colonial territories. The British realized then that it could not oppose the

Chinese claim nor grant independence to Hong Kong. Nonetheless, the British had to consider such a consequence and think of their own interest, which was to avoid future possible large influx of their British subjects from Hong Kong. They then began to consider amend the British Nationality Act.

So in 1976 HMG published a Green Paper, in which it was suggested to amend the terminology "British Subjects: Citizens of the United Kingdom and Colonies" to "British Overseas Citizens" and to strip by decree their right to reside in the United Kingdom. As a side note, the de-colonization of British colonies after the Second World War created many independent states in the British Commonwealth. Those British subjects of African and Indian origin who did not wish to become citizens of the newly established independent states could become British Overseas Citizens with no right of abode in Britain.

Sir Yuet-keung Kan and I in our UMELCO roles called on London in the summer of 1977 for the celebration of the Silver Jubilee of Queen Elizabeth. We took the opportunity to register our strong protest with the Labour Government Minister of State, Lord Goronwy-Roberts, at the proposal robbing our people of their right of abode. I recall Sir Yuet-keung, a senior lawyer, complaining to the Minister:

> "We are Hong Kong born citizens of Britain. We did not make that decision to have been Hong Kong born. We committed no crime. We made no mistake. We don't have a vote or say in the British Parliament. Yet the British Parliament will decide to abolish unilaterally and arbitrarily our birthright. This deprivation is neither humane nor democratic."

Over the next several years the UMELCO lobbied Britain furiously but failed, and only succeeded in convincing the United

Kingdom to create a new class of British subjects known as "British Dependent Territory Citizens" and the BDTC passports. This piece of travel document later further evolved into the even more dubious "British National (Overseas)" or the BN(O) passports, as a result of the Sino-British Joint Declaration on the future of Hong Kong.

Readying for Beijing

China sent from Jiangsu Province a Politburo member and provincial Party Secretary, Xu Jiatun, to replace Wang Kuang as the Director of the Xinhua News Agency on 17 May 1983. He was the most senior official from the Mainland ever appointed to head the *de facto* Chinese "embassy" in Hong Kong. His appointment reflected the seriousness with which China attached to the post and to winning over the people. Xu arrived by train, sporting a pair of tinted glasses, which stood him out from the usually stodgy Mainland cadres.

I first met Xu on 15 August 1983, accompanied by fellow Executive Councillors, Lydia Dunn (later Baroness) and Lee Quo-wei (later Sir), at a dinner hosted by the Chinese University Vice-Chancellor, Ma Lin, at his chancery. Dunn, a Swire senior executive, alumnus of St. Paul's Co-ed. College and the University of California, Berkeley, joined the Legislative Council in 1976 and the Executive Council in the beginning of 1983. Lee, a very prominent banker, had been a legislator since 1968 and Executive Councillor since 1976. He resigned from both posts in September 1978 for health reasons but rejoined the Executive Council in August 1983.

At that dinner I left early because I had to see Governor Sir Edward Youde off that evening for his flight to London. Nonetheless, we had arranged for regular secret rendezvous with Xu in the future. We did meet quite regularly later about once a month at a third person's location to avoid the media. After each meeting I reported to the Governor the essence of our discussions, and I believed Xu would do likewise and inform the Government in Beijing.

Near the end of 1983 we had established a certain rapport with Xu. He indicated to us that the Chinese leaders in the capital would like to talk with us about the Hong Kong issue. We tacitly agreed in principle but we had to mull it over more carefully, learn in advance whom we might be meeting, and plan the trip. But in the meantime every one had to keep the whole plan confidential lest it would alarm or arouse too high an expectation. The matter was left at that with no further progress.

Until the end of April 1984 Xu at a secret meeting told us that we were expected to go to Beijing on 10 May. But we had a conflict of schedules since we had to travel to London at the same time for the parliamentary debate on Hong Kong. Hence we were not able to meet the wishes of Xu. This, I believe, had created bad feeling between Beijing and us. In retrospect, I doubt that the Chinese had forwarded the invitation deliberately to make us choose between visiting London or Beijing and expected us to give them priority.

We came back from London on 23 May, met Xu once more, and were not clear whether the invitation to Beijing was still open since the Chinese leaders were vehemently opposed to our position paper published during our London trip. Nonetheless, we told Xu that we would love to go but we also had three requests. First, the delegation to Beijing should include Lobo in his capacity as the Senior Member of LEGCO. Second, we should go in the name of the UMELCO delegation. Third, Xu should let us know the name of the Chinese leaders meeting with us in Beijing. Xu hesitated for a moment, saying it would be difficult and the matter was left unresolved.

We had further talks for a couple of times before Xu and his deputy, Li Chuwen, invited Lee, Dunn and myself to lunch on 15 June at their premises for making the final arrangement for the visit to Beijing. Time was pressing for we had already arranged that afternoon a press conference to announce our pilgrimage to the Chinese capital. There was, however, a hitch. Xu said his government wanted us to go not as a UMELCO delegation but as private individuals. If we could agree to that, we could count on meeting with Deng Xiaoping, which was a very high honour. But, again, Xu did not want us to announce meeting Deng in advance. We wrangled over these two points until after three in the afternoon but still both sides could not compromise.

I thought of a way out of the impasse. I said I wished to phone our UMELCO office from the meeting room, sensing that they would overhear what I was going to say. Then I called and told the UMELCO office loudly that the session with Xu had been futile, the trip to Beijing would be aborted, and the press conference cancelled. Xu then did budge somewhat and eventually we agreed that each side could say what one would like to say. So then our trip to Beijing was on as scheduled.

Hard Talk with the Supreme Leader

After long and hard bargains with the Xinhua Director, Xu Jiatun, for the past few months, we three members of the UMELCO (Lydia Dunn, Lee Quo-wei and I) eventually went to Beijing on 21 June 1984 to meet the supreme leader, Deng Xiaoping. We were accompanied by the Hong Kong Xinhua Deputy Secretary General, Yang Qi, and on arrival checked into the Jianguo Hotel on Beijing's main thoroughfare, Changan Street.

This was my first visit to Beijing. Looking around during the ride from the airport to the hotel, we did not see many new and tall buildings until Changan Street. The roads were wide but jammed with bicycles, especially at the junctions. Traffic in the city centre was chaotic, even more so than in Hong Kong. I was not impressed and felt that the capital had a long way to catch up with its urban development.

The next evening at our billet we met for the first time the Secretary General of the Hong Kong and Macao Affairs Office, Lu Ping. Lu, a graduate of St. John's University, has been living in Hong Kong some time ago and speaks Cantonese. We briefed him about our speaking notes used for our session with the supreme leader scheduled for the following morning. The objective was to allow some extra time for the Chinese Government to consider and respond during the official meeting.

At the appointed time officials whisked us to the Great Hall of the People's Sichuan Room to meet a Sichuan native son Deng Xiaoping. Waiting for us were the Hong Kong and Macao Affairs Office Director, Ji Pengfei, his Deputies, Li Hou and Li Zhongying, and the Secretary General, Lu Ping. We brought along our secretaries, Wilfred Tsui and Ho Shing-him, to keep records and they sat further back in the room with Xinhua's Yang Qi. In retrospect, we were very fortunate to have the two able secretaries to keep verbatim records as we had disputes later in Hong Kong with the Xinhua Director, Xu Jiatun, on the substance of our discussion with Deng.

Deng enthroned in his customary armchair, with a spittoon on his side, puffing on a cigarette, was the first to speak, "I welcome you to Beijing in your individual capacity. I understand you have a number of opinions, to which we are willing to listen." Now, with the global media recording our visit for the news and for posterity, I

Plate 2.13 *The author meeting Chairman Deng Xiaoping in Beijing, 1984.*

could not back down. So, I summoned the pluck to respond, "We three Unofficial Members of the Hong Kong Executive and Legislative Councils are very honoured for this opportunity to call on Chairman Deng and other national leaders." Soon as those subtle greetings had been uttered, with Deng not recognizing our formal status and we insisting on this, officials started to usher out the large media contingent for the meeting to commence.

Deng then started to say, "Feel free to say whatever you want to, but I would like to say something first.... You know the Sino-British talks well, we will resolve the problem with Britain, which will not be subject to any interference. There have been talks of the so-called 'three-legged stool'. No three legs, only two legs." My immediate reaction at that point was that Deng was applying the traditional Chinese arranged marriage of their children to the determination of Hong Kong's future. Subsequently the phrase "three-legged stool" became the jargon frequently used by the Chinese to discourage any input from Hong Kong people in the talks.

Deng was resolute and absolute, continuing to express his rather threatening view, "As far as sovereignty is concerned, it will be resumed in 1997 regardless of the Sino-British talks and reactions from all sides. I have told the British Prime Minister that if major unrest occurred in Hong Kong before 1997, we would reconsider the timing and ways of taking back Hong Kong."

We then presented our case as cogently as we could to Deng while he was still attentive. Our presentation was supposed to be in three parts, a preamble and two main themes. In the preamble we expressed support for China's recovery of the sovereignty of Hong Kong in 1997, making it a Special Administrative Region with a high degree of autonomy to be administered by local inhabitants and with the existing system unchanged for 50 years after 1997.

For the first theme, we with diffidence told Deng about and explained in some details the people's lack of confidence in Hong Kong, both before and after 1997. I said, "People remain anxious and worried, and are filled with uncertainties. This anxiety is not limited to those with money. They affect workers and ordinary citizens alike. This is a fact and we feel it our duty to reflect this situation honestly. This would lead to a loss of confidence, an exodus of professional and talented people, an outflow of capital, and a lack of investment, resulting in economic recession in Hong Kong. As regards the period after 1997, there are three main worries. First, people are worried that instead of genuinely being administered by the people of Hong Kong, the future government of the HKSAR would actually be governed from Beijing. Second, people fear that the middle and lower level cadres who are responsible for the implementation of China's policy over the HKSAR may not be able to accept the capitalist systems and lifestyle of Hong Kong. Third, while people have faith in Chairman Deng and the present leadership, people are concerned that the future policy of China may change and that future leaders may revert to extreme left policies."

In addition, I emphasized that I was not speaking for my personal interests as I, like Mr. Lee, would be near 80 years of age by 1997 and there was nothing more I would ask for.

As this point before I began to speak on the second theme, Deng interrupted me and made his response. He specifically mentioned three major areas, the state of confidence in Hong Kong, the 13-year transitional period, and the administration of the Hong Kong SAR. First, it was about the confidence in Hong Kong. He spoke in his typically blunt style, "Generally speaking, you said Hong Kong people don't have confidence. Actually it is your opinion. It is you who have no faith in the People's Republic of China."

With the confidence issue summarily dismissed, he then tackled the subject of the transition period and said, "In regard to the 13-year transition period, the problem does not lie in Beijing. Our worries are no less than yours. That is why we propose to set up the Joint Liaison Group. It is for these 13 years that this body will have to be set up in Hong Kong. I do not doubt that there will be unrest in Hong Kong during the 13 years. The question is whether the unrest is major or minor. We do not want to see any major unrest.... If there were more serious disruptions, I have told the British Prime Minister, Mrs. Margaret Thatcher, we would consider recovering the sovereignty and the right of administration over Hong Kong earlier (than 1997)."

The third area Deng specifically referred to was the administration of the Hong Kong SAR after 1997 and he elaborated, "As regards the question of who will rule Hong Kong in the future, I want to draw a line. Members of the future Hong Kong Government and its affiliated bodies should basically be patriots. Their mission is to rule Hong Kong well. I have said many times that Beijing would not send people to Hong Kong. The Central Government has the power. No matter how they are nominated or elected, the Hong Kong officials will be appointed by the Central Government. This is a procedure. Other than stationing troops in Hong Kong, we will not send anyone to administer Hong Kong. This policy is clear and will not change. The Central Government won't take a single coin from Hong Kong after 1997."

Deng then ended the meeting saying, "The duration of the discussion is long enough. I want to take a rest. If you have other opinions, you can discuss them with my colleagues."

As we had scheduled a working dinner with the Director of the Hong Kong and Macao Affairs Office in the evening, I then on behalf of the delegation submitted a copy of our memorandum and presented a souvenir to Deng.

The three of us returned to Hong Kong on 25 June and immediately held a press conference to reveal what we had said to the Chinese leaders and more importantly what Deng had told us plus our interpretation of his message. I reported to the media,

Plate 2.14 *The press briefing after the UMELCO Delegation to Beijing, 1984.*

"Chairman Deng did not believe what we had told him was the real opinion of Hong Kong. He did not believe we really reflected to him the public state of mind. He did not believe there was a crisis of confidence in Hong Kong. He said China would look after the interest and standing of Hong Kong."

The press conference proved too inflammatory for Xu, who had invited us to Beijing. He refuted our claims and stressed that Deng had never said he had ever questioned that there ever was this crisis of confidence. He accused us, particularly myself, of distortions. The tit for tat subsequently triggered more mutual accusations from Xinhua and the UMELCO. The row got very serious but eventually both sides cooled down and agreed to publish separately its own record of verbatim conversations that Deng and us had in Beijing, allowing the public to draw their conclusions.

Whilst I thought that this argument would remain a mystery in history, unexpectedly a newspaper reporter in January the following year drew my attention to a news release by an official news agency in Beijing. On 2 January 1985 the China News Agency issued a report on the publication of a book containing a collection of the past speeches of the supreme leader, Deng Xiaoping. In the report there was an account which read, "The essence of Deng's speech when he on 23 June 1984 met Chung Sze-yuen and others had been included in the new book titled *Building Socialism with Chinese Characteristics* published on the New Year Day 1985. It contains a revealing passage saying that, 'With regard to the so-called Hong Kong people are afflicted with the confidence crisis, I do not believe that is the true feeling of the Hong Kong people.'" Accordingly, we were eventually vindicated by Deng himself.

Craft of Story Telling

Rhetoric is a neglected art form, at least to those of us who are not Cicero reincarnates. Candour is fine but sometimes talking straight elicits the opposite effect. This is why a skill orator employs nuances, similes, allegories, and parables to let his listeners draw their own inferences or none at all. This was what Dunn, Lee and I applied to the Hong Kong and Macao Affairs Office Director, Ji Pengfei, when we had a working dinner with him on 23 June 1984 after our session with Deng Xiaoping in the morning. Among others present were the Deputy Director, Li Hou, and the Secretary General, Lu Ping.

Prior to the dinner we had quite a long session to explain and discuss with our hosts in great detail the second theme of our memorandum containing the three main proposals by which China could allay the fears and assuage the doubts of the people of Hong Kong. The first proposal was that the Sino-British Agreement had to be detailed and binding and contains provisions that the Basic Law would be based on the terms of the Agreement. Ji, after hearing our explanations, quite readily agreed.

The second proposal was that the Basic Law should be drafted in Hong Kong by local representatives and representatives from Beijing. We said drafting the Basic Law in Hong Kong would help to enhance confidence and make use of the local expertise and talents. Ji's final response was that the Chinese Government would consider it.

A substantial number of Hong Kong residents were either refugees from the Mainland or their children. They had their personal experience or knowledge of the recent upheaval history on the Mainland. For the past 30 years or so the record of the Chinese Government had not been exemplary, having shifted policies at a whim. The caprice and the horrific consequences eroded what little trust the people of Hong Kong had in the Chinese Government. Instead of blurting out such a harsh spiel, we used an analogy, which had a special poignancy to so many Chinese.

So before we proceed to explain the third proposal we told Ji and his colleagues a fictitious story. We said, "The people of a small village is about to resettle to a place where flooding had occurred about once in every ten years during the past three decades. In order to secure confidence of the villagers being resettled there, a flood protection dam is built to ensure that their future livelihood will not be threatened."

We said to Ji how much we hoped the Chinese leaders could understand the scarred psychology of the people in Hong Kong and, therefore, give them some assurances, a peace of mind. We suggested that the Chinese Government should form a Basic Law Legal Committee comprising Chinese people of international standing and reputation. The Committee, we further proposed, should be empowered to advise on the drafting of and subsequent changes to as well as to monitor the implementation of the Basic Law. Ji, after pondering our suggestion, said the Chinese Government would seriously consider our request when drafting the Basic Law.

Just how "seriously" was borne out on 4 April 1990 when the Chinese National People's Congress promulgated the Basic Law and established the Committee for the Basic Law of the Hong Kong SAR with three provisions:

(1) Affiliation: To be a working committee under the Standing Committee of the National People's Congress.

(2) Function: To study questions arising from the implementation of Articles 17, 18, 158 and 159 of the Basic Law of the Hong Kong SAR and submit its views thereon to the Standing Committee of the NPC.

(3) Composition: Twelve members, six from the Mainland and six from Hong Kong appointed by the Standing Committee of the NPC for a term of office of five years. The Hong Kong members shall be nominated jointly by the Chief Executive, President of the Legislative Council and Chief Justice of the Court of Final Appeal.

While the "Basic Law Legal Committee" we envisaged is not identical to the "Basic Law Committee" that has since been established, the two are similar in their purpose.

When I wrote the memoirs in 2001 Hong Kong had already returned to China for more than three years, and our visit to Beijing and its controversial ending had become part of Hong Kong's history. Chairman Deng had passed away, unfortunately, just four months before Hong Kong's return on 1 July 1997. Xu Jiatun, one of the key players in the saga, had fled to the United States of America in the early 1990s under the protection of Uncle Sam. As for the three of us, we were happy that our observation was prescient and the three proposals had come to pass. Dunn is now a Life Peer in the British House of Lords joining the ranks of Margaret Thatcher whereas both Lee and I continue to live in the Hong Kong SAR, some say we have changed side.

Public Support for the Beijing Trip

Whilst we were pondering over the criticism from the Chinese leaders in Beijing that our views were not necessarily those of the people of Hong Kong, the *South China Morning Post* on 6 July 1984 published another opinion poll by Survey Research Hong Kong Limited. This survey was conducted to gauge public support for our visit to Beijing.

The pollsters interviewed at random 1,010 people, aged 19 and above, from a wide cross-section of the community. The poll was conducted by telephone between 28 June and 1 July, three days after our return from the Beijing mission. Of the total respondents, 529 were men and 481 women. White-collar workers accounted for 189, blue-collar workers 491 and the rest were either retired, housewives, students or unemployed.

It was found that:

(1) Some 79 per cent of the respondents supported the UMELCO delegation to Beijing.

(2) The UMELCO's three proposals received a positive support.

  (a) 74% agreed that the Sino-British Agreement must be detailed and binding and contain a provision that the Basic Law will be based on the terms of the Agreement.

  (b) 78% agreed that the Basic Law should be drafted in Hong Kong jointly by local representatives and representatives from Beijing.

Plate 2.15 *The UMELCO Delegation to Beijing, in front of the Temple of Heaven, 1984.*

(c) 61% agreed that a committee of Chinese people of international standing and reputation should be appointed by China to monitor the implementation and advise the drafting of and consider subsequent changes to the Basic Law.

(3) Some 67 per cent of the respondents thought there was a problem of confidence in Hong Kong.

Before we visited Beijing, we did not invite public opinion. But afterwards we received a lot of praise for our trip to Beijing. The *South China Morning Post* lauded us for accurately reflecting the views of the people, an accolade that was especially satisfying as we had faced so much antipathy for our efforts from some quarters. The *Post* in its editorial on 6 July commented that this poll served to emphasize the point that has been disputed in Beijing, in London and even in Hong Kong: that while the Unofficials might not represent the people of Hong Kong and while they might not fully reflect the people's views, they were able to articulate the concerns of a large number.

The Joint Liaison Group

When China proposed to the British during the diplomatic talks the formation of the Sino-British Joint Liaison Group (JLG) for the transition period, it evoked fear that the entity would invite Mainland meddling in local affairs whilst Hong Kong was still under British administration. The Executive Council, whilst sharing this fear, recognized the need for such a liaison body with which the two governments could discuss matters of sovereignty transfer during the last years of transition. Consequently, we accepted the principle of establishing the Sino-British Joint Liaison Group but wished to consider carefully its terms of reference.

I remember distinctly my EXCO colleague Li Fook-wo raising the issue of potential, if inadvertent, interference. The disquiet was enough to prompt Britain and China to spell out clearly the functions and reaches of the Group in the Sino-British Agreement. In particular, at his request, the British were able to convince the Chinese to insert a clause in Section 6 of Annex II of the Joint Declaration. It reads in part: "The Joint Liaison Group shall be an organ for liaison and not an organ of power. It shall play no part in the administration of Hong Kong or Hong Kong SAR. Nor shall it have any supervisory role over that administration."

I also recall my colleague Maria Tam suggesting that the life of the Group should have a "mirror image" life and operate for "x" years before and after 1997. But the British thought that the Chinese would balk at such an extension and was reluctant to raise it at the negotiating table.

The British Foreign Secretary, Sir Geoffrey Howe, came to Hong Kong on 27 July 1984 *en route* to his second visit to Beijing. At the EXCO meeting with him we pressed him again very hard to raise with the Chinese the "mirror image" concept. We pointed out that it would be a form of residual British presence and should enhance the acceptability of the Agreement by Hong Kong people. Sir Geoffrey was receptive to the idea and argument but did not promise to raise the issue with the Chinese.

Sir Geoffrey, who had been in Beijing to put the finishing touches to the Sino-British Agreement, which was to be initialled in September 1984, returned to London via Hong Kong to brief the Executive Council on 1 August. A few minutes before entering the Executive Council Chamber, Sir Geoffrey gave me a small piece of paper, which read, "I didn't care about the opposition of my advisors and did broach to the Chinese the possibility of prolonging the life of the Joint Liaison Group beyond 1997. The Chinese agreed that the Group could exist until 1 January 2000."

He later told me that all his advisors were against raising the issue with the Chinese, but when he felt the cordial and friendly atmosphere at the meeting, he wanted to have a go at them so that he could face the Unofficial Members afterwards. He was pleasantly surprised that the Chinese, after asking for a brief recess, came back to the negotiating table and readily agreed to extend the life of the Joint Liaison Group till 1 January 2000 without any ado. I then said to him, jokingly, that he should have followed up and bargained for a longer period, if not to the extent of the "mirror image".

Political Gambit

The negotiations were long and laborious. Both sides, their nerves frayed, in the end agreed on a constitutional arrangement for the territory, but each side laid its own gambit and the dangling issue continued to jangle and rankle.

Britain accepted China regaining sovereignty under Article 31 of its Constitution allowing for a Special Administrative Region. The SAR would enjoy a high degree of autonomy, rule of law, liberty, way of life and a capitalist economic system for 50 years beyond 1997 while relinquishing responsibility for foreign affairs and defence to the Central Government.

At the time Hong Kong was a British colony and its Governor, appointed by Her Majesty, held almost absolute, autocratic power. He, as the envoy of the Queen, commanded the military, lorded over the government, presided over the Legislative Council, and appointed all its members along with those in the Executive Council. He could refuse to heed the advice of both Councils and ratify any bill passed by the LEGCO, which he could also dissolve.

But once Hong Kong returned to China, the economic and other systems would stay much the same while the political one would change dramatically, becoming more democratic. The Chinese wanted the SAR Chief Executive to be returned by consultation and sanctified by the Central People's Government (CPG), and the Legislative Council to be elected or appointed.

The Chinese Government later agreed that the Chief Executive would be selected by election or through consultation for appointment by the Central Government. But the Chinese strenuously opposed to the British proposal that the LEGCO would be constituted by direct geographical election.

Britain, with the support of the Executive Council, was intransigent on this point, counting on direct elected legislators thwarting Chinese interference and checking their influence on the Chief Executive. China, perhaps, considered this direct geographical election as means by which the United Kingdom could continue to exercise some sway over the territory. Both sides could not nudge any closer to a final settlement on the intractable political question.

It was rumoured that Deng Xiaoping, however, insisted on British wrapping up the negotiations before the 35th Anniversary of the Chinese National Day on 1 October 1984. We also recalled the warning by the former British Prime Minister, Edward Heath, in September 1983 that Deng would like to complete the Sino-British talks in September 1984.

Around summer 1984 the talks had reached consensus on most of the main points, other than on politics with both sides sticking to their principles on the direct elections. Time was running out and so the Chinese made another opening gambit in the chess game that is diplomacy.

China decided to couch or cloud the issue by deleting the adjectives "direct geographical" that qualified the noun "election" which was further changed to the plural form "elections". This implied people could be enfranchised in different ways to choose their legislators who might be returned via geographical, functional and Electoral College constituencies. The result would be a much more diluted, perhaps anaemic, form of electoral mandate.

Earlier on both sides recognized the difficulty in putting the solution into the main body of the Joint Declaration and agreed to continue discussion in the Joint Working Group established around June 1984 and worked continuously for almost three months in Beijing to resolve the remaining problems. Dr. David Wilson (later Lord and Governor from 1987 to 1992) was leading the British team. For this reason, the method of formation for the Hong Kong SAR Legislative Council was not contained in the main body but rather the Annex I of the Joint Declaration.

Agreement Became Declaration

The term "Sino-British Joint Declaration" entered the lexicon of diplomacy at Chinese insistence. Both Britain and the Hong Kong Executive Council initially and all along had thought of labelling the accord the terminology of "Sino-British Agreement".

The British had proposed the nomenclature "Agreement" to the Chinese who, however, objected to the title, as far as we were aware, for two reasons:

(1) China never accepted the validity of the unequal treaties ceding Hong Kong and leasing the New Territories to the United Kingdom back in the Victorian era. The People's Republic, therefore, would not need to reach "agreement" with the British to resume the exercise of sovereignty over Hong Kong.

(2) Once the People's Republic of China has exercised its sovereign control over Hong Kong again, it would not require British "agreement" to propagate its policies towards the Hong Kong SAR.

But since both sides reckoned their friendly ties were strong, the Chinese were willing and prepared to sign a "Joint Declaration" with the British. The semantic acrobatics, however, vexed some of the members of the Executive Council, who feared that such an oddly phrased compact might not have any binding and legal validity, and therefore pressed the British to clarify the difference between the two terms. Her Majesty's Government then brought in experts in diplomatic law who confirmed to us that the pact by the name of "Joint Declaration" was legitimate and equally binding between the two signatories.

To be double sure, the Executive Council suggested that the document be submitted to the United Nations for registration. The two signatories concurred and, on 12 June 1985, after the ratification by the two respective parliaments, tendered the Joint Declaration to the World Body where it stands as an eloquent testament to the reconciliation of two former foes.

EXCO's Final Mission to London

Britain and China had their 22nd and final round of negotiations on 6 and 7 September 1984. They concluded the session with a lot of mutual congratulations for the painstaking progress over the past couple of years since Thatcher's visit to Beijing. Most members of the Executive Council, and also the Hong Kong people, we believed, endorsed the framework of the Joint Declaration but, surprisingly, many were more disappointed with the British than with the Chinese. They felt the United Kingdom had shirked its responsibility towards the British subjects in Hong Kong.

The Unofficial Members of the Executive Council accompanied Sir Edward Youde to London for the fifth and last time to meet with

Plate 2.16 *The Hong Kong Executive Council, 1984.*

the Prime Minister prior to her Cabinet discussed the draft Sino-British Joint Declaration. We left Hong Kong on 17 September and met Thatcher at 10 Downing Street on 19 September at 6 p.m. Also present at the meeting were Foreign Secretary Sir Geoffrey Howe and Minister of State Richard Luce.

In the session with the Prime Minister I, on behalf of the Unofficial Members of the Executive Council, reminded her of the UMELCO visit to London in May and, most compelling, the four requests in our position paper we had submitted to her. I said that, according to opinion polls conducted independently, most of the Hong Kong people supported the position paper. The draft Joint Declaration, though was not perfect, did more or less meet the first three requests. On the contrary, it was the last request, that is, to safeguard the rights of the British nationals in Hong Kong, which was disappointing. We urged the British Government to deliver on the fourth and final request, which was in its power to grant and as a part of its sovereign and moral obligation.

With such a misgiving expressed, the Unofficial Members of the Executive Council endorsed the embryonic Joint Declaration and undertook to recommend it to the people of Hong Kong.

Dunn's Embarrassment

We, the Unofficial Members of the Executive Council, were very strung out in London in 1984 by the enormous pressure and at times frosty reception. We decided one evening to take a furlough by touring the cosmopolitan city of hedonistic pleasures.

The UMEXCO at that time usually stayed at Knightsbridge's Sheraton Park Tower Hotel near the world famous store Harrods and in the bustling shopping district. One early evening one of our colleagues suggested to have Chinese cuisine for dinner, the best of which could be had at Soho, the "Red Light" district. About seven of us subsequently hailed a couple of cabs, which, however, got separated in the ensuing traffic jam. In my taxi rode Oswald Cheung, Li Fook-wo and Lydia Dunn, who fancied spiked heels, modish clothes, and a stylish coif, which nearly proved her undoing.

In Soho after getting off from the taxi, we decided to spread out to locate our other colleagues riding in the other cab. Rather without chivalry, we left Lydia in the corner under a lurid lamp-light to wait for our return. I sprinted across the street and on the other side I gazed back at Lydia who was daubing her face with her makeup kit. I traipsed around for a few minutes and couldn't locate any one from the other cab. I then returned to check on Lydia and spotted a man of Middle Eastern extraction sidling up to Lydia, from what I could gather, propositioning her, mistaking the future Baroness for a hooker. I was desperate as I charged back across the street, shrieking, "She is mine, she is mine." The John seeing gallant me dashing towards Lydia slunk away into the night.

One day we, who abandoned her to that street corner, would kid her how we might have in our haste ruined her life by stopping her from perhaps marrying an Arabian prince. In fact, she did blame me afterwards for threatening away that Middle Eastern gentleman, who could be, though with very slim chance, an Arabian prince, a sheikh or sultan.

False Alarm

Not only Lydia Dunn had her close scrape in London; I too had a jolt. By the summer of 1984, a few sticking points aside, the negotiations were still in progress when I, together with other Unofficial

Members of the Executive Council, accompanied Sir Edward Youde to the British capital for meetings with the Prime Minister and other British officials. Alone in one afternoon I remained at my hotel room to pore over confidential documents. My concentration was suddenly interrupted by a knock at my door, which I opened to see three Englishmen. One of them I recognized as an aid to the Governor. He introduced the other two as agents of the British Ministry of Intelligence or MI5. They then invited themselves into my room, speaking to me in a hushed, conspiratorial tone.

One of the heralds told me that they had received news from the Special Branch of the Hong Kong Government about a plot being hatched against me. He then asked me whether I was aware of having a love affair with any woman or a financial dispute with any party, which could have a motive for the plot. My answer was a definite no. I then asked in turn the source of the Hong Kong Special Branch's tip-off. The other agent said the news had been traced to the Hong Kong Branch of Xinhua News Agency. I then found the whole story too incredible.

But the shadow of doubt hanged over me and so after my return to the Colony, I consulted with the Royal Police of Hong Kong. I was advised to take certain precautionary measures as a matter of prudence and so I did. After the lapse of about three months, nothing had happened and I gradually returned to my daily routines.

The Hand Shake

The Commendation

The chief Chinese negotiator Zhou Nan and his British counterpart Sir Richard Evans wrapped up their formal deliberations on Hong

Kong and initiated the draft Sino-British Joint Declaration at noon on 26 September 1984 in Beijing. In Hong Kong a total of 3.6 million copies of the draft Joint Declaration were distributed to the public. The British printed 800,000 copies in English and 1.6 million copies in Chinese, whereas the Chinese printed 400,000 copies in English and 800,000 copies in Chinese.

The Unofficial Members of the Executive Council, after meeting with the British Prime Minister returned to Hong Kong and on 28 September conducted a press conference to recommend the draft to the people. The purpose was to explain to the public why the UMEXCO endorsed the draft Joint Declaration and commend it to the people of Hong Kong.

Plate 2.17 *The author with Dr. Allen Lee at the Summer Palace, Beijing, 1984.*

The UMEXCO assessed the acceptability of the Joint Declaration based on the four major criteria outlined in the UMELCO position paper of May 1984, which had received overwhelming support in the community. In our opinion, the Joint Declaration, on the whole, did meet substantially our major requirements. In addition and in assessing acceptability, we said we had considered the alternative, particularly for those who could not leave or did not wish to leave.

Of course, there was another alternative, which was no Joint Declaration. The likely consequence of this choice would be a unilateral declaration by China. We said, "A unilateral declaration may not contain all the details we require; may not be binding; may not provide any assurance or an undertaking about the future Basic Law. It almost certainly would not safeguard the rights of Hong Kong BDTCs."

The UMEXCO further pointed out that, in addition, there were in the draft Joint Declaration many positive features which were to be welcomed. We quoted, for example, the promise of an elected

Plate 2.18 *The Hong Kong Delegation attending the 35th National Day Celebration in Beijing, on the Great Wall of China, 1984.*

legislature; continual renewal of land leases in both the New Kowloon and the New Territories; the right of Hong Kong people to travel freely in and out of the SAR; and the various freedoms which we hold so preciously in Hong Kong.

We also emphasized the fact that the draft Joint Declaration contained much more details than many people expected at that time indicated the efforts of both Governments to meet the concerns of the people of Hong Kong. We therefore believed that a mutually binding agreement freely negotiated and entered into between the two sovereign states and providing a workable framework, is much to be preferred to no agreement.

Finally, we said, "It is our belief that what we have today is the best agreement possible and one which we, the Unofficial Members of the Executive Council, can commend to the people of Hong Kong in good conscience."

A Minor Rebuff

The draft Sino-British Joint Declaration had in fact incorporated most of the recommendations of the Unofficial Members of the Executive and Legislative Councils. Even then when the legislature debated the draft Declaration, it failed to secure an unanimous support.

For three days — 15, 16 and 18 October 1984 — the Legislative Council debated the compact. The Senior Member of LEGCO, Roger Lobo, submitted the motion, which in essence read, "That this Council endorses the draft Agreement on the Future of Hong Kong between the British and Chinese Governments and commends it to the people of Hong Kong." Some 27 legislators spoke with considerable eloquence and emotion in what might well be the most important oration of their political careers. When all the words were said there were two legislators, barrister John Swaine (later Sir and President of the Legislative Council from 1991 to 1995) and unionist Chan Kam-chuen (later migrated to Canada) did not endorse the proposed treaty by abstaining.

Swaine berated the British for "negotiating with China with one arm tied behind their backs" because the British had already demonstrated their lack of commitment to the territory by robbing their subjects of their right of abode in the United Kingdom through a series of immigration and nationality acts. He regarded the draft Declaration as the best of a bad deal and abstained from voting. Chan repeated the argument that the people of Hong Kong could not trust the Chinese Communist Party and a piece of paper would not lessen the decades of psychological terror. He too abstained from voting.

The Hong Kong Government did not stand idle while the legislators and Executive Councillors waded through the issue as it formed a special task force, chaired by a High Court Judge, Simon Li, to monitor public opinion and report direct to the Administration. At the same time, the UMELCO also wanted to have their own assessment of the public opinion and used the money contributed by some individual members to commission Survey Research Hong Kong Limited in conducting a separate independent opinion poll covering 6,000 persons of 18 years and over. The survey concluded that the vast majority supported the draft Joint Declaration. Some 90 per cent of the respondents in the poll found the treaty was far preferable to none. The 18 District Boards, established to keep their ears close to the figurative ground, also backed the accord.

UMELCO's Reaction to the Declaration

When the Unofficial Members of the Executive and Legislative

Councils heard that the parliamentary debates on the draft Sino-British Joint Declaration would be held in early December 1984, we decided to send a delegation to London. The purposes were to reflect the views of the Hong Kong people to members of both Houses and attend the debates. More specifically, we wanted to remind the British Government not to sacrifice Hong Kong's interest for its own and not to tolerate Chinese meddling during the transition.

The delegation checked into our London haunt, the Portman Intercontinental Hotel, in the heart of London on 1 December with many questions on our minds. On the surface we, the UMELCO, except for the two dissenters, were for the treaty but, at heart, we were also ambivalent about the agreement and anxious about the future. As time passed our disquiet became palpable, eclipsing our reasons for hope.

Roger Lobo and I headed the squad that included, for the record, Lydia Dunn, Lee Quo-wei, Maria Tam, Allen Lee, Andrew So, Cheung Yan-lung, Selina Chow, Chan Ying-lun and Rita Fan. We met separately Foreign Secretary Sir Geoffrey Howe, Minister of State Richard Luce, the Parliamentary Foreign Affairs Committee, the Parliamentary Hong Kong Group, and a large number of Members of both Houses.

At each of these meetings we began by giving a run down on the reaction of Hong Kong people to the draft Joint Declaration, the outcome of the debate in the Legislative Council, the support of the 18 District Boards as well as the Urban Council and the Heung Yee Kuk. We also cited the positive results of the independent opinion poll commissioned by the UMELCO. On the whole, we concluded that the people of Hong Kong accepted the draft Joint Declaration.

We also talked about the development of the representative government during the 12-year transition. We expressed caution

Plate 2.19 *The third UMELCO Delegation with Prime Minister Thatcher in London, 1984.*

against any rapid or radical changes, which might put at risk Hong Kong's *raison d'être*, that is, stability and prosperity. We stressed that most people in Hong Kong believed that only if stability and prosperity were maintained in the transition period prior to 1997 could there be any hope that stability and prosperity would be continued for fifty years after 1997. We asked HMG not to sacrifice Hong Kong to placate China or bolster Britain's own interests.

We also presented to them a litany of eight concerns and two demands that had been issued in an UMELCO statement on 29 November, which was released just before our leaving Hong Kong. The eight concerns were:

(1) Anxiety about interference from the Chinese Government;

(2) Worry about conscription in the Hong Kong SAR;
(3) Concern about other countries not recognizing the new form of British passports;
(4) Doubt about the preservation of existing human rights and personal freedoms;
(5) Fear about stationing of PLA troops in the Hong Kong SAR;
(6) Resentment about the BDTC status could not be passed on to the next generation;
(7) Reservation about the possible incompatibility between the Basic Law and the Chinese Constitution;
(8) Concern about China might not implement the Joint Declaration's terms and renege on its treaty obligations.

The two demands were:

(1) The people of Hong Kong should not only be consulted but be involved in the drafting of the Basic Law;
(2) The people of Hong Kong should participate in the Sino-British Joint Liaison Group.

All these eight concerns and two demands we had confided in Sir Geoffrey and Minister Luce and so we did not repeat in their entirety when we met with the Prime Minister on 5 December at 9.30 in the morning. Thatcher heard not only an abbreviated reference to the eight concerns but every syllable of the two demands plus the two items below:

(1) A new form of British passports;
(2) The Hong Kong ethnic minorities being able to bequeath their British status to their descendants.

The House of Commons sat on the afternoon of 5 December for

Plate 2.20 *Governor Youde meeting the Japanese Prime Minister in Tokyo, 1984.*

the debate on the draft Joint Declaration with us in attendance in the gallery. The points we had raised with them were the focus of discussion in the Parliament, which agreed with us about the people of Hong Kong taking part in the drafting of the Basic Law and in the operation of the Joint Liaison Group, not as observers but as contributors. The Commons unanimously ratified the draft Joint Declaration.

Both Lydia Dunn and I had to leave London in the mid-course of the mission on 9 December to accompany Governor Sir Edward Youde on an official trip to Tokyo to court the Government and businessmen of that country for support. Lobo stayed behind as the leader of the UMELCO delegation and attended on 10 December the debate in the House of Lords. It also ended up with a unanimous sanction of the draft Joint Declaration.

Plate 2.21 *The Sino-British Joint Declaration Signing Ceremony in Beijing, 1984.*

On the Plane with Thatcher

By 10 December 1984 the draft Sino-British Joint Declaration had basically passed all its hurdles in Britain. The work on the treaty had gone from a trial of patience to triumph for every body as well as a testament to bilateral co-operation. Prime Minister Margaret Thatcher, with another laurel to her name, travelled to Beijing, this time in an exultant mood, and on 19 December 1984 at the Great Hall of the People signed on the dotted line along with Premier Zhao Ziyang. Beaming over the proceedings were the treaty's architect Deng Xiaoping and President Li Xiannian. From Hong Kong a party of about one hundred attended the ceremony, including 12 representatives of the UMELCO.

After the mandatory rounds of toasts and fetes I returned to the hotel in time to receive news that Thatcher wanted me to fly on her official jet from Beijing to Hong Kong the following morning and to spend the night in Diaoyutai compound, both the first time for me. I gladly accepted the invitation and stayed overnight at the Chinese Government's sprawling estate that had catered for some of the most famous leaders, including Richard Nixon and of course the British Prime Minister.

Early the next morning, on 20 December, I went with my British minder to the airport and boarded the aeroplane, which was impressively unassuming with its sleeping cabin and private lavatory as well as a small meeting room plus an office in the front. At the middle of the aircraft were seats for the Prime Minister's accompanying staff, and on the back was mainly the press. I sat near the front. The journalists, I was told, had to pay for the passage with the attendant privilege of a chance to interview key figures.

The Prime Minister later invited me to her airborne office to

Plate 2.22 *The Chinese leaders with the Hong Kong Delegation in Beijing, 1984.*

Plate 2.23 *Prime Minister Thatcher addressing the Legislative Council, 1984.*

discuss future British and Chinese ties and also the transition of Hong Kong for about 20 minutes. I do not recall all the details except that we generally talked about developments ahead. She then assured me that Britain would do right for Hong Kong and hoped that the UMELCO could well put its collective mind at ease.

The Highest Knighthood

The British and Chinese Governments resolved the fate of Hong Kong through negotiations and made history. Governor Sir Edward Youde, at a time of jubilation, informed me that the United Kingdom would honour me for my contributions to the process by awarding me one of the highest knighthoods — the Knight Grand Cross of the Most Excellent Order of the British Empire or G.B.E. in short. The

Queen would also confer on the Senior Member of the Legislative Council, Roger Lobo, the more humble Knight Bachelor that I had received six years back. But I did not receive that ultimate G.B.E. medal from H.M. the Queen in the Buckingham Palace until four years later.

The United Kingdom has a very comprehensive and complicated system of honours. But for Hong Kong, one of its colonies, the following three categories were generally used:

(1) The Most Distinguished Order of St. Michael and St. George, in which there are three classes and for which women as well as men are eligible:

Knight/Dame Grand Cross	G.C.M.G.
Knight/Dame Commander	K.C.M.G. or D.C.M.G.
Companion	C.M.G.

Members of the first two classes are entitled to be called "Sir" or "Dame".

(2) The Royal Victorian Order, in which there are four classes and for which women as well as men are eligible:

Knight/Dame Grand Cross	G.C.V.O.
Knight/Dame Commander	K.C.V.O. or D.C.V.O.
Commander	C.V.O.
Member	M.V.O.

Members of the first two classes are entitled to be called "Sir" or "Dame".

(3) The Most Excellent Order of the British Empire, in which there are five classes and for which women as well as men are eligible:

Knight/Dame Grand Cross	G.B.E.
Knight/Dame Commander	K.B.E. or D.B.E.

Commander	C.B.E.
Officer	O.B.E.
Member	M.B.E.

Members of the first two classes are entitled to be called "Sir" or "Dame".

(4) There is one lowest Order of Knighthood called Knight Bachelor. Recipients of this order are entitled to be called "Sir" but have no initials after their names.

The British, generally speaking, bestowed the first category of honours on government officials, the second on those who provided services to the Royal Family, and the third on government officials, citizens with exemplary public services and noted philanthropists.

Sir Edward told me in December 1984 that the British Government was prepared to recommend me to the Queen for the highest of the honours under the Most Excellent Order of the British Empire to add to my first knighthood, Knight Bachelor, received in 1978. I would then became the second ethnic Chinese in Hong Kong ever to be bestowed a double knighthood after Sir Yuet-keung Kan.

Though thrilled by the laurel, which was so rarely bestowed, I had to defer accepting the citation because taking it so soon after the negotiations might suggest impropriety or an over eagerness to take credit. Sir Edward agreed with my reason and decision. The Queen delayed decorating me with that GBE Knighthood until after my first political retirement in 1988.

Preventing Sabotage

No sooner than the signing and sealing of the Sino-British Joint Declaration we in the UMELCO were back to London for another tilt, this time to defend the nationality status of Hong Kong British subjects. In May 1984 we submitted a petition paper containing, *inter alias*, four proposals, one of which was an appeal to the United Kingdom not to shirk its responsibility for British nationals born in Hong Kong.

This issue was touched on by Foreign Secretary Sir Geoffrey Howe who, during the House of Commons debate on the Joint Declaration on 5 December 1984, announced that Britain would return Hong Kong to China in 1997 and would handle the question of nationality as a part of its obligations.

The British Government on 10 January 1985 published the Hong Kong Bill set for the debate in the House of Commons 11 days later. This piece of legislation was meant to sanction the switching of the British Dependent Territory Citizen (BDTC) passport to the British National (Overseas) (BN(O)) travel document, which would continue to have effect after 30 June 1997, an arrangement acceptable to the Executive Council.

But a Member of Parliament, Enoch Powell, famous or infamous almost 20 years earlier for his bigoted "River of Blood" speech calling for the end to immigration into the country, threatened to postpone the Hong Kong Bill indefinitely. We in the UMELCO felt compelled about stopping the xenophobe's ploy that, if effective, could affect the Sino-British Joint Declaration and stall the transition of the BDTC to the BN(O).

To thwart Powell's sabotage, the UMELCO decided to rush a small delegation of three — Peter C. Wong, Maria Tam and myself — to London to lobby the Members of Parliament for the Hong Kong Bill. Peter and Maria (both lawyers) went first, arriving in London on 16 January, to start the lobbying work. I, happened to be in Beijing at that time for the signing of the Daya Bay Nuclear Power Joint Venture, met up with the pair three days later. We, accompanying

Plate 2.24 *The Farewell Party to mark the end of the Exclusive Appointment System for the Legislative Council, 1985.*

Governor Sir Edward Youde, spoke with Sir Geoffrey and Minister of State Richard Luce in the morning of 21 January before attending the debate in the Commons in the afternoon.

We, in the galley of the Parliament, were very pleased when the Speaker of the House rejected Powell's motion and, consequently, the Hong Kong Bill was passed without any problem.

The Grand Finale

British and Chinese friendship flowered after the Sino-British Joint Declaration's inking. The ambience was euphoric in June 1985 when Premier Zhao Ziyang made an official visit to Britain where he attended a banquet hosted for him by his Joint Declaration co-signatory, Prime Minister Margaret Thatcher, at her official residence 10 Downing Street.

Attending the state banquet were some sixty very distinguished guests, including prominent politicians, diplomats and businessmen having some kind of connection with the People's Republic of China. The Governor and the two Senior Members of the UMELCO were among those present. At the cocktail reception I spoke with Premier Zhao, Foreign Minister Wu Xueqian and the top Chinese Joint Declaration negotiator Zhou Nan. We talked about Hong Kong's future and its stability and prosperity. In some way that was the zenith of Chinese and British rapprochement, a height that proved rather impossible to maintain.

Chapter 3

The Long Transition

Honeymoon Period

The Three-act Play

Britain and China signed their Joint Declaration in December 1984 agreeing to return Hong Kong from the former to the latter on 1 July 1997, a transitional period of twelve and a half long years.

While the two countries converged on the fate of Hong Kong in principle, their missions diverged during the transition. For China the priority was to draft and pass the Basic Law to establish the Hong Kong Special Administrative Region and to effect the "One Country Two Systems" from 1 July 1997. The British mission was to evolve the colonial political system of 1984 to the self-rule of 1997 whilst maintaining Hong Kong's prosperity and stability.

If I were to write a drama for the transition, I would have designed a three-act play. The first act covers the period from January 1985 to June 1989. This was the "co-operative phase" and marked the Joint Declaration's honeymoon. The British Government in the United Kingdom and its adjunct in Hong Kong collaborated reasonably well with the Chinese Authorities. The Joint Liaison Group made steady progress and Britain and China communicated mostly well. I retired from the Executive Council in September 1988, which somewhat coincided with the end of this honeymoon period.

The second act covers the period from the Tiananmen Square incident, which deeply affected the people of the Colony. The British Hong Kong Government subtly abandoned its era-long neutral stance and tolerated "anti-Communist" activities. The Unofficial Members of the Executive and Legislative Councils applied pressure on the United Kingdom, which relented and modified its Nationality Act by extending to 50,000 elite families of Hong Kong British subjects full British Passports that entitle them to live in the "home country". Ignoring Chinese protest, the British sped up democratic reform in the territory and, in March 1990, incorporated the spirit of the International Covenant on Civil and Political Rights into Hong Kong's own human rights legislation. The mutual recrimination marked the episode as the "period of distrust".

Early in 1992 the British Government announced the recall of Governor Sir David Wilson (later Lord) perceiving him to be too accommodating to China, and replaced him in July 1992 with former Conservative Party Chairman, Chris Patten, who had lost his Bath parliamentary seat early in the year. Two months later the new Governor returned to London to secure the blessing from both Prime Minister John Major and Foreign Secretary Douglas Hurd for his blueprint of accelerated political reform. The programme sought to change radically the electoral procedures for the District Boards and Urban Councils in 1994 and the Legislative Council in 1995, plus revamping the composition of the Executive Council as well as divorcing the Legislative Council from the Executive Council. Patten delivered his first Policy Address to the Legislative Council on 7 October, ten days after providing the gist of his address to the Chinese Government in Beijing and rejecting its request for immediate consultation. This was the beginning of the third act and could be branded as the "confrontational phase", which did not end until British rule did on 30 June 1997.

Secret Meetings with Xu

Throughout the Sino-British negotiations the Xinhua News Agency Director in Hong Kong, Xu Jiatun, and his deputies met about monthly with Lee Quo-wei, Lydia Dunn and me, all Unofficial Members of the Executive Council. These secret sessions, during which we exchanged views freely, petered out after the Joint Declaration was signed in December 1984 but resumed eleven months later though much less frequently than before. The need for such meetings was partly because the accord did not resolve all the issues germane to the transition from colony to the Special Administrative Region. Some of these hurdles could not be resolved in the meetings of persons but not of minds. The Chinese side also wanted to test its rhetoric on us inside the room and broadcast the same on the outside through its media.

We came together once more at the suggestion of Xu on the evening of 22 November 1985 at the old Bank of China Building, whose penthouse has since been converted into a stylish club replete with period photographs and posters. Xu this time brought along with him his two deputies, Qiao Zonghuai (now China's Representative at the United Nations Human Rights Commission) and Mao Junnian (the only local recruit rising to the deputy status). Dunn by then had been promoted to be the Senior Member of the Legislative Council, succeeding Sir Roger Lobo, who was knighted in the 1985 New Year. The legislature itself was moving step by step towards elections and gradually away from appointments.

The British had then started, although some say belatedly, to

Plate 3.1 *The UMELCO dinner for Director Xu Jiatun of the Xinhua News Agency, Hong Kong, 1985.*

prepare Hong Kong for the autonomy that China had promised in the Joint Declaration. They did so by shifting power to the people gradually and ideally with China's blessing. The Colonial Government, less than a year after the signing of the Joint Declaration, restructured the Legislative Council in which 10 members were officials and 46 were not. Until then the Governor had appointed everybody but in the summer of 1985 the Government allowed 24 of the 46 "unofficials" to be elected via "functional constituencies", that is, guilds and professional associations.

Once the three of us, Dunn, Lee and myself, sat down with Xu and his two deputies we halted the bantering. Xu immediately launched a tirade against the Hong Kong Government for flouting the Joint Declaration and rushing in a representative system of government. He said the accord had committed the British to govern Hong Kong effectively rather than to let them tinker, experiment and fork administration over to the local people, a job apparently for the Chinese to do according to their time table.

Xu also talked about troop deployment and nationality, issues that riled the Chinese side. He was specially offended by the Commander of the British Forces who suggested in public that Hong Kong should establish its own militia to assist the police, in case of need, to maintain law and order. The Director bristled at the temerity of such a proposal, saying Hong Kong had no need of its own garrison. In the first instance, Xu said, the British should not withdraw their garrison before 1997. After 1997 the People's Liberation Army stationed in Shenzhen could always be summoned to help police the Hong Kong SAR in case of absolute emergency. (Later Deng castigated officials of his who accepted that no PLA troops would be posted in Hong Kong. The supreme leader, and Chairman of the Military Commission, said where China deployed its soldiers inside its own territory was a manifestation of its sovereignty that could never be compromised.)

Xu also opposed the White Paper on the British National (Overseas) travel documents that would offer a new lease to the British Dependent Territories Citizen passports. He felt that the BDTC passport was sufficient for the transitional period and should simply expire in 1997. As for the Hong Kong SAR passport, he suggested that arrangement could be made for the British Hong Kong Government to commence its issue on behalf of the SAR Government a few years before 1997.

Both sides had had these tense but yet also instructive meetings from then on until 1 September 1988 when I retired from the Executive Council. These sessions, however, went from frequent to sporadic. Each time I would faithfully record our impressions and the information gleaned from the talks and report to the Governor.

While the talks sometimes waxed and waned as the subjects changed, the most volatile topic during the early days of the transition remained the political reforms of 1988. By then the Chinese side added another regular attendant to the talks, Li Chuwen, a Deputy Director of Xinhua (now an advisor to the Shanghai Municipal Government). A climax of sorts came in at the meeting on 6 March 1986 when Xu quoted to us the conclusion drawn by the visiting Deputy Director of the Hong Kong and Macao Affairs Office, Lu Ping, who was in Hong Kong about a month ago. Lu was the Secretary General in the early 1980s, then promoted to the Deputy Director in the mid-1980s and in November 1990 to the Director, a post he occupied until his retirement in 1997. Xu said Lu had met and talked with over a thousand people and concluded that the majority did not support direct election.

The Chinese were incensed that the British had provided for more elected legislators in the 1985 White Paper than that stated in the 1984 Green Paper given to them by the British. They were convinced that the crafty British had deceived them, and an insult was added to injury when the other side also advanced the next political review from 1988 to 1987. This, Xu considered, was a unilateral action, which betrayed the spirit of co-operation underscored by the Joint Declaration.

We explained that a Green Paper was merely a consultative document for public discussion. After revision as a result of the consultation process it became a White Paper or a policy document. As there had been many calls for faster democratization, the resultant White Paper was purely a reflection of that popular demand. The next election of the Legislative Council would be in 1988 and the political review had to be advanced to 1987 in order to allow sufficient time for the legislative process.

Soon after the Hong Kong Government published the Green Paper on political reform in May 1987, Xu and his deputy Li Chuwen invited the three of us to a meeting on 25 May at the Stanley Villa compound. The complex consists of six newly built town houses recently bought by Xinhua, which was expanding its presence to cope with its much more divergent work. The Deputy Director said

Plate 3.2 *The author speaking at the Dragon Boat Festival Dinner in London, 1986.*

he had read the latest Green Paper which, while modified to include some Chinese suggestions, was still too radical. Li argued that the appointed members of the Legislative Council had a stabilizing effect on society and should be retained until 1997. In fact, he continued, China would wish to retain some form of the appointment system beyond 1997.

We rebutted their charge by mentioning the Joint Declaration's Annex I, in which it is stated that the legislature of the Hong Kong SAR shall be constituted by elections. There was no way that the appointment system in any form could be retained after 1997. We said the Hong Kong Government was doing no more than the introduction of a gradual democracy so as to provide society and the institutions time to prepare for the eventuality sanctioned in the Joint Declaration.

But our explanation did not sway the implacable Chinese side, which insisted that the speed of democratization should be slowed down. The Hong Kong Authorities eventually yielded to Chinese objection and, with the majority support of the Executive Council, delayed the introduction of direct election to the Legislative Council by three years to 1991. I remember during the discussion we quoted the Chinese slang, "A short sharp pain is preferable to a long-drawn suffering", meaning that if direct election were put off to 1991 there would be an uproar, but it would soon die down. On the other hand, if direct election were introduced in 1988 it would be more difficult and troublesome for the Hong Kong Government to govern in the next few years.

The last time I met the Chinese side in my capacity as the Senior Member of the Executive Council was on 8 June 1988, almost three months before my first retirement. The Director of the Hong Kong and Macao Affairs Office, Ji Pengfei, and his two closest aides,

Li Hou and Lu Ping, happened to be in Hong Kong and joined the talks. We discussed several issues and one of them was about the establishment of the Hong Kong SAR Government. We said, as Executive Councillors, we knew that the British had proposed to the Chinese the way of forming the HKSAR Legislative Council, by permitting those elected in 1995 according to the Basic Law prescriptions to serve through the transition and beyond 1997. We believed this arrangement would ensure continuity and enhance confidence. This was the beginning of the "through train" concept.

Ji replied that in the establishment of the HKSAR, China would observe two basic principles, one was for the country to reassert sovereignty and the other for achieving a smooth transition. He said they wanted as few changes as possible but thought that legislators elected in 1995 would still have to step down from the proverbial train, if only symbolically, and pay obeisance to the new order before re-boarding.

We did not want to dwell exclusively on just one issue and so we shifted the subject, saying we had some concerns about certain articles of the draft Basic Law. We conjured up the scenario of a Hong Kong resident charged with breaching national security and, according to the draft Basic Law, the HKSAR Authorities should arrest and hand him over to the Central Government for trial. We also raised another concern that the HKSAR courts must seek the interpretation of the Basic Law from the Central Government before the court could pass verdicts on questionable areas of the law. Ji said he was aware of these concerns and assured us that he would relay them to the Central Government.

During the period between 1985 and 1988 I met Xu many times but these few mentioned above remain the most vivid and relevant.

Sir Edward's Death — An Omen

Sir Edward Youde, who had sworn in as the 26th Governor of Hong Kong on 20 May 1982, suddenly died in his sleep on 5 December 1986 at the British Embassy in Beijing, working to the very end. His untimely passing struck me, in retrospect, as ominous.

During the greater part of his four and a half years of governorship Hong Kong was in an unsettling state. He was deeply involved in the Sino-British negotiations on the future of Hong Kong and, after the signing of the Joint Declaration, had initiated the difficult work of the transition. Though his tenure was not long, he had won the hearts and minds of the Hong Kong people.

Sir Edward had treated me, his Senior Member of the Executive Council, as a friend and we spoke to each other frequently. One day he told me that, with the Joint Declaration signed, he was able to take a vacation in the summer of 1986, returning to Britain partly to tidy his estate, which he had neglected during the past years. Sir Edward, perhaps with premonition of his death, said he felt much relieved because, having settled the domestic business, he would now be ready to take care of Lady Pamela, whatever happened to him. As always the Governor spoke of his wife with total respect and tenderness.

Sir Edward made history with the Joint Declaration. He also made the same as the first incumbent governor to have died in office. The whole community felt bereaved and the outpouring of grief reflected the affection in which he had been held. More than perhaps he himself had realized, he had woven himself into the fabrics of Hong Kong society, and not just for the elite but, more movingly, for the ordinary people.

On the day of the funeral, 9 December, mourners crowded

Plate 3.3 *The funeral procession of the late Governor Youde, 1986.*

both sides of the sombre street, many weeping, to glimpse at his passing hearse — a converted military jeep covered with a Union Jack. The cortege wended its way slowly down from the Government House at Upper Albert Road, turning into Lower Albert Road, passing through the courtyard of the Central Government Offices, before halting at St. John's Cathedral. Then the church bells tolled — a peal resonant throughout the financial district that had ceased its bustle in his memory.

Sixteen pallbearers carried Sir Edward in his final journey in Hong Kong. Among them were the Chief Justice, the Commander of British Forces, and the past and present male members of the Executive Council who had worked with him. I joined their ranks and during the short but solemn journey I recalled the most momentous times, now filed away. The Queen, the Prime Minister and the Foreign Secretary had sent their condolences as did the Chinese leaders. The Acting Governor, Sir David Akers-Jones read the eulogy in English and I, as the Senior Member of the Executive Council, did the honour in Chinese. Lydia Dunn, the Senior Member of the Legislative Council, rendered an evocative reading of "In Praise of Famous Men".

Sir Edward was returned to his native Wales for burial but his spirit remained in Hong Kong with us and in the public consciences. The *Ming Pao* in an editorial on 6 December 1986 compared the late Governor to the great statesman in the Three Kingdoms period, Zhuge Liang, who had pledged to work diligently on state affairs until death. Whilst the scales of their responsibility — Sir Edward with Hong Kong and Zhuge with China — differed, the substance of the men was the same for which the apt words are "total dedication". I share the editorial's sentiment to this date.

Sir Edward's Vision

While Hong Kong was engrossed in the Sino-British negotiations and their slings and arrows, Sir Edward Youde had another preoccupation, which was a mark of his vision. The Governor concentrated on the future, even though that proved tragically short for him personally, not only with the Joint Declaration but also with the technological and economic transformation of society. His foresight would serve Hong Kong well as his part in the Sino-British talks did in another way.

Throughout the 1950s and 1960s the territory was suffering from the lack of technicians to meet the growing needs of the booming manufacturing sector. The Government in 1968 therefore established the Polytechnic Planning Committee to explore the idea of a

Polytechnic and appointed the Executive Councillor and Chairman of South Sea Textiles, Tang Ping-yuan, to chair it. I, as the head of the Federation of Industries and a Legislative Councillor, was drafted to be the Committee's second in command. Unfortunately, Tang died two years later, just weeks before the Committee could complete its report. We who were in it out of respect for the late chairman did not fill the vacancy while finishing the submission. The report advocated for the Polytechnic which was then incorporated in July 1972 with me chairing its governing board and the industrialist and legislator, James Wu, as the deputy. The Polytechnic graduated into a university in 1993 and is flourishing in its centrally-located Hunghom campus in Kowloon.

The export-driven manufacturing sector prospered right into the 1970s, accounting for a third of the gross domestic product, bringing wealth to Hong Kong and fuelling the property boom. The Polytechnic expanded spectacularly, enrolling more than 10,000 full-time students by then, but still it could not cope with the rising demand. The Government in 1982 appointed the Polytechnic Governing Board to form another Planning Committee to consider a sister institution, which I chaired with the legislator cum Hong Kong Electric General Manager, Chen Shou-lum, as the vice-chairman. To cope with the urgent need a decision was made for the second polytechnic, known at the time as City polytechnic, to enrol students in 1984 in a temporary campus at the newly completed Argyle Centre in Mongkok. The City Polytechnic later moved into its purposely-built campus in Kowloon Tong and in the early 1990s was upgraded into the City University of Hong Kong.

Towards the end of the 1970s China opened its door to the outside world and implemented its economic reform. Later it established a Special Economic Zone in Shenzhen, adjacent to Hong

Plate 3.4 *The Hong Kong Polytechnic, 1986.*

Kong and based, in part, on the Hong Kong model. Shenzhen had the advantages of ample and cheap land and labour at a tenth of those in Hong Kong. This of course was extremely attractive to the Hong Kong based export-oriented labour-intensive manufacturing industries. When Britain and China inked the Joint Declaration in December 1984 the boundaries between Hong Kong and Shenzhen began to blur. Sir Edward foresaw Hong Kong and the Mainland symbiosis and knew the territory had to face a paradigm shift by replacing the exiting, senescent industries. He would do his part to usher in the high-tech revolution. The Governor in Council in September 1985 asked the University and Polytechnic Grants Committee (now the University Grants Committee) to explore the feasibility of a third university after the Chinese University and the University of Hong Kong.

In March 1986 the Executive Council received the positive report of the Grants Committee and the need for such a varsity was by then beyond doubt. This proposed University of Science and Technology (UST) would have to be different from its two predecessors and its suggested cachet was a focus on science and technology, as its name implied, plus management and postgraduate training. Sir Edward tapped me to chair the UST Planning Committee and the legislator for the Engineering Functional Constituency, Cheng Hon-kwan, as the number two. The Governor had a keen interest in the UST and consulted with me often about its progress. Though the terms of reference for the Planning Committee were for the varsity to admit the first batch of students in September 1994, this was still not soon enough for Sir Edward, who wished the project could proceed faster to meet Hong Kong's technological demands. He hoped that I could find some ways to speed up the work of the Planning Committee.

Plate 3.5 *The 15th Anniversary of the City University of Hong Kong, 1999.*

The Royal Hong Kong Jockey Club (now without the "Royal") shared the view of the Government and trumped up HK$2 billion for the construction. The building of the campus under the able supervision of the Jockey Club took an impressive short time of three years, considering all the complications and architectural revisions. The UST began enrolment in September 1991, three years earlier than the original target, accepting the initial batch of 600 students for the phase one of the campus. The inaugural class of graduate students completed their studies in 1993.

From the onset the UST boasted a renowned faculty and, within a decade, was deemed by the *Asia Week* magazine in year 2000 as one of the ten finest universities in Asia, situated in a scenic cove of the Clear Water Bay. The actual ranking was number seven. In the following year, its Business School was ranked by the *Financial Times* newspaper in London as the top in Asia and 48th in the world. This was no mean achievement indeed. The credit must go to the founding President, Professor Woo Chia-wei, a celebrated physicist in his own right and the first ever ethnic Chinese president of a major American varsity, San Francisco State University with an enrolment of 25,000 students.

Sir Edward's vision was thus fulfilled with a university having its mission specified by the Governor in Council as "To advance learning and knowledge through teaching and research, particularly, (1) in science, technology, engineering, management and business studies; and (2) at the postgraduate level; and to assist in the economic and social development of Hong Kong."

A good start, though, does not necessarily imply a smooth sailing thereafter. Policy and execution must be complimentary to

Plate 3.6 *The Hong Kong University of Science & Technology, 1995.*

each other and people involved must share the same goal and vision in order to achieve an overall success. Regrettably, the University Grants Committee has since strayed from the principle of giving priority to need and values, but instead, allocated funds "equitably" to all the varsities. Consequently, the UST was not able to offer more places at postgraduate level in the past years as its mission stipulated. This, to me, is unfortunate and a retrograde policy that has caused Hong Kong to further lag behind the competition in advanced science and technology.

Myth of the UST Cost Overrun

Since I have mentioned Sir Edward Youde's vision in establishing the University of Science and Technology, it would be appropriate for me, as someone caught up in the imbroglio from day one, to deal with the so-called "cost overrun" in the building of the UST campus.

The Director of Audit in 1991 alleged massive cost overrun. His charge was misleading and based on a false premise. During that year Hong Kong introduced for the first time direct geographical election into the Legislative Council. Budding politicians took the opportunity to play up the controversy and attacked the establishment. The UST and those involved in its building thus became the scapegoat in this political drama.

Back in June 1986 the UST Planning Committee was established and chaired by me with Cheng Hon-kwan as the deputy. We conducted a campus design competition and, in November 1987, handed over one of the winning designs, Dr. Simon Kwan's architectural plan for the Clear Water Bay campus, to the Royal Hong Kong Jockey Club (RHKJC) for cost estimation. Earlier the Jockey Club had pledged to donate HK$1.5 billion to the project and, for that reason, was appointed by the Hong Kong Government as the Project Manager responsible for supervising the construction of the campus. At about the same time the University Planning Committee and the Jockey Club also jointly formed a Campus Project Management Committee headed by the Chairman of the Jockey Club, Sir Gordon MacWhinnie, to co-ordinate the efforts of the two bodies. The RHKJC's Chief Executive, Major General Guy Watkins, was designated supervisor of the day to day operations of the project.

The costs for the phases one and two of the UST campus were then estimated to be HK$1.93 billion, inflation included. This "estimate" was based on Dr. Kwan's architectual plan but using the unit cost incurred in building the City Polytechnic campus at that time. There was no budget *per se*, only rough figures that acted as a guideline. The Government, nonetheless, quoted this most preliminary estimate when it approached the Legislative Council Finance Committee on 4 May 1988 for funding approval before it could accept the Jockey Club's donation. The Administration also assured the legislators that it would make up the difference if the project costs exceeded the Jockey Club's donation.

What no one could have anticipated at that time was that construction costs would inflate by 150 per cent within three years from 1987 to 1989 because of the property boom and the fast-rising inflation in Hong Kong. By the end of 1989 when the RHKJC was ready to receive tenders, it noticed with alarm the high cost escalation.

Concurrently Professor Woo Chia-wei, the designated President, took up his post in 1988 and together with his teams of American academic consultants studied the design, scope and scale of the campus. They found great inadequacies in both academic and research space for a tertiary institution specializing in science

Plate 3.7 *A bird's-eye view of the Hong Kong University of Science & Technology, 2000.*

and technology and emphasizing research and postgraduate teaching. The architects and other experts had to rush in, to reconfigure and expand the building area. The Government, after consulting the University and Polytechnic Grants Committee, agreed to this expansion and submitted to the Finance Committee of the Legislative Council on 1 June 1990 the "budget" of HK$3.548 billion, again including inflation. At the same time the RHKJC had raised its donation to $1.96 billion. Legislators, after pondering the explanation for the large increase in the "budget" over the earlier "estimate", eventually approved the budget of $3.548 billion without any objection. Martin Lee was the only legislator abstained in voting. At the time, June 1990, the campus construction had only just started with the laying of the foundation and was much too soon to conclude what the final costs would be.

The Director of Audit in his report of October 1991 compared the 1990 "budget" of $3.548 billion with the 1988 "estimate" of $1.93 billion, and called it "a huge cost overrun". This was a sensational charge, which affected public confidence in the UST.

Construction work for the phases one and two of the UST campus continued and completed on schedule in the middle of 1993 for $3.244 billion, some $304 million, or 8.6 per cent, less than the approved budget. There has never been any cost overrun. The generally accepted definition of cost overrun is the actual construction cost incurred exceeding the budgeted cost, and not the budgeted cost exceeding the estimated cost.

The whole plan for the UST campus was vindicated eventually by Anthony Walker, Professor of Surveying at the University of Hong Kong. In his book published in 1994 titled *Building the Future*, he analysed in depth the UST project and drew a number of conclusions. Two of these were particularly relevant. One was that the unit cost of the UST campus was broadly comparable to those similarly scaled buildings in Hong Kong at that time. The second was that the university campus represented reasonable value for money, that is, it did not cost more than it should have.

In passing I would like to mention that in 1999 the architecture design of the UST campus became an entry into the Contemporary Chinese Architectural Art Exhibition in Beijing and won an Innovative Art Award.

One of the major objectives of both the UST Planning Committee and later the Governing Council was to make the UST one of the world's first class research universities and, to this end, it simply had to have adequate funding for campus facilities. The beneficiary would be the younger generations and Hong Kong as a whole. No matter how one looks at this particular issue of the so called "cost overrun", a phrase against which I resent, no one could deny all the money spent was proper and for the good of the University and the younger generation. The SAR Chief Executive, Tung Chee-hwa, in his second Policy Address in 1998 emphasized the significance of science and technology for the future of Hong Kong. The UST will no doubt continue to contribute to this transformation of the community; and for this, we have to be thankful to the late Sir Edward Youde for his wisdom and foresight.

Basic Law Conundrum

Drafting the Basic Law was a monumental enterprise entailing a complexity even more baffling than that had confronted the pioneering American Constitution framers in Philadelphia in the torrid summer of 1778. This was what someone familiar with the American process had told me, which was probably true. The thirteen colonies of the United States, having expelled the British, had basically a blank sheet of parchment on which to jot down their rules and aspirations.

Those from the Mainland and Hong Kong who partook in the exercise had to observe the guidelines of the Chinese Constitution, the Joint Declaration, and also the prevailing conditions and traditions of the territory. The State Council of the Chinese National People's Congress (NPC) began the exercise by naming 58 members to the Basic Law Drafting Committee (BLDC), comprising approximately equal numbers from the Mainland and the territory. Those from the Mainland side were chosen for their political status and knowledge of the Chinese Constitution. Whereas those so selected from Hong Kong were picked for their public standing, patriotic credential, expertise, and understanding of what made the territory tick.

The NPC deputized these 58 in July 1985 and a few months later nominated 180 to the Basic Law Consultative Committee (BLCC) so that these individuals of prominence could advise the drafters. In the beginning a lot of time was spent in thrashing out the procedures, then in 1986 the structure of the Basic Law was decided. Specialized groups were established to facilitate discussion, and by the second half of 1987 they resolved and compiled 57 specialized reports that would form the skeleton of the draft Basic Law. The drafters then pored over the points, editing line by line, agonizing over semantics and syntax, before publishing the first draft in 1988 for public consultation, which drew about 72,000 responses. Having collated these views, they returned to the drawing board and churned out the second draft that was pruned of some of the earlier inconsistencies and contradictions before giving the public another chance to react in 1989, attracting this time over 6,000 comments. At this stage the Mainland had experienced one of the worst upheavals

Plate 3.8 *The Swearing-in Ceremony for Governor Sir David Wilson, 1987.*

in recent memory that culminated in the soldiers clearing the Tiananmen Square of protesters and squatters while Hong Kong had gone from euphoria, empathy and despair over that student movement.

Set against this dramatic backdrop, with several Hong Kong drafters resigning, the Basic Law was finally promulgated on 4 April 1990 at the third session of the Seventh NPC Plenum. This Basic Law is a covenant between the Special Administrative Region (SAR) and the Chinese People's Republic. It has specific and explicit clauses safeguarding the Hong Kong SAR's capitalist economy, Common Law jurisprudence and financial system as well as the freedoms of association, religion, expression, property ownership and demonstration. These guarantees appear especially remarkable considering what had transpired on the Mainland in 1989 and the system that still continues up north.

Throughout the period of the Basic Law drafting the British Hong Kong Government was not a passive observer to the proceedings. On the contrary, the Authorities contributed to the Basic Law by co-operating with China and passing relevant information as well as technical advice to the drafters through the Sino-British Joint Liaison Group (JLG). This was done in the spirit of mutual assistance and confidence.

Whilst the Annex I to the Joint Declaration had outlined in reasonably details on many areas and systems, nonetheless, the text on the political system for the SAR was not, as it lacked depth and suffered from excessive latitude. This can be seen in the Sub-section I of Annex I to the Joint Declaration, which is reproduced below:

> "The government and legislature of the Hong Kong Special Administrative Region shall be composed of local inhabitants. The chief executive of the Hong Kong Special Administrative

> Region shall be selected by election or through consultations held locally and be appointed by the Central People's Government. Principal officials (equivalent to Secretaries) shall be nominated by the chief executive of the Hong Kong Special Administrative Region and appointed by the Central People's Government. The legislature of the Hong Kong Special Administrative Region shall be constituted by elections. The executive authorities shall abide by the law and shall be accountable to the legislature."

China, not being democratic, did not have the experience and expertise to draft the political system. On the other hand, the Chinese also did not trust the British to craft a governing system for the SAR. The drafter from the Mainland, who tended to be more conservative, and those from Hong Kong, who tended to be more liberal, wrangled furiously over the issue, especially the methods of election for the Chief Executive and the legislature. The 1989 tempest on the Mainland just aggravated the disputes, prompting several drafters to quit in protest.

The British had as a custom left their colonies with democratic political systems very similar to the Westminster model but without the appointed House of Lords to perform the initial checks and balances on the directly elected legislature. Such an exit was thought by the enlightened in the United Kingdom to be a gift to the natives. However I regret to say how many of these former colonies did not flourish with democracy that was immature, that was hasty, and that did not have time to take root in the community. These newly independent countries subsequently lapsed back into nepotistic rule or tyranny, if not anarchy. My caution offended those who had suddenly awaken to the virtues of democracy and could not get enough of it. But then the truth is more often than not a hard and bitter medicine.

I have often cited Britain as an example of how successful democracy had to evolve rather than be grafted on in one go. The United Kingdom, which describes its legislature as "the Mother of Parliaments", still has the Queen appoint people to the House of Lords to check and balance the Commons. The Lords only lost their veto power in 1911 and even today they still have the power to delay the Commons passing their bills. The implicit message is that the country requires some sterling individuals — not only peers but also statesmen and persons who have succeeded in other endeavours — to temper the populist zeal of politicians with eyes fixed on the polls rather than the national interest.

The former Executive and Legislative Councillor, Lo Tak-shing, a learned Oxford graduate and lawyer, in his capacity as the BLCC member, advocated a bicameral system similar to that in the United Kingdom only to have his wise counsel rejected. Nonetheless, the Basic Law drafters eventually conjured up a format of separate voting for the SAR legislature. The current practice is that motions and bills initiated by members themselves could only be passed if these had the majority support of the two sets of legislators — one lot for the functional constituencies and the other basically for the geographical and directly elected constituencies. Such a beast, odd looking as it may be, actually gets the work done. A donkey it may be but it has earned its fodder. A bicameral system the SAR may not have in name but has in fact.

Democracy in Gestation

The Basic Law drafters eventually reached a compromise after years of haggling on the political system for Hong Kong, the Special Administrative Region under the Chinese Constitution. They decided not to emulate the British but rather to follow the American example with allowances for the uniqueness of the territory, whose only political experience had been colonial autonomy with minor concessions to the will of the people.

Democracy takes various forms, some of which are hybrids and none is static. But in the English speaking world two main formats prevail — one is the British Westminster model and the other is the American presidential cum congressional paradigm.

Most former British colonies initially adopted by default the British example without an appointed upper house, which Hong Kong had made a calculation to avoid as the result of Chinese initiative during the Sino-British negotiations. Back home the British entrust power to the elected House of Commons checked in turn by the appointed House of Lords. The party, which holds the majority of seats in the House of Commons, forms the government, whose nucleus is the cabinet. Should a party fail to secure an absolute majority, it may cobble together a coalition, which, by nature, is wobbly. (Some countries opt for preferential voting that may go several rounds until a clear winner is elected. The British stay with the "first past the post" system of election, even though some people, particularly the Liberal Party, are advocating "proportional representation".)

A British ruling party is totally powerful — despite ritual deference to the Constitutional Monarch and the House of Lords. This power is manifest through patronage, the votes it commands in the Commons, and an apolitical, obedient civil service. There have been calls in the United Kingdom from time to time to abolish the House of Lords or, short of that, the deprivation of their residual right to delay legislation, thus reducing that chamber into simply a talk shop.

The Prime Minister has the authority to ask the Queen to

Plate 3.9 *The Hong Kong Executive Council, 1987.*

dissolve the Parliament and call fresh elections, usually when he thinks his popularity has reached zenith and the opposition is in disarray, with of course the symbolic consent of Her Majesty the Queen. Quite often elections are declared after reading the new budget in which the voters are nicely "bribed".

The American system is one of rigorous checks and balances, at least on paper, and the credit for that must go to the framers of the Constitution with their abiding distrust in absolute authority. The result is that more often than not the president may be from one party and the majority in the Congress from another. The Congress is in turn divided into the House of Representatives, with geographical constituencies determined more or less by population, and the Senate, with each state, large or small, serving up a pair who, again, may be of opposing parties. Thus rivalry is institutionalized and power is not monopolized.

The governance of the U.S. is separated into the executive and legislative branches as well as being monitored by the judicial branch in which the Supreme Court alone can interpret the Constitution and its verdict is final. Some are saying after the most recent (year 2000) presidential electoral fiasco, in which the Supreme Court ruled in favour of President George W. Bush, all the three pillars have become politicized.

The president's party seldom holds the majority in the Congress and even if it did dissenters are many and the whips may not get them in line for controversial issues. The head of the State can veto legislation, a power that may be overturned by two thirds majority in the Senate which in turn exercises a similar restraint on the House of Representatives.

The U.S. also staggered its congressional and presidential elections, unlike the British who have theirs in one go. The timing of these elections is not according to the expediency of party politics as is the case in the United Kingdom but according to a constitutionally stipulated calendar of quadrennial balloting.

The American governance would be impeded in perpetual stalemates if not, however, for the president's stature and power of persuasion. President Bill Clinton faced a hostile Congress for much of his two terms of office and yet got most of his bills passed and policies adopted. This is because, like his predecessors, he had the political skills to coax his opponents along. Congress often postured but eventually caved in to the pressure and to the fear of reprisal from a disenchanted electorate. The incumbent President, George W. Bush, like the previous Presidents, such as Ronald Reagan and George Bush Senior, has to deal with skilfully an opposition controlled Congress which was testament to the success of their system.

The Basic Law of the Hong Kong SAR opted more or less for the American model but with some elements modified to suit our own requirements. The following are some of the salient features of the SAR political set up:

(1) The Chief Executive and the legislators have different terms of office and are mostly not elected in the same year. This is similar to the U.S. system.

(2) When a legislator accepts a government appointment and becomes a public official, he would have to renounce his seat. This again is similar to the U.S. system with separation of power between the executive and legislative branches.

(3) The time of elections in the SAR is basically fixed as in the U.S., rather than subject to political timing.

(4) Unlike the British Prime Minister, the SAR Chief Executive can only serve two terms of 5 years each, which is similar to the U.S. system of term limits.
(5) The Chief Executive, similar to the American President, can veto legislation unless two-thirds majority in the legislature overturns it.
(6) The SAR electoral systems are totally different from those practised by both the American and British.
(7) The standing orders and procedures of meetings are different from both the British and American practices. One significant difference is that the SAR officials, who are not legislators and have no vote, are the only ones allowed moving bills and motions for the Administration.

It is therefore obvious that the future development of the Hong Kong SAR political system should basically be in the following three areas:

(1) The method of electing the Chief Executive;
(2) The composition and voting system for the legislature;
(3) The standing orders and procedures for the operation of the legislature.

Another Chinese Invitation

The Basic Law Consultative Committee was formed in the latter part of 1985 to assist the Basic Law Drafting Committee. It had to include a broad range of people to give it both credibility and visibility, qualities which could be tapped in the Executive and Legislative Councils. It is therefore not surprising that some of the Councillors received invitations to join. Lydia Dunn had just taken over from Sir Roger Lobo as the Senior Member of the Legislative Council.

Since Lydia Dunn and I were then Senior Members of the two respective Councils, we naturally got a call. The two of us, with the invitations in hand, then pondered the request from the Chinese Government for several days, just as I had the entreaty for me to participate in the Chinese People's Political Consultative Conference in 1982, only to have me refuse the honour.

Dunn and I agreed that since we were both senior advisors to the Hong Kong Governor and were privy to sensitive documents, including papers pertaining to Sino-British relations, we might diminish our roles were we to join the BLCC. Even though at that time, in 1985/86, the relations between the two countries were cordial, neither of us could preclude any possible conflict or contention in the future. If there were any leak of classified information one day, however inadvertent, the blame for that would rest with us and affect our public standing. Much as we wanted to contribute to the Basic Law, we finally resisted.

The decision of ours has somehow leaked to the press and led to public discussion for a while. It has also prompted the *South China Morning Post* to pen a gratifying editorial titled "The Wooing of Mr. Xu Jiatun" on 5 March 1986 praising our wisdom. The commentary read in part:

> "Indeed one reason why Sir S. Y. Chung and Miss Lydia Dunn have not joined the advisors on the Basic Law could be that they do not wish to associate themselves with a move which could ultimately undermine the body they now represent. Their position is to serve Hong Kong's interests today and they do that by not compromising the institutions they represent and with which they are likely to be associated for several more years.
>
> "If they were seen to be hedging their bets people might well wonder whether they could continue to be effective represen-

tatives fighting for the retention of the system that Hong Kong has devised and which it hopes to carry into the next phase of its existence.

"Sir S. Y. Chung and Miss Dunn were right to stand apart and indeed will be respected more, both by Chinese representatives and the people of Hong Kong for not taking their place on the Basic Law bandwagon. The Basic Law has to come, but they are in a better position to advise and recommend from outside its ranks than inside. Certainly they will be heard with greater respect."

Period of Distrust

The Shock from Tiananmen

Just as the public was evaluating the second draft of the Basic Law, trouble brewed in Tiananmen Square. I noticed right away that both Britain and the Hong Kong Government had deviated from their earlier, sensible position of not aiding and abetting forces hostile to the Communist Authorities on the Mainland. The change alarmed sober thinking people who accepted that the security of Hong Kong rested in part in not meddling in the domestic affairs of China. This condition was true long before the Communist ascendancy, and the neutrality had allowed the Chinese Governments of whatever ideology to tolerate a British colony on their sovereign soil.

The event that led to the Chinese national tragedy and the confidence crisis in Hong Kong began with death in April 1989 of the former Chinese Communist Party General Secretary, Hu Yaobang. The late leader had won over some in the country by his liberal thinking. He was specially revered for his refusal two years

Plate 3.10 *A rally held in May 1989 at Statue Square in support of the student movement in Beijing.*

earlier to quell university student demonstrations over dismal dorm conditions. His death was mourned and it also became a catalyst for the expression of mass discontent.

Students, who had been spared the wrath of the Government because of his intervention, expressed their deepest grief and also outrage against the party elders. They thronged the cenotaph at Tiananmen and draped the shrine to the heroes of the revolution with a mount of wreathes, refusing to disperse when ordered to do so. The mourners-turned protestors demanded that not only the party restore Hu posthumously to the pantheon of revolutionary martyrs but also tackle corruption and promote democratic reform as the dead General Secretary had sought. They were determined to defy the Government and finish the business of Hu.

Many in Hong Kong who had been watching the drama being played out on local television, which gave the unfolding story ubiquitous coverage, began to sympathize with the students in Beijing. Many Hong Kong people had been victims of the Communist Government and were particularly supportive of the anti-government movement. Then the support-student movement started and quickly spread to the streets leading to the first major demonstration of a million people on 21 May. Xinhua headquarters in Happy Valley was the focus of the fury. Each time the Government up north upped the tempo of its rhetoric, the demonstrations intensified in Hong Kong. The cycle kept escalating and there was now no way for either side to back down.

The Communist Politburo met and then in late May denounced the demonstrators after the virtual ouster of Premier Zhao Ziyang who had proposed a compromise. The development ignited an already combustible situation as the students in Beijing intensified their campaign, drawing supporters in from the factories and countryside as well as arousing tremendous fever in Hong Kong. Calls for donations rang out and were immediately answered as ordinary people gave cash and contributed two hundred new and beautiful red and blue tents. This material support arrived in Beijing on the eve when the students were preparing to leave Tiananmen on the following day, thus reversing their earlier decision and prolonging the siege. A Hong Kong unionist and an engineering graduate, Lee Cheuk-yan, was one of those who ferried supplies and money to the Tiananmen squatters. Security Bureau agents arrested Lee and confiscated, he claimed, over one million dollars cash before releasing him after several days in detention and signing a confession.

The troops, after two abortive attempts to clear the square peacefully, on the night of 4 June finally advanced into the symbolic centre of China and drove out the reeling demonstrators. The footage of carnage shocked Hong Kong into a serious depression and another rally of a million people, now in grief, poured onto the streets. They now stared into their future, to the date of reckoning of 1 July 1997, as they would stare into the abyss.

Until the spring of 1989 the Colonial Administration had sedulously curbed activities that might be construed as provocative or subversive against the Mainland Authorities by whatever name. I was told that the British at the turn of the twentieth century even banished Dr. Sun Yat-sen, the father of the Republic, from the colony at the behest of the Qing Government. I also know from my own experience the Hong Kong Special Branch in the 1970s routinely detained and deported without trial suspected agents and provocateurs from Taiwan numbering about ten a year at the approval of the Governor in Council. The draconian decree against outside agitators was the way for Hong Kong to ward off interference from the Chinese Government and it worked.

I had retired from the Executive Council just under a year before the Tiananmen incident but I remained focussed on what was happening up north and down here. I detected the Government's shift of policy against others using Hong Kong as a staging post for conspiracy against China in May 1989. The editor Wang Bingzhang of the ardently anti-Communist publication *China Spring*, circulated overseas among the exiles, came to Hong Kong and gave a televised interview in which he slanted the Communists and discussed how to support the Tiananmen students. To me such provocation was very alarming. I then approached Governor Sir David Wilson to ask him if he had known about the incident. Sir David, previously a political advisor to Governor Lord MacLehose in the late 1970s, said he had been on vacation when the *China Spring* editor stormed through Hong Kong. I approached Sir Run-run Shaw, Chairman of the Television Broadcast to obtain a copy of the news interview and sent it to Sir David at the Government House. A few days later I saw the Governor and queried him why a visa had been issued to a known anti-Communist person of such a high profile. The Governor said the visa was not issued by the Hong Kong Government but rather by the British Embassy in the U.S.A. Nonetheless I was surprised that Wang's name was not on the stop list in the Immigration Department, and expressed my concern to the Governor. I urged Sir David not to let Hong Kong abandon its long-held policy of neutrality that had served Hong Kong so well.

The Tiananmen affairs not only mortified the public faced with reunification eight years away but it also prompted the Unofficial Members of the Executive and Legislative Councils to try to revive confidence in Hong Kong with two proposals to the British Government. The UMELCO first wanted to appeal to the United Kingdom to let in the three million Hong Kong-born British nationals, a right of residency denied by a series of immigration and nationality acts of the British Parliament in the 1960/70s. The UMELCO organized a delegation, which went to London during June 1989 to lobby both the British Government and the Members of the Parliament.

The UMELCO would also request that Britain speed up democratic reform, specifically by revising the White Paper on Representative Government by doubling the proposed number of directly elected seats in the Legislative Council to 20 in 1991. They further advocated total direct elections by 1995, regardless of Chinese objections. The two Senior Members of the UMELCO, Dame Lydia Dunn (who was awarded a D.B.E. in the 1989 New Year) and Allen Lee went to London in early 1990 to lobby the British Prime Minister, Margaret Thatcher, who had signed the Joint Declaration of 1984 for the return of the territory to China.

I remember on 5 July 1989 Dunn and Lee invited me to lunch at the Mandarin Hotel to thrash out a strategy to buoy confidence and mitigate the damages done by the Tiananmen incident. Both were less cautious than I was as I counselled them against abandoning Hong Kong's historic neutrality towards Chinese politics and explained that the demonstrations in Beijing were much more than a simple student movement. It was, in my assessment, a part of the Communist Party power struggle. Were Hong Kong to continue to meddle in China's affairs, it would provoke a reaction and jeopardize the future for most people who would have no choice than to stay in the territory. I continued to explain that even if the forces against the Chinese Government were successful this time, what about the next time? I also doubted that the British Government would ever allow in three million refugees from Hong Kong, given the UMELCO's own experience in May 1984. Finally I advised Dunn and Lee to resist the temptation of a harder stance and, instead, to appeal to the people to calm down and watch the development with fewer emotions. The head must rule the heart.

In the end I was unable to sway Dunn and Lee. They held firm to their opinion. Lee later told me that they both did faithfully relate to their colleagues at the UMELCO my views, which nonetheless were rejected, as my former associates courted disaster without even knowing the implications.

Seeds of Confrontation

During the years of 1989 and 1990 the Unofficial Members of the Executive and Legislative Councils focussed on selling the package of right of abode and faster democratic reform to Britain to help restore the flagging confidence in Hong Kong. They were successful in the short run, having convinced Britain in December 1989 to issue 50,000 full family passports that benefited between 200,000 and 300,000 individuals. Even here the victory was pyrrhic since these passports were given only to the elite — senior civil servants, prominent businessmen and professionals — and denied to the majority of the residents. The inherent discriminatory quota only aggravated class tensions.

The British Government also succumbed to the UMELCO lobbying by expanding the number of directly elected seats in Legislative Council for 1991 from 10 to 18 and raising that total again to 20 by 1995, above and beyond what the Basic Law had earlier prescribed as the proper pace of reform. Even such concessions failed to appease some proponents of democracy.

I felt, as satisfying as these achievements were for the UMELCO, the strong pressure exerted by the UMELCO for accelerating the process of democratization could actually sow the seeds of confrontation between China and Britain in later years (1992 to 1997) to the detriment of Hong Kong. The British Prime Minister, Margaret Thatcher, in her memoirs, *The Downing Street Years* published in 1993, recalled that in 1990, her final year in power, how her Government had come under strong pressure, from what I gather she meant the UMELCO, to accelerate the process of democratization in Hong Kong. Her political instincts, still not rusty even as her enemies closed in on the "Iron Lady", told her that 1990 was the wrong time for any rift or row with China. She felt that the leaders in Beijing were extremely nervous, if not paranoid. She decided that Britain would need to wait for calmer times before making moves for faster democratization in Hong Kong.

The actual words as contained on page 495 of her book are:

> "So in 1990 we legislated to give British citizenship to 50,000 key people in the Colony and their dependants.... We were also brought under strong pressure immediately to accelerate the process of democratization in Hong Kong. There were, in any case, strong moral arguments for doing so. But all my instincts told me this was the wrong time. The Chinese leadership was feeling acutely apprehensive. Such a step at that moment could have provoked a strong defensive reaction that might have undermined the Hong Kong Agreement. We need to wait for calmer times before considering moves towards democratization within the scope of the agreement."

Thinking back, I suspect the Prime Minister's calculations had contributed to the recall of the more accommodating Governor, Sir David Wilson, and the appointment of someone less accommodating, more vocal and aggressive, someone by the name of Christopher Patten, even though that decision was made by her successor, John Major.

The Third Chinese Invitation

China in 1991 has learned a lesson from the British over the airport imbroglio and would not be so gullible again. There were also rumours that Britain was going to replace the incumbent Governor with a more aggressive person. Thirdly the year 1997 was approaching and China would need more support from the local people for a smooth transfer of power from the British to the Chinese. These considerations, I believe, were the spur behind China appointing the local people as its advisors on Hong Kong affairs.

Lu Ping, formerly Secretary General and later Deputy Director, has since November 1990 become the Director of the State Council's Hong Kong and Macao Affairs Office. He was visiting Hong Kong in early 1992 and on 11 January attended a dinner hosted for him at the Island Shangri-la Hotel by the Business and Professionals Federation of Hong Kong (BPF). I was then a member of the Federation's Advisory Council and had earlier accompanied a delegation led by its Chairman, Vincent Lo, to Beijing. Lo during the drafting of the Basic Law was a prominent member of the Basic Law Consultative Committee leading a group of young businessmen and professionals. In 1990 members of this group formed themselves into the BPF headed by Lo, who is the owner of the Shui On Group of Companies dealing with property development and building construction. At the banquet I was sitting next to Lu and during our discussion the Director told me that China would appoint a small group of advisors on Hong Kong affairs and would like me to join.

I had previously turned down two Chinese invitations. The first was an invitation to the Chinese People's Political Consultative Conference in 1982, and, the second, an invitation in 1985 to serve on the BLCC. The reason was that, back then, as the Senior Member

Plate 3.11 *Visit of the Business and Professionals Federation of Hong Kong to Beijing, 1993.*

of the Executive Council, I dreaded a potential conflict of roles. By 1992 the situation was different, as I no longer had such misgivings, having retired from the Executive Council three and a half years ago. I had also retired from active business and owned no interest on the Mainland. The Joint Declaration was more than seven years old and the future of Hong Kong had been mapped out. I also realized, at the age of 75, I might not have long to go but still wanted to serve Hong Kong.

Like the previous occasions I mulled over the invitation and, unlike the last two times, accepted the challenge. This prompted some critics to deride and decry my decision, calling me all sorts of colourful names. I brushed off these slurs and insults because my conscience was clear. When I had embarked on the public service, I had never considered myself as an agent of the British or, later, of the Chinese Governments because my loyalty was always to my native Hong Kong.

On 3 March 1992 the Chinese Government announced the appointment of 44 Hong Kong Affairs Advisors to the Hong Kong and Macao Affairs Office and the Hong Kong Branch of Xinhua News Agency for a term of two years effective from 12 March 1992. China later added three more batches of advisors until we numbered 186. The appointments were later renewed until 30 June 1997. The induction for the first batch took place in Beijing on 11 March at the Great Hall of the People with a grand ceremony presided over by Premier Li Peng. The event was televised in Hong Kong which again got tongues wagging that somehow I had "changed sides", a charge that was as juvenile as it was wrong.

We, advisors to China, were not an organization. We served in our individual capacity. We were free to speak our minds. So as an advisor I, on 1 June 1992, sent a dissertation of over 7,000 characters to Lu of HKMAO and Zhou Nan, Director of HKXNA. This discourse entitled "Sze-yuen Chung's Views on Hong Kong's Political System", was my first written submission to the Chinese Government. The essay was divided into nine sections:

(1) Hong Kong's post-war political development.
(2) Western political models.
(3) The value of political parties in a democracy.
(4) The political system in the Basic Law.
(5) An analysis of the electoral results in the Hong Kong SAR.
(6) Similarities and differences between the HKSAR and U.S. political systems.
(7) Trends of political reform in Hong Kong.
(8) How British HKG would govern HK during the latter part of the transition.
(9) Conclusion.

Lu Ping on 27 July 1992 sent me a reply, commented thus:

"The paper on political systems has made a study of the history of Hong Kong's political development, its present situation, and also a comparison with those of the West. You have made valuable research into the subject. Many of the constructive suggestions in your paper are meaningful and can assist in effecting a smooth transition and efficient transfer of administration as well as upholding of stability and prosperity of Hong Kong. This paper is a good reference for our work. I thank you and welcome you continue offer your valuable opinions."

During the ensuing five years till the hand-over in July 1997, I had altogether made a total of 15 written submissions to both Lu Ping of HKMAO and Zhou Nan of HKXNA.

Airport Turbulence

That the territory needed a new airport to replace Kai Tak was sounded as far back as in the 1970s as jumbo jet travel came of age. The Hong Kong Government, however, kept postponing the inevitable, despite increasing complaints against the noise in the middle of a densely populated residential area as well as increasing concerns on the growing air traffic congestion.

The decision about building the new airport was actually one of the two major measures by which the Government in October 1989 hoped to bolster confidence in the territory after the Tiananmen incident in Beijing. Governor Sir David Wilson in his annual Policy Address of that autumn proposed doubling the first-year first-degree places at universities and polytechnics to about 15,000 in 1995 or 18 per cent of the relevant age group of 17 to 20. The Government also committed itself of spending about HK$127 billion on a replacement airport at Chek Lap Kok on Lantau Island. It would be a two-runway airport capable to operate 24 hours a day. When completed it would be able to handle 80 million passengers a year, which was three times the capacity at Kai Tak. The new airport was scheduled to open the first of the two runways by the early part of 1997.

The Sino-British relations were rather testy at that time and furthermore the Administration believed it could have the new airport ready before the British handing back the territory to China on 1 July 1997. It was then thought it could proceed without gaining Chinese approbation, which proved to be folly. As the Government started to discuss with banks and financial companies with regard to loan financing for the project, these commercial institutions, however, disagreed. It was pointed out that even the project could be completed on time, the debts would still have to be repaid when

Plate 3.12 *The Hong Kong International Airport, 1998.*

Hong Kong became a Special Administrative Region and China had to be consulted and agreed as the loan guarantor.

So reluctantly the Hong Kong Government, through Britain, negotiated with China on the airport project after the 1989 incident. The Mainland Government, however, was not happy with the late approach by the British and not in a co-operative frame of mind. The talks stalled and the bickering commenced as the two sides niggled and haggled. The British, sensing time was slipping away, dispatched the former ambassador to China, Sir Percy Cradock, to Beijing in June 1991 to prod the process along. Sir Percy eventually reached a tacit agreement with the Chinese host and together initiated on 30 June 1991 the "Memorandum of Understanding Concerning the Construction of the New Airport in Hong Kong and Related Questions", which was announced four days later. The two sides sealed the deal, or so it appeared, on 3 September when the

British Prime Minister, John Major, became the first Western leader to call on Beijing after the Tiananmen incident when he and Premier Li Peng signed the accord at the Great Hall of the People. It was thought that the new airport issue was satisfactorily resolved and that work could be commenced immediately and completed prior to the transfer of sovereignty in July 1997. But this assumption was wrong. Though the work on the airport could begin, the wrangling continued. It was a long story, let me explain!

The British had in the beginning told the Chinese that the new airport would cost $111.2 billion (at March 1991 prices) or $164 billion (at money of the day). The British also assured the Mainland leaders that they would not deplete Hong Kong's treasury for the scheme and promised to leave behind at least $5 billion in reserves as at 30 June 1997 for the Special Administrative Region. The Chinese were wary, suspecting that the project was a means for Britain to plunder the territory's accrued wealth before the retreat. The British to placate them then pledged to bequeath at least $25 billion to the SAR by 1 July 1997. The Chinese eventually and reluctantly accepted this offer and also agreed that, unless the British were to incur debts for the project exceeding $5 billion beyond 30 June 1997, the British did not have to consult the future sovereign. So these were the major financial terms in the agreement.

On 4 March 1992 the Hong Kong Government introduced the annual budget to the Legislative Council projecting spectacular surpluses that would, by 1 July 1997, top up the reserves to $78 billion, more than three times of what had been bargained and agreed in the Memorandum of Understanding signed only six months ago. The British raised even more eyebrows and hackles when they told the Chinese that, according to March 1991 prices, the airport construction costs would rise by 14 per cent and the affiliated airport rail link costs by 85 per cent. The startled Chinese were very dismayed by such cost escalation and then asked the British to cap the cost spiral but the British refused.

Far from a distant observer, I was later drawn into the dispute, first, in my capacity as a Hong Kong Affairs Advisor to the Chinese Government and later as a member of the Preliminary Working Committee for the transfer of sovereignty.

My role as an advisor to the Chinese Government was taken up in early 1992 when I was one of the 44 so chosen. The appointment certificate presentation ceremony for the advisors took place in Beijing on 11 March 1992 at the Great Hall of the People. After the ceremony I stayed behind in Beijing and joined the delegation of the Business and Professionals Federation of Hong Kong led by its Chairman, Vincent Lo. I was a member of its Advisory Council. The Hong Kong and Macao Affairs Office Director, Lu Ping, hosted a dinner for the delegation on 14 March and we talked about the airport project. Lu was infuriated by the British attitude and felt they were dishonest. He particularly referred to the estimates of the reserves as at 30 June 1997. Lu reckoned it was dubious and absurd for the British to promise initially only $5 billion in reserves for the SAR in 1997, which was equivalent to only four per cent of the total government annual expenditure of $120 billion for the coming fiscal year. He dismissed the $5 billion inheritance as "chicken's feed", and said it was only after hard bargain that the British eventually raised the amount to $25 billion. Lu found it incomprehensive that the British could within six months raise the reserve for 1997 to $78 billion. I was astonished by the vehemence of the Director as I calmly explained to him the practice of evaluating large projects in the business world. I said we normally employed three sets of estimates, one was optimistic, the other pessimistic and the third most probable. I reckoned the British were playing safe when they promised only $5 billion, which was probably the pessimistic figure. I suggested that China asked for the other two sets of estimates before reaching any conclusion.

When I got back to Hong Kong I told Sir David Wilson my exchange with Lu, who felt China was being fleeced, and wondered whether the Government had three sets of reserve estimates. The Governor after checking with the Financial Secretary replied there was only one estimate and added that the confusion about the reserves could have stemmed from the dramatic 1991 recovery of the property and stock markets. He said the recovery, however, occurred after giving the figure to the Chinese in February 1991 and brought to the treasury a totally unexpected windfall. Just as the Government was raking in more money, it was also spending less as government engineering projects, particularly those core projects for the airport, had been delayed. Factoring in all these variables, the Governor said, the Financial Secretary, Sir Piers Jacobs, concluded that the reserve could be much over $75 billion by July 1997.

Not long after my talk with Lu Ping in Beijing, there were rumours that Sir David Wilson would soon be replaced. The rumours suggested that Prime Minister John Major, feeling humiliated by his September trip to Beijing, would appoint someone much more belligerent towards the Chinese than had Sir David, a career diplomat and China expert. China, hearing this rumour and in turn, would probably use the airport project as leverage and the ensuing bickering would shrill and incessant.

Chris Patten replaced Sir David Wilson in July 1992 and announced his political reform in October 1992. China was further aggravated by this British move and reacted by speeding up its own preparation for recovering Hong Kong by, for one, establishing in the middle of 1993 the Preliminary Working Committee (PWC). The Committee was sub-divided into five specialized groups each responsible for a specific policy area. One of these, the Economic Specialized Group, in November 1993 launched four study panels to delve into four subjects with one focussing on the airport. The Chinese agreed that a new airport was crucial to the SAR's ambition to be a hub of Asian aviation and wanted the Economic Specialized Group to advise it on a number of areas including controlling costs, monitoring progress, shaping future management, and the formation of the Airport Authority. The Study Panel on Airport had seven members and I was its convenor. The other members were Nellie Fong, Vincent Lo, Shao Youbao and Lau Wong-fat from Hong Kong, and Gao Shangquan and Wang Qiren from the Mainland. We first discussed in depth the financial aspects of the project and made the following four recommendations to the Chinese Government:

(1) Loans taken out by the Provisional Airport Authority and the Airport Railway Corporation should be treated as government loans. China should request the British to inject more capital into the project and minimize the debts.
(2) China should agree to the request for land grants related to the airport rail link but details should be assessed annually by the Sino-British Land Commission in accordance with market conditions.
(3) Strengthen the supervision system for construction work and cost control as well as establish a cost-monitoring unit under the Airport Authority.
(4) Make realistic estimates for a budget that could be needed to cover construction cost for uncompleted works and claims from contractors beyond 1997.

The Hong Kong Government similarly made its own moves and published in January 1994 a White Paper Bill on the Airport Corporation for public consultation with the intention of turning the Airport Authority into a corporation. The study panel immediately pored over the Bill and with the help of the Secretary for Economic Services of the Hong Kong Government, Gordon Siu, eventually submitted to the Chinese Government twenty proposals grouped into three categories, namely:

(1) China should insist on the establishment of a board of directors and the retention of the name "The Airport Authority" as stipulated in the Memorandum of Understanding. The appointment of those directors of the board straddling 1997 should be made jointly by both Governments. Any major mortgaging, acquisition of assets outside the airport, and raising loans should be agreed by the board of directors and approved by the Financial Secretary. Fees and charges should be approved by the Governor in Council.

(2) China should strengthen the Authority's internal regulatory mechanism, such as the provision of separate posts for the chairman and the chief executive with clear delineation of authority and responsibility. Strengthen the structure of the board so as to expedite its process of decision-making and install its mechanism of checks and balances.

(3) China should restrict the Authority's scope of activities, such as it could engage in business only related to airport operations and within the airport boundaries. Any activity outside the airport boundary should need prior approval of the Government.

So after nearly a decade of pitching and yawing, controversies and consternation, the work on the airport was eventually completed a year late in July 1998. It was officially opened by the Chinese President, Jiang Zemin, on 2 July and then opened for business on 6 July. Unfortunately the baptismal for Chek Lap Kok turned from celebration to confusion and fanfare to farce as computer breakdowns created chaos causing delays in passenger flights and cargo shipments for a week. The Legislative Council later established a Select Committee to investigate the matter resulting that the contract of its Chief Executive, Dr. Henry Townsend, was not renewed, and both its Chairman, Wong Po-yan, and the Chief Secretary, Anson Chan, in her capacity as Chairman of the Government's Airport Steering Committee, criticized.

Birth of the Liberal Party

Hong Kong started to democratize its legislature in 1985 immediately after the signing of the Joint Declaration. Nonetheless direct geographical election was not introduced until 1991 as a minority in the chamber. The 1991–95 Legislative Council comprised three senior ex-officials (the Chief Secretary, the Financial Secretary and the Attorney General), 18 appointed members, 18 directly elected and 21 elected from the functional constituencies, making a total of 60.

Back then only the United Democrats (which later joined with Meeting Point to form the Democratic Party) were the ones organized politically to contest elections and shape an agenda. They also boosted 14 members in the legislature, making them an articulate and formidable force. The other 40 odd legislators were mostly not politically affiliated and seemed in contrast to be passive — at least

Plate 3.13 *Celebration of the 4th Anniversary of the Liberal Party, 1998.*

as portrayed in the press which slanted towards the eminently quotable and approachable United Democrats.

I retired from the Executive Council as the Senior Member in September 1988, passing the mantle to Lydia Dunn, who in her turn surrendered her leadership in the Legislative Council to Allen Lee. By 1991 democracy was the trend sweeping through Hong Kong and some legislators found it untenable, if not also awkward, to have Lee, an appointed politician, to remain the Senior Member of the Legislative Council. The friction between Lee and the United Democrats became so frequent that Lee graciously resigned in early 1992, leaving the position vacant and the job would be phased out as the Council turned into a free for all.

The United Democrats grew bolder, more assertive and more aggressive, claiming to have the mandate of the people and scorning the other legislators who did not ascend from the rough and tumble of electoral politics. Lee and his fellow LEGCO colleagues Steven Poon, Selina Chow and Stephen Cheong knew that they had to rally some of their fellow legislators if they were to have a chance against the United Democrats' onslaught. The quartet then canvassed the other appointed legislators and friendly representatives from the functional constituencies to form the Co-operative Resource Centre, a think tank, research unit, and brain trust for a future political group. But the Centre still could not fend off the attacks from the United Democrats who had mastered the tactics of the political pantomime, public ridicule, and punch lines.

Lee and Poon then approached me for counsel and I conjured up an analogy to motivate them into doing more than forming the Centre, a salon for kindred spirits. I compared their plight to a group of 10 or 15 people locked into a lion's cage. If they ran around on their own, they would be an easy meal each for the beast. Should they gang up against the predator, they stood a chance, if even several of them might be mauled. The gist of the allegory was "united we stand, divided we fall".

The contributors to the Centre were genteel people, unlikely to use the previous metaphor to go out to slay a lion. Guts and grit were what these individuals, and individualists, needed. They shared a dislike for the United Democrats, who constantly disparaged them, but dislike was no substitute for a common philosophy and common ambition. The lot of them might co-operate enough to defend but not to conquer. I suggested to Lee and Poon to abandon any pretence of being above politics and, instead, form a proper political party with its belief, vision, discipline and platform.

The two agreed and, with others, notably Selina Chow and Ronald Arculli, found the Liberal Party in 1994 amidst howls of derision from the media, which sided with the United Democrats and their allies. They were reluctant or cautious at first because their constituency, the professionals and businessmen, were wary of politics and China was biased against any party, other than its own. But the Liberals persevered and today, under the leadership of James Tien, it has become the third largest party and, more often than not, holds the decisive votes. Nonetheless the Liberals still have a long way to go before it could achieve its true status as an influential political party.

Period of Confrontation

Patten Realigned the Executive Council

The British Prime Minister, John Major, replaced the seasoned diplomat, Lord Wilson, with the crony Chris Patten, who had lost his own Bath seat in the 1992 general election. However, as the Chairman of the Conservative Party, he had led the party to win the general election, earning the gratitude of John Major. One of the very first major changes he had made within a few months of his arrival was to divorce the Executive Council from the Legislative Council. But Patten was not really the author of the separation. The initiative for that ought to go to some individuals from Hong Kong, including Vincent Lo, the leader of the Business and Professionals Federation of Hong Kong. Lo together with some of his colleagues in BPF had travelled to London in May 1992 to lobby Patten quietly before the Englishman came to the Colony to be its last Governor.

Patten arrived in Hong Kong on 9 July 1992, six days after Lord Wilson had departed, refusing to wear the ceremonial regalia — including sash and ostrich plumed pith hat — for the occasion.

He was the first and the only head of the Colony who was not knighted. He arrived together with two comely daughters, Laura and Alice, and wife Lavender, a lawyer. He and his family seemed too busy to observe the fusty conventions and made right away a refreshing impression. Breaking the colonial tradition, he also brought along with him two personal assistants from outside Hong Kong.

Only two weeks into office the strong-minded Governor made known his political stance that his Government would be executive-led, which came as a relief to many who did not want the Legislative Council to have too much sway. His Government would be transparent as well as responsible to the people. He also maintained that he would not form a party in the Legislative Council to provide support to the government. The Governor promised that his inaugural Policy Address in October would focus on the political development of Hong Kong.

During this period the Senior Member of the Executive Council, Dame Lydia Dunn, rounded up her colleagues and "convinced" them to join her in tendering their resignations to Governor Patten so as to give him a free hand to reshape the Cabinet. Patten accepted all the resignations, except one — that of Dunn who was "re-appointed" as the Senior Member among a new crew. This outcome had created resentment among some of her former colleagues.

I, as a Hong Kong Affairs Advisor, faxed to the Director of the Hong Kong and Macao Affairs Office, Lu Ping, and also the Director of Xinhua News Agency in Hong Kong, Zhou Nan, on 25 July 1992 an analysis of the shifting situation. I outlined how Patten had three possible options to realign his Executive Council and predicted he would eventually settle for the one modelled in part after the system in the United States. He would, I reckoned correctly as it turned out, delineate a clear separation of the executive and legislative branches. He would not appoint any legislator to his Cabinet, which would comprise professionals, academics and businessmen. These people would be willing to serve Hong Kong but did not wish to face electors and would assist Patten to formulate policies pragmatically for the overall good of the colony. This arrangement on the surface would bring the political situation back to those pre-1985 days.

But, alas, the situation was not so simple as the political chemistry in Hong Kong had since 1985 changed irrevocably. The Colony by 1991 had a majority elected legislature with nearly one third of its members geographically directly elected. These directly elected members considered themselves as representatives of the people. I pictured in my analysis a scenario in which the Executive Council might adopt a policy for the overall interest of Hong Kong but contrary to the wishes of the voters of a strong party in the legislature. The *de facto* "royal opposition" would then attempt to block the bills behind such a policy and force a showdown. Patten, versed in the adversarial politics of parliament, would have to lead his Executive Councillors and government officials to lobby the people through the media to counter his opposition in the Legislative Council. Nonetheless, it would be difficult to predict the outcome of these political battles.

I told Lu and Zhou in my submission that if Patten were to persist and heed the advice of Vincent Lo's group, which had made the suggestion to him in London, he would jeopardize the collaboration between the EXCO and the LEGCO for the past generation. One obvious and apparent consequence of this decision of the new Governor would be the dissolution of the UMELCO Office, established some thirty years ago.

The Governor invited me on 6 August 1992 to his residence, the Government House, to discuss his political plans. I presented him with a comprehensive analysis of the various options and recommended to him, despite its repercussions, the model of separating the EXCO from the LEGCO. I said that it was the only way out for him under the obtaining circumstances at that time. We spoke for longer than two hours, drawing observations from my nearly 30 years of political experience in Hong Kong, a city in which he had made a splash but about which he knew little. The Governor then saw me out with appreciation for my comprehensive appraisal of the situation and said, whilst he had not reached any final conclusion, he would probably adopt the model I had recommended.

Eventually he ended up separating the EXCO from the LEGCO and appointing a new team to the EXCO with consequential dissolution of the UMELCO Office, first formed in 1963.

Patten's Political Reform

The first Chinese Chief Justice, Sir Ti-liang Yang (later put himself forward as a candidature for the Hong Kong SAR Chief Executive) swore in Christopher Francis Patten as the twenty-eighth and the last Governor of Hong Kong on 9 July 1992. Only two months into his tenure the politician returned to London to consult Prime Minister John Major and Foreign Secretary Douglas Hurd on his political reform agenda, which they approved. Secured with the British Cabinet's blessing, he came back more self-confident and more determined to confront the Chinese Government.

Patten proceeded to shake up the political establishment in the colony with his maiden Policy Address. His reform package contained two major components, one was to re-jig the arrangements for the 1995 Legislative Council elections and the other was to abolish the appointed seats to the 18 District Boards and the two Municipal

Councils. The British Ambassador to Beijing, Sir Robin McLaren, on 26 September 1992, presented Patten's Policy Address to the Chinese Foreign Ministry, ten days before its delivery in the legislature and without any allowance for discussion or review.

The Chinese pored over the speech and were appalled by the proposed 1995 electoral arrangements that did not "dovetail" with the Basic Law as the British had promised they would. The Foreign Ministry then asked the British to postpone the reading of the political segment of the address and negotiate a settlement. The British side agreed to negotiate but only, it said, after the speech had been read on 7 October without any deletion or elision on the issue of reform.

There were five main features to the package that Patten was to unveil:

(1) Lower the voting age to 18 from 21 years.

(2) Change the current "double-seat, double-vote" system (with each elector given two ballots for two representatives) to "single-seat, single-vote" format for the geographical constituencies.

(3) Replace all district board and municipal council appointments with directly elected members.

(4) The nine new functional constituencies shall be elected on a different basis from the 21 existing functional constituencies. These are to be returned not by a narrow, often organization, federation or group-based electorate but by a broad, inclusive franchise. Generally speaking, the current functional constituencies might have voters numbering in the hundreds to tens of thousands. The proposed new system was in fact direct election on the occupational basis, with an estimated number of voters of about 2.7 million in these new nine functional constituencies.

Plate 3.14 *Governor Patten's Open Forum for his political package, 1992.*

(5) The Election Committee picking ten representatives to the Legislative Council will comprise exclusively directly elected district board members.

The reform was in fact a slap on the face of the Chinese Government and its reaction understandably would be furious. I reflected on the situation and assessed the Chinese bottom line for these five proposals:

(1) China would not quibble with lowering the voting age to 18 years since that complied with the existing practice on the Mainland.
(2) China would not object to discussions about the modest changes to the election methods for the geographical constituencies because it had not reached a decision on this issue.
(3) China would strongly oppose the abolition of the appointed seats to both the district boards and the municipal councils.
(4) China would be strenuously against the introduction by stealth of *de facto* universal suffrage in the guise of the new functional constituencies.
(5) China would not accept such a formation of the Election Committee and would regard the British proposal as a breach of the previous understanding.

Two days after Patten defiantly read his inaugural Policy Address, that is on 9 October, I wrote him a four-page letter, reminding him that the Election Committee he had suggested differed from that outlined in the Basic Law. I stressed that his programme, if implemented, would derail the "through train" arrangement for legislators to straddle the 1997 as envisaged in the Basic Law and agreed by the British. I said his carrying on would impair British and Chinese relations, damage Hong Kong's interests, and wreck the smooth transition founded on trust and continuity. Patten promptly replied on 16 October, rebutting my claims and saying that the composition of the Election Committee for 1997 was not specified in the Basic Law. However history has since proven that I was right in my assessment.

I retired from the Executive Council in September 1988 and therefore was not aware of the mutual understanding between the two Governments on the composition of the Election Committee through the exchange of letters between the British and Chinese Foreign Ministers on this subject in early 1990. Patten should have known the existence of these important letters, but if he was not, then the responsibility for this mistake must lie on both his aids in the Hong Kong Government and his colleagues in the British Foreign Ministry.

My conclusions proved prescient for the Chinese got so riled up by the Policy Address that, soon after, it refused to talk to the British until they had withdrawn the political package. This was the climate of reproach that clouded Patten's first and only visit in October to Beijing during his five years of governorship in Hong Kong. In the Chinese capital the Governor met the Hong Kong and Macao Affairs Office Director, Lu Ping, who was frosty, if not hostile. Neither side would budge.

Britain and China then fought out their dispute by once more mounting propaganda blitzes on 28 and 29 October respectively through the release of the 1990 seven exchange of diplomatic letters. The correspondents dwelled mainly on ensuring a "through train" for the legislators to minimize disruption to the transition in 1997, as well as the number of directly elected seats allowed and the formation of the Election Committee.

I read those documents carefully and concluded that the British had made a commitment from which they subsequently reneged, a serious breach of diplomatic faith. I agreed with the Chinese view that the British had shifted their position and wanted to implement, as former Prime Minister Thatcher said in her memoirs, speedier democratic reform at calmer times.

The British had not exhausted their manoeuvre even in the "simultaneous" release of the seven exchanges, opting to publish these together with a rather biased synopsis on 28 October, a day before the Chinese could do so. Her Majesty's Government apparently figured that by pre-empting the other side it could gain the momentum in the battle for public opinion. Once again, the Chinese had learned another lesson from the British on diplomatic cunning.

As the row worsened the British further poured oil onto the fire. The Hong Kong Colonial Government in March 1993 gazetted the reform proposal which coincided, planned or not, with the sitting of the National People's Congress and the Chinese People's Political Consultative Conference in Beijing. The timing and the contents so incensed the Chinese side that they used their media to condemn Patten, denouncing him as an agitator and a villain for all history.

While the rhetoric reached a crescendo, and the markets quivered, the British and Chinese Governments suddenly and jointly announced in early April that they would negotiate in Beijing starting on 22 April. The situation appeared to have calmed, but it was calm before the storm. These talks went on for nine months and 17 rounds, only five rounds less than in the negotiations over the Joint Declaration, and with no "happy ending" for the travail. The haggling stopped in November 1993 with both sides finally conceding that there was no chance of a breakthrough. The Hong Kong and Macao Affairs Office on 3 December 1993 published a terse, 3,000-character statement explaining and blaming the failure on the intransigence of the other side.

Several months later, in March 1994, the Chinese Government affiliated Joint Publishing (HK) Company published a book entitled, *Facts About a Few Important Aspects of the Sino-British Talks on the 1994–1995 Electoral Arrangements in Hong Kong*. In the account the Chinese Foreign Ministry spokesman discoursed on the 17 rounds of talks lasting from April to November 1993 and explained why these had failed. The book disclosed that the Chinese side had acquiesced to the British demand on the abolition of the appointments to the district boards and municipal councils, even though the future Hong Kong SAR could restore the practice. The Chinese had also agreed to dropping the voting age to 18 and accepting the arrangement for total universal franchise to the elections of the district boards and municipal councils. Just as the protagonists were on the verge of signing a first stage agreement, the British added new demands. (Earlier the British and Chinese Governments had agreed to split the negotiations into two stages. The first stage was to deal with the district board and municipal council elections whereas the second with the Legislative Council elections.) Most outrageous for the Chinese was the British insistence that not only the district boards and municipal councils were to be elected in 1994 via the proposed system of "single-seat, single-vote" so should the Legislative Council election in 1995.

What galled the Chinese too was that on 2 December 1993 Patten had read a statement to the Legislative Council saying and explaining to his advantage why the talks had stopped. The Governor ascribed the failure in negotiations to the Chinese not agreeing to "single-seat, single-vote" for the LEGCO geographical constituencies. This was consistent with the Chinese statement. The Governor also revealed that, whilst the Chinese might no longer oppose Britain scrapping the appointed seats to the district boards and municipal councils before 1997, they held out the possibility of resurrecting these in Hong Kong after 30 June 1997. This emphasis, with the finger wagging at China's "intransigence", was an insult to the Mainland Government. Not only did the talks not achieve an accord, these had actually worsened the acrimony.

Whether or not the Patten reform had technically contravened the seven exchange letters in early 1990 between the two Foreign Ministers is a subject for historians, but what is glaring wrong to me was Britain attempting to meddle in the affairs of Hong Kong, the Special Administrative Region, which China would never countenance as a matter of pride, or principle. The British could not expect to set a political course outside the scope of the Joint Declaration and compel China to stick to it when the territory was no longer under their jurisdiction beyond 30 June 1997. In short, as long as China does not violate the Sino-British Joint Declaration, Britain had no right to intervene.

I had at times discussed with British officials why they insisted on abolishing appointments to the district boards and municipal councils when in their own country they still maintained their appointment system in the House of Lords comprising aristocrats, dignitaries and retired politicians. While the Lords had been shorn of the veto power since 1911, the upper chamber could still block or delay legislation for up to a year. I queried how they could justify their appointments while revoking these for the colonial district boards and municipal councils. Unlike the United Kingdom with its Magna Carta dating back centuries, the territory had but a decade of democratic experience of any form. The British could never explain the disparity, the double standard, to my satisfaction.

The fortune of the Lords depends of course on the whims and expedience of British politics. The Labour Party in 1970s had advocated the abolition of the Lords only to have been thwarted by the Conservatives, which saw advantage in cramming that house with their own out of service grandees. But, alas, the Tories were not exactly enamoured of the Lords at one stage after the Labour Government of Harold Wilson had sent up its own batch of loyal retainers. The Tories in 1978 had proposed restructuring the Lords by making two thirds of them elected but still with a third appointed. Even this half-hearted reform was not carried out.

I also reminded the British that before Patten was himself appointed to be the last Governor of Hong Kong he, as the Chairman of the Conservative Party under John Major, did not champion reforming or removing the Lords. The new Governor then promptly confronted the Chinese about political appointments, a morally dubious stance, since when a person cleans up he should start at home.

During 1993 I had been a guest at the Government House talking with the Governor alone a few times. I remember telling him one time about his work as the last Governor of Hong Kong with only a few years to go. I suggested that he should co-operate with the Chinese Government in the spirit of the Sino-British Joint Declaration and act as a "caretaker governor". His swift response was that he would not have come to Hong Kong with that kind of work in mind.

Justified or not in its actions, the Colonial Government in January 1994 tabled in the Legislative Council the reform package for the district board and municipal council 1994 elections that would be a prelude for the same in the next LEGCO polls in 1995. The bill on district boards and municipal councils was easily passed without protracted debate on 23 February.

The Government, victorious, then put forward the bill for the

Legislative Council reform but received tremendous resistance in the Council. Eventually with the personal assistance of the Prime Minister, John Major, Patten's reform package narrowly escaped from the fate of being amended by the Liberal Party by a mere majority of one vote on 29 June 1994. I have more to disclose on this battle later. With the passing of this bill on LEGCO reform, Sino-British confrontation not only continued but also intensified until 30 June 1997.

Anatomy of a Dispute

The British and Chinese Governments jointly announced in early April 1993 that negotiations over Governor Chris Patten's proposed political reform would begin on 22 April in Beijing. There were mixed feelings by the public, some were optimistic, others pessimistic. But still, all in all, there was hope.

Four days before the talks were to commence I faxed a 3,000-character discourse, titled "British and Chinese Strategies over the Arguments on Hong Kong's Political Structure", to Lu Ping and Zhou Nan. In this article I examined their disparate tactics, steeping my assessment in my knowledge of their histories and inclinations. I suggested that Patten had been clever in exploiting the grey areas in the Basic Law to undermine the consensus between the two countries, speed up democratic change to his advantage, and wreck any chance of a political convergence in 1997. I figured he would unleash a furious campaign of propaganda, based on the motto of "fairness, openness and acceptability to the Hong Kong people" to win over the Hong Kong public, sway the British media, and garner international support.

Were Patten to succeed, then he could claim credit for an honourable British retreat and pose as a saviour of the people he scarcely knew. The United Kingdom could then say it had passed Hong Kong's administration to the democrats over the objection of China. Patten was, I stressed, prepared to take unilateral action with Executive Council approval and put the proposal to the Legislative Council in which he had appointed several members close to his thinking and roused the public through a sympathetic press. He would lobby legislators furiously, postured and mocked, using all the possible avenues at his disposal. Twitting China was easy when it came at somebody else's expense. Even if the majority of the legislators did not succumb and amend his package to complement the Basic Law, he could still claim moral victory, saying he had allowed the people of Hong Kong to decide, despite Chinese bluster. Thus Governor Patten had written a very clever political script in which he would be the winner whatever the outcome.

I told the two directors, Lu and Zhou, that I, now an outsider to the process unfolding in the Executive and Legislative Councils Patten had divorced, was not optimistic at all. I felt the British would not budge and the Chinese could not give, and failure was inevitable. I wished my prognosis had been wrong for once.

I then tried to provide some comfort to the Chinese officials by saying that every democratic society would periodically have to face the trauma of transition when one political party yielded to another after losing in a general election. Hong Kong's situation was analogous to such a trauma and could cope with the shock, one of the many it would have to face in the future, and it was in coping that would toughen the character of this society.

I also said to Lu and Zhou that, irrespective of the outcome of the negotiations, Patten would have to put his political reform package to the Legislative Council in the form of a bill for endorsement. The Chinese side at that stage could lobby directly and indirectly the legislators to change the bill in accordance with the Basic Law's doctrine. I further gave the Chinese officials the consolation that, even if this attempt were to fail, the setback would not be terminal. I specifically repeated what I had suggested two months ago in Guangzhou, which was the need for the Chinese to establish a "Sovereignty Transfer Planning Committee" to advise the Chinese Government on matters of this sort.

Finally I urged the Chinese not to be too distracted by Patten or obsessed with political continuity, which might be less virtuous than touted, and, instead, focus on preserving a stable and prosperous Hong Kong. I implored them to help buoy Hong Kong's economy which, ultimately, mattered a lot more than a temporary political setback. I asked them to concentrate on overseeing the construction of the new airport, expanding the container terminals, and increasing the land supply so as to forge the future of SAR. The Chinese should institute an effective monitoring mechanism of all these projects to ensure that the SAR's inheritance was not looted or squandered and this would earn the gratitude of the people, if not right away, then certainly in time.

I spelt out those points to salve the wounded ego of the Chinese Government and nudged it towards a constructive response to the British provocation. Lu, Director of Hong Kong and Macao Affairs Office, appreciated that and wrote from Beijing on 3 May 1993: "Your letter of 18 April was received. We note your analysis of the motives of Chris Patten and assessment of the possible British tactic in the talks to come as well as your suggestions on what China should do in the circumstances. These are very useful and an invaluable reference. I thank you."

I am now jotting down those snippets of memory for this book and noticing that many of my predictions had come to pass:

(1) Sino-British negotiations failed by the end of 1993 and the two Governments went their separate ways.
(2) When Patten tabled his bill in the Legislative Council in the middle of 1994, the Liberal Party Chairman, Allen Lee, led his members and allies to amend the package to make it conform to the Basic Law provisions, failing by only one vote and failing because of treachery.
(3) China agreed to the new airport construction and to the increase of land supply to shore up the economy that helped the transfer.
(4) Whilst the "through train" was derailed, the transition proceeded smoothly and was universally praised.

A Blessing in Disguise

The Sino-British talks on Patten's political proposal had been going on for the greater part of 1993, but at the end of November and after 17 rounds the talks eventually faltered. There was naturally great disappointment among many in Hong Kong. But after careful thought I concluded that the failure to secure a settlement could be a blessing in disguise for it freed the Chinese Government to pursue its own course and formulate its own election methods for the legislature.

The Preliminary Working Committee (the precursor to the Preparatory Committee) for the Special Administrative Region, of which I was a member, convened its second plenary session in Beijing on 9 December 1993. Foreign Minister and Committee Chairman, Qian Qichen, a seasoned diplomat of measured words and a cool temperament, delivered the opening address. Not once did he appear ruffle by the unravelling of the partnership with Britain for Hong

Plate 3.15 *The author addressing the 2nd plenary session of the Preliminary Working Committee in Beijing, 1993.*

Kong's transition. Then after Qian spoke, Vice Foreign Minister and the Chief Negotiator for the Chinese side, Jiang Enzhu, announced that the discussions with the British had stalled. (Jiang in July 1997 became the Director of the Liaison Office of the Central People's Government in the Hong Kong SAR after a brief spell as the Chinese Ambassador to Britain.) He impassively ascribed the failure to the United Kingdom insisting on applying the "single-seat, single-vote" format for the 1994 district board and municipal council elections to that for the 1995 Legislative Council election without consultation with China.

I took my turn at the lectern on 11 December and addressed briefly the issue of the political system for the SAR as mapped out in the Basic Law. I said, while on the surface it was disappointing that the talks had failed, nonetheless, it could be a blessing in disguise in the long run. I then proceeded to explain and describe the two major political models in the English-speaking world.

The British one revolved around the Parliament, whose upper chamber was appointed and lower house was returned on the "single-seat, single-vote" basis of universal suffrage. The dominant party formed the government beholden to the majority in the House of Commons and in theoretical command of an apolitical civil service which executed the policies. With this political model the "single-seat, single-vote" voting system would help to produce a majority party in the legislature, thus minimizing the possibility of having a coalition government.

The other political model, epitomized by the American, was marked by a clear separation between the legislative (divided into the Senate and the House of representatives in the United States) and presidential branches, which checked and balanced one another. This system was favoured, I said, by the U.S. and many continental European countries. There the chief executive formed the government and drafted the policy initiatives for the legislative branch to reject or enact, with or without amendment, into law. The judiciary then interpreted these laws according to its reading of the national constitution.

I then proceeded to talk about the political system for the Hong Kong SAR. According to the Basic Law the SAR would follow the American system by vesting the power of government in the executive branch and instituting checks and balances in the legislative assembly. The government would be an executive-led and yet face restraints. The "single-seat, single-vote" voting format would tend to produce a majority party in the legislature and would impede the operation of an executive-led government, as I cautioned. The "proportional representation" voting system, a concept many continental European countries championed, would be more suitable as it would minimize any one party dominating the future legislature, as I asserted. Hong Kong, for the sake of stability, had to have a strong executive who would be able to lead, execute policies, and take responsibility. I then concluded:

> "The breakdown of the Sino-British talks would let China reconsider on its own the electoral method for the Legislative Council. China could now go it alone, without the British intervention, and ensure a strong and effective executive-led government for the Hong Kong SAR. For this reason I declared earlier that the breakdown of the talks could be a blessing in disguise."

History has since proven me right. China did abolish the "single-seat, single-vote" system that the British had adopted for the Legislative Council and instead opted for the "proportional representation" format to dull the advantage of the anti-China Democratic Party, their allies, and forces hostile to the Chinese Communist Party. The SAR now has a reasonably powerful office of the Chief Executive which, while more accountable than any colonial governor, is answerable to an electorate with representation of very wide interests. Hong Kong is better served as a result.

Patten Saved from His Waterloo

After the collapse of the Sino-British talks on Patten's political proposal, the Governor submitted his reform package to the Legislative Council for the final voting on 29 June 1994. Legislators of the Liberal Party led by Chairman Allen Lee and allies wanted to amend the proposal enough to conform to the Basic Law. Whether or not they succeeded hinged on the crucial vote of Martin Barrow, a legislator, Chairman of the Hong Kong Tourist Association, and a senior executive of Jardine Matheson & Company, the last connection being the most pivotal.

Allen Lee disclosed to me that Barrow, a tall, patrician figure, went to his office at the end of 1993, declared his interest in the "through train" for the Legislative Council. He offered to co-operate with the Liberal Party as well as the independent ones and those leftists of liked mind. The Englishman said, however, his support depended on Lee getting from the Hong Kong and Macao Affairs Office Director, Lu Ping, to spell out what might be acceptable to the Chinese Government. Lee thought the entreaty reasonable and then consulted his Liberal Party colleagues who gave him the support to press ahead with the plan.

Lee and his deputies, Selina Chow and Ronald Arculli, then secretly travelled to Beijing to speak with Lu about the conditions for boarding the "through train". The Director said, for the train to run, the nine new functional constituencies must be returned like the already established ones with a specific, narrow franchise and the Election Committee should comprise four sectors as the Basic Law stipulated.

The three Liberals then returned to Hong Kong and, during the following months, thrashed out with Barrow and others an amended reform proposal that would incorporate those points Lu had cited. They arranged with legislator Howard Young, a member of the Liberal Party and representative of the Tourism constituency, to propose the alternative plan for political development. Lee and associates lobbied furiously and, with Barrow's vote tallied, reckoned they could squeak out a victory against Patten. So with cautious optimism, they watched the final voting of both Patten's package and their own amendment on Wednesday, 29 June.

Two days before the voting, that is, Monday, 27 June, Lee

received a phone call from Barrow, who blurted out, "I am sorry, Allen, I will have to abstain from voting." The Liberal Party Chairman was stunted by the volte-face and asked, "How come? You were the first suggesting me to have a deal with Lu Ping and the amended version had many of your proposals. How come you are now going to abstain?" Barrow again repeated his apology, saying he had "great difficulties" but did not elaborate. Lee, nonetheless, could guess what the reasons were for the eleventh hour betrayal.

Patten, Lee believed, had got wind that his proposal was to be rejected and so made a call to Prime Minister John Major to lean on Jardine Matheson Chairman, Henry Keswick. Although Keswick and Patten were not in good terms but the doyen could not snub the Prime Minister, and Barrow in turn could not act against the wishes of his boss. But there was more to the story from another source, Steven Poon, a Liberal Party Vice-Chairman and a legislator from 1991 to 1995.

After Lee hung up on Barrow, he called a crisis meeting with Poon, Chow and other Liberals. Poon said to me that they remained puzzled at Barrow's sudden switch and so he volunteered to find some answers from his British contacts. Poon, a professional engineer, had been the General Manager of the China Light & Power utility, which had bought a lot of machinery from the United Kingdom. Poon thus had good contacts in the British political and business circles. Both Lee and Poon simply had to sate their curiosity and identify the real culprit.

Poon on the early evening of 27 June, which would be about 11 o'clock in the morning London Summer Time, telephoned the Chairman of General Electric Company, Lord Prior, who had been a Cabinet Minister during Margaret Thatcher's days as Prime Minister. He told the life peer about the treachery and said how a Jardine

Matheson's back down on the amendment to the Patten package would damage the Sino-British relationship. He stressed that had Jardines stuck with Patten from start to finish the repercussions from China might have been less severe. What no one would forgive was the final hour betrayal. Lord Prior agreed with Poon's assessment and promised to call Jardines Senior Director, Sir Charles Powell, who, before joining the firm, had been Thatcher's private secretary in the 1980s. About half an hour later Lord Prior phoned back to Poon, saying he had just spoken to Sir Charles who had been humming and hawing. The General Electric Chairman asked Poon to ring Sir Charles directly.

Poon then immediately phoned Sir Charles, explaining to him how unwise Jardines was, urging him to persuade Barrow to get back on their side. But Sir Charles would not budge and was evasive, insisting that it was Barrow's own decision. Poon figured it was futile to dicker with Sir Charles and to appeal once more to Barrow because the matter was now obvious not theirs but that of the British national policy to move the Patten reform and wreck co-operation with China. Poon then informed Lee of his London telephone conversations. Both sensed that the Governor must have had intelligence sources telling how precarious his package was as legislators marshalled their forces to thwart or change it. Patten had to have phoned Major to lean on or trade favours with Barrow's ultimate superior.

After Barrow's reversal, Lee tabulated that the vote on the package was now deadlocked at 29 to 29. He figured his best bet now rested on his swaying two independent legislators, the unionist Pang Chun-hoi, a member of the Kuomintang, and Hui Yin-fat, the representative of the Social Welfare constituency. Lee approached Pang, whom he did not know well, and Hui, a good friend. He went to meet Hui on Tuesday evening, the eve of the voting day, and pleaded with him for 90 minutes, dwelling on every conceived advantage of a "through train" for every one. Hui was sympathetic but could not vote for the amendment because, as Hui claimed, his constituents, the social workers, were unanimously for the Patten package. Sensing failure, Lee phoned Lu who, Lee believed, in turn rang up Hui and Pang but still the pair would not relent.

On voting day Chan Sui-kau, a garment tycoon and the uncle of the industrialist Chan Wing-kee, came to the Legislative Council Building to make a desperate effort to lobby Pang. Even though the conservative businessman Chan and the stalwart unionist Pang were from two different and opposing camps, they had worked together for ten years in the Labour Advisory Board and had mutual respect. Chan met Pang in Room 220, and the textile magnate thought at one stage that he had succeeded in coaxing Pang along.

But back then even the walls had ears. Patten, holed up in the Government House, while the Legislative Council debated its future, heard every murmur through the constantly updated reports of his private secretary, Bowen Leung, now ironically posted to Beijing as the Hong Kong SAR representative in the national capital. The situation was unbearably tense because some could change sides in the last minute. And it did happen.

His nerves on edge, Young, in whose name the amendment was recorded, finally could not hold his composure and berated those who could bolt. Several of course were looking for an excuse to do just that and Young's reproach provided the pretext. As legislators were ready to vote on the amendment, Simon Ip of the Legal constituency chastised Young for having been "rude" to the independents and would now abstain rather than go with the revision as he had promised. The final count on the amendment was 29 against to 28 for. The "through train" skidded off the rail. Patten won the battle but lost the war.

Allen Lee also disclosed to me that two weeks before voting he had spoken to Martin Lee, Chairman of the Democratic Party, to lobby him and his block to reject the Patten package. Allen told Martin that if the Democrats were to back the Government's package they would have themselves to blame for giving China the free hand to decide on a political system to its own liking. The "proportional representation" system favoured by China proved harmful to the Democrats and it still does. But irony being supreme, the Democrats ended up being the authors of their own misfortune and could not say they had not been warned. I agree with Lee's analysis, whose conclusions have since been confirmed by events. The Democrats are now losing out in the directly elected seats. They are also suffering from internal disputes with regard to precedence on the party's electoral candidates lists.

Preliminary Working Committee

The Preparatory Committee (PC) for the Hong Kong Special Administration Region was a product of the Sino-British Joint Declaration. The Preliminary Working Committee (PWC) for the Hong Kong Special Administrative Region was the fruit of British and Chinese discord.

I was instrumental, to some extent, in the establishment of the PWC, as I had suggested it in early 1993 in, of all places, Guangzhou, the capital of Guangdong Province and about 90 miles north of Hong Kong. By then every body could sense that the political through train was about to be derailed because of Governor Chris Patten's reform package. On 6 February, at the invitation of the

Plate 3.16 *The author accepting the PWC Appointment Certificate from the NPC Chairman, 1993.*

tycoon Henry Fok, a stalwart patriot and Vice-Chairman of the Chinese People's Political Consultative Conference, a number of Hong Kong Affairs Advisors boarded a real through train for the ride from Hong Kong to Guangzhou. We went to attend a ceremony of the White Swan Hotel, one of the best of its kind in the capital.

There at the hotel before us — Vincent Lo, Cha Chi-ming and a few others including myself — were the Directors of the Hong Kong and Macao Affairs Office, Lu Ping and Xinhua News Agency Hong Kong Branch, Zhou Nan. We met and discussed the Hong Kong situation. I said the Hong Kong Affairs Advisors, acting individually, would not be of much use to the Chinese Government, and proposed that China should set up a "Sovereignty Transfer Planning Committee". Its functions were, as the name implied, to advise the

Chinese Government on matters of sovereignty transfer during the transitional period. Such a Committee, however, must not be an alternative centre of power or a challenge to the British Colonial Administration. Lu and Zhou were quite receptive of the idea.

I returned to Hong Kong and jotted down the gist of what I said at the meeting and then faxed it to Lu and Zhou on 14 February. My written proposal suggested that China should establish such a committee or think tank as soon as possible but it had to be absolutely shorn of any administrative power in Hong Kong so as to be acceptable to the people of Hong Kong. The work of this committee should cover three main areas:

(1) To prepare the planning and preliminary work for the establishment in 1996 of the Preparatory Committee;
(2) To study and conduct public debate on how to maintain an apolitical civil service;
(3) To advise the Central Government actions to be taken to effect a smooth transfer of power in 1997.

As for the composition of members for this Planning Committee, I suggested that it should include:

(1) Former government officials and former members of the Executive and Legislative Councils;
(2) Persons who are trustworthy, knowledgeable and pragmatic;
(3) Young democrats and up and coming persons.

The Chinese Authorities did not respond and I thought the matter was left at that. A few months later, on 5 June, Zhou Nan invited me to his headquarters at Happy Valley where he told me the Central Government would establish a Preliminary Working

Committee and wish me to join. The offer was now on the table but there were no details to what the PWC entailed or what were its exact terms of reference. I was puzzled. Then the Standing Committee of the National People's Congress on 2 July sanctioned the establishment of the PWC and announced its membership of 57, with 30 from Hong Kong and the rest were officials from the Mainland.

The Vice Premier and Foreign Minister, Qian Qichen, was named the Chairman. This Committee would also feature a prominent cast of Vice-Chairmen, namely, Vice Foreign Minister Jiang Enzhu, Hong Kong and Macao Affairs Office Director Lu Ping, Hong Kong Xinhua News Agency Director Zhou Nan, NPC Standing Committee Secretary General Zheng Yi, all from the Mainland. From Hong Kong there were three former Basic Law drafters — Ann Tse-kai, Henry Fok and Justice Simon Li.

The PWC got into action very quickly by spawning five specialized groups, each responsible for a specialized policy area, namely, political, economics, legal, culture and security. I joined the political and the economic groups. Each specialized group had a pair of convenors, one from Hong Kong and the other from Mainland. They were for the record:

(1) Political: Leung Chun-ying, Xiao Weiyun.
(2) Economic: Nellie Fong, Gao Shangquan.
(3) Legal: Simon Li, Shao Tianren.
(4) Culture: Ng Hong-mun, Wu Jianfan.
(5) Security: Rita Fan, Wang Shuwen.

The Committee held its first plenary session at the Great Hall of the People on 16 and 17 July to considerable fanfare and media interest. Then in early 1994, additional 13 members were appointed to the Committee, eight from Hong Kong, to round up the roster at 70.

Three years later in 1996 at a National Day Celebration Dinner I sat next to the Deputy Director of Hong Kong Xinhua News Agency, Zhang Junsheng (now President of Jiejiang University in Hangzhou). We exchanged conversation about the work of the PWC over the years and its contribution to the smooth transition. He said it was fortunate that I had proposed to the Government the establishment of the PWC, without which the work of the Preparatory Committee, under the Sino-British confrontational atmosphere, would be extremely difficult.

Little Tricks

The Preliminary Working Committee decided during its inaugural plenary in Beijing in July 1993 to establish a liaison office in Hong Kong, regardless of British objections. Such an office not only projected a presence in Hong Kong but also enabled the PWC to receive submissions, letters and phone calls from the public on matters pertaining to its work. It would further serve as a meeting venue for its Hong Kong members. This sounded reasonable since there was not much purpose in talking about Hong Kong in the abstract from a distance.

The catch was that the PWC had to register such an office with the British Hong Kong Government in accordance with the Societies Ordinance. Knowing Governor Patten's unbridled hostility towards the PWC this would provide an opportunity for the Colonial Government to ban or restrict its operations. Xinhua News Agency in Hong Kong, responsible for aiding the PWC, therefore refused to comply with the registration of the PWC office. The two sides, the British and the Chinese, again reached an impasse and once again they postured, not only to strike an attitude but also to score some propaganda points. Xinhua's External Affairs Department, thereby, on 18 August forwarded a speaking note to Hong Kong Government's Acting Political Advisor, John Ashton, to seek not only exemption from registration but also, much to the gall of the British, assistance.

The Colonial Administration through a third party reminded Xinhua that to ignore or flout the provisions of the Societies Ordinance was obviously illegal. A PWC that was not registered with the Societies Office could be deemed an unlawful organization, more or less on a par with the Triads. If this were leaked to the press, the media would have a field day with the technical niggles.

Xinhua Deputy Director, Qin Wenjun, asked me in October 1993 to help the PWC over the hump. I then spoke on 1 November to the Chief Secretary, Sir David Ford, on how to defuse yet another explosive situation. At that time the Sino-British talks on Patten's political reform were not going well. Sir David, a mandarin who had begun his career in the Royal Army, pondered my request overnight and faxed a letter to me on 2 November asking Xinhua to furnish him with four pieces of information. The Chief Secretary needed to know:

(1) The name of the office.
(2) The name of the officers of the office.
(3) The objects of the office.
(4) The address of the premises.

I relayed this request to Qin who, on 11 November, provided me with the information, including the name of the head of the office, Xinhua Deputy Secretary General, Chan Wei, and the address, Room 1501, China Building, Queen's Road Central. On 15 November I passed the letter from Qin to Sir David. The Chief Secretary answered quite promptly on 27 November, and said, *inter alia*, "... the Societies Officer has now confirmed that he is satisfied that all the requirements of the Societies Ordinance have now been met (albeit in a somewhat unusual way)."

With that, ended an embarrassing episode, as Sir David further said in his letter to me: "We have therefore averted the potentially very difficult problems which would otherwise have risen. I am glad to have been able to see this achieved before my departure."

Sir David Ford retired at the end of 1993 and was succeeded by Mrs. Anson Chan, the first Chinese and the first woman to occupy that high office. Unfortunately she was not only unhelpful but rather hostile to the PWC and its members. There will be more on this in the next section.

British Enmity with the PWC

The Standing Committee of the National People's Congress in July 1993 established the Preliminary Working Committee as a Chinese response to the British reneging on their Joint Declaration pledges. For this reason, it aroused a great deal of resentments from Her Majesty's Government and its Hong Kong Branch. The British, likely at Governor Chris Patten's prompting and the directive of Prime Minister John Major, ordered the colonial civil service (which was supposed to be apolitical) not to co-operate with the PWC, practically declaring it an enemy organization.

The new Chief Secretary, Anson Chan, a loyal mandarin, dutifully issued a circular of 6 October 1994 to her sub-ordinates, instructing them not to deal with the PWC. She stated in the opening paragraph that the PWC was a consultative body of the Chinese

Government and was different from the Preparatory Committee. Chan then got pedantic, saying, because neither the Joint Declaration nor the Basic Law mentioned a PWC, it was superfluous. This was bigotry and also a case of twisted logic. Neither the Joint Declaration nor the Basic Law prescribed Chris Patten's drastic political reform and yet the civil service was told to promote as well as implement it.

The circular said the Administration would not (and could not in a compact community like Hong Kong) forbid officials from meeting and mingling with the PWC members in social functions but it prohibited any of them from attending meetings organized by the PWC or its sub-groups. Civil servants were also not allowed to act as advisors to the PWC or its sub-groups. The civil service unions reluctantly obliged. By putting the entity into purdah, the Hong Kong British Government had hoped but failed completely to stifle the PWC.

But still the circular cast a long shadow, discouraging civil servants from making even courteous, if banal, exchanges with the PWC members during parties and banquets. The officials became wary or aloof, fearing any inadvertent contact might compromise their positions and, worse, jeopardize their careers.

Many of the PWC members were prominent citizens holding important positions locally. These PWC members, for example, included Li Ka-shing, Chairman of Cheung Kong Group; David Li Kwok-po, Chairman of Bank of East Asia; Vincent Lo, Chairman of Shui On Group; Wong Po-yan, Chairman of the Provisional Airport Authority; Lau Wong-fat, Chairman of the Heung Yee Kuk; Woo Chia-wei, President of the UST; and so on. There were also former members of the Executive Council such as Rita Fan, Maria Tam and Lo Tak-shing as well as incumbent legislators, namely, Ngai Shiu-kit, Tam Yiu-chung and Philip Wong.

Executive-led Government

The Preliminary Working Committee's Political Specialized Group had discussed a number of times the so-called "executive-led government structure" as depicted in the Basic Law. The objective was to help the Special Administrative Region retain and refine such an executive-led administration that would be efficacious, open and accountable. Many members including Chinese officials optimistically thought the issue was already settled since the Basic Law, promulgated in April 1990, had already enshrined the principles of an executive-led administration in the SAR. Others who understood the qualities behind the Hong Kong success during its colonial days and knew the chemistry of a strong, effective, executive administration, did not share such premature optimism. Professor Lau Siu-kai and I obviously belong to the doubting minority group not just by way of theory but more so by participation in and observation of how the colonial apparatus worked. We believed the SAR Government would have difficulty maintaining the executive order because of the mounting resistance to it from those with an alternative agenda. What made Hong Kong tick was a consensus that society should focus on economics and not be obsessed with politics, a consensus that was unravelling.

During the earlier colonial days the Legislative Council had both officials, that is mandarins, and "unofficials", that is private citizens who were appointed and answerable to the Governor of the day by whatever name. Power flowed from the executive, the envoy of the Queen. Before 1976 officials even outnumbered unofficials. This ensured that, come what may, the Governor got what he wanted through the LEGCO. Even all the unofficials should defy him, the officials with the majority could always outvote the unofficials. Thus the Governor, the master of patronage, enjoyed the prerogative of first placing his favourites in the LEGCO and then re-enforced that advantage with the official majority. This official majority, let alone the ultimate power of veto, he never had to wield throughout my time as a legislator and Executive Councillor.

I sensed that such an archaic arrangement had to be changed and so, in 1976 in my capacity as the Senior Member of the LEGCO, I persuaded, Governor Sir Murray MacLehose to add more "unofficials" and subtract officials from the assembly. I presented him with a teaser, saying if all civilian appointees to the LEGCO were to disagree with him on an issue, would he abide by them. Sir Murray, after a pause, said he would. I then suggested that since he obviously trusted his "unofficials" he could improve his own public image by naming more private citizens than civil servants to the LEGCO.

Imagine, I said, if the police spotted someone toting a butcher knife in broad daylight and sauntering down the street, would the constable pre-emptively stop, frisk and arrest this suspect or let him go because he had no incriminating evidence, no swag, on him and claimed not to be hell-bent on robbery, bedlam or some form of felony? The police would of course book him or at least take away his butcher knife. The Governor heeded my advice for a pre-emptive reform for, after 1976, he installed in the LEGCO more "unofficials" than officials, even though there was no public outcry against the previous structure. He had began an irrevocable, democratic trend.

His successor Sir Edward Youde ushered in not only more civilians into the assembly after Britain and China signed the Joint Declaration in December 1984, but also introduced elected members. This then furthered the democratic process that his predecessor had nurtured. The British Hong Kong Administration introduced elections to the LEGCO, albeit of the functional constituency kind, in 1985. But still elected members accounted for only a third of the total, leaving of course the appointed, both officials and unofficials, in the majority for the period between 1986 and 1991 when the Basic Law was being drafted. Such a LEGCO composition had no serious impact on the executive-led system, even though the once staid assembly did get a whole lot livelier, which naturally increased the television news rating, whether or not it improved the quality of the bills passed and the debates held.

The big shake-up only came in 1991 when directly-elected legislators were introduced and at the same time elected members became the majority. Four years later in 1995 all the appointed species, including both officials and unofficials, were extinct. This was when the Government felt for the first time serious pressure from the once docile LEGCO wherein the atmosphere had been leisurely, like that of a country club, and legislative business got done with a minimal acrimony and maximum efficiency. No, not that there was an absence of discord but the disagreements were resolved in private rather than out in the open because, back then, what had mattered was not public perception or theatre but effect. Legislators of yore were not really sycophants or rubber stamps. They held their own views and priorities and, being successful in their private sector careers, possessed enough self-confidence not to have to toady to anyone. In some ways those legislators were more capable of individual thinking than are many contemporary politicians, forever ignoring their private qualms and parroting party lines.

Abruptly the Administration in the early 1990s had to lobby for support and alter bills to the restive legislators' liking. Even then members did amend or vote down proposed legislation and, in 1994, even had the unprecedented temerity of denying the Governor the vote of thanks for his annual Policy Address. Civility and manners, whatever these might be called, went out the window along with the once almost compulsory attire of dresses for women and suits for men. Some populist or rebellious legislators just affected the style and argot of the streets as a statement of their refusal to be co-opted into the "establishment". Posturing and uttering sound bites became the norm.

Governor Chris Patten, who had willed the LEGCO to be more democratic or confrontational, only got his reform package saved from being amended by one vote through the intercession of the Prime Minister, John Major. The once vaunted executive-led system was clearly breaking down and, whilst the decay made for more interesting news, it did not make for better government. The Administration began to lose the respect, however once grudging, of the people. This was vexing to those who cherished decorum, order, efficiency and common sense.

The Basic Law stipulated that the SAR legislature would be constituted by election of various means and methods. These elected members of course had to advance the interests of their constituents. They not only had to represent their voters but must appear to do so since image mattered so much, mattered sometimes more than substance.

Hong Kong is not an independent country but a SAR of the People's Republic of China. The Chief Executive (CE) himself is afflicted with dual loyalty. He had to abide by the voters, few though they were and are still now, and also the larger community, and at the same time discharged his duty to the Central Government, which appointed him at the recommendation of the Selection Committee. To complicate an already confusing situation, China in formulating the rules for the election of the CE, also forbade any CE candidate with political affiliations. Those who had such ties must resign forthwith from the party, even though it could lend him and his administration support in the LEGCO. The President of the United States, for one, professes to rule for the non-partisan, national interests and yet he had his own party. Nonetheless he could induce defectors from the opposition to rally to his cause in the Congress and Senate.

The power of the SAR legislature, like that of the other parliaments, is considerable. While the legislative assembly cannot initiate or formulate government policy *per se*, it can amend and repeal laws. The LEGCO can vet and pass (or not) the budget as well as oversee the revenue and expenditure. The members can be more than a nuisance because they can stall the government.

The Basic Law, in promoting an executive-led administration, is wise enough to retain a power from the colonial era by way of its Article 74, which states that legislators can not move private members' bills that affect public expenditure, political structure and government operations. Those legislators who want to encroach on this administrative prerogative must acquire the written consent of the Chief Executive, which is unlikely.

The Basic Law Annex II also lists in detail the LEGCO voting procedures on bills and motions. The very elaborate, sometimes perplexing, composition of the Council and its electoral methods also prevent domination by any one party. These instruments should be helpful in maintaining an executive-led SAR Administration.

Taking all these factors into consideration, I reckon the Basic Law by itself alone does not provide sufficient safeguards for an executive-led government and need some supplementary provisions. One way is for the Chief Executive to command some consistent and substantial, if not majority, support in the legislature to do his work better. It is suggested that the second clause of the Election Rules should be abolished, specifically the point about "The Chief Executive candidature can only be accepted in his personal capacity. People who belong to a party must quit the party when declaring his intention to run." As I write these memoirs the first Chief Executive, Tung Chee-hwa, is hobbled without consistent support in the now highly politicized legislature and this has eroded public confidence in his office and in his leadership. Furthermore it is just like adding salt to injury, as he is also lack of support in the executive branch from his own men sharing his vision, advocating and defending his policies, and faithful to him.

Looking forward, it is imperative that the SAR Government should seek a proper law for political parties, and at the same time encourage their healthy development. The Government should also do more to raise the standards of social and civic education, to nurture young political talent, and to encourage more able and civil people to take part in politics. Only then can the SAR look towards to a bright, democratic and dynamic future under an executive-led administration.

Reckless Driving

The Chinese Government invited Hong Kong Affairs Advisors and Preliminary Working Committee members to a resort near Sanya, Hainan Island, for a holiday from 16 to 18 December 1994. The tropical setting would relax the perpetually tense people and induce them to think more creatively than in the confine of bustling conference halls and crowded hotel lounges. Strolling along the esplanade, Hong Kong and Macao Affairs Office Director Lu Ping and I inadvertently strayed from the pack. We stragglers, therefore, had only each other to talk to and it was then that Lu told me that the Sino-British Joint Liaison Group might form an expert group to oversee the Hong Kong British Government in drawing up the 1996–97 and the 1997–98 budgets. The Director said his Government wanted me to be advisor to the expert group and hoped that I would accept.

This plan was officially announced in early 1995 and the group would be called, "The Expert Group on the Transitional Budget and Related Matters". China appointed to it, besides Mainland officials and economic specialists as members, some Hong Kong members of the PWC Economic Specialized Group as advisors. Right away the detractors of the PWC began to moan about some of us gaining monetary benefits from learning the fiscal secrets of the Hong Kong Government. The tarring of the PWC had by then become a nervous tick with some people. Even some Hong Kong officials groused.

South China Morning Post columnist Fanny Wong (now Mrs. Mike Rowse and an employee of the Independent Commission Against Corruption) wrote an article on the subject. She harped on the conflict of interest issue and asked the Chinese Government to act cautiously.

On the same day that Wong's column appeared I faxed to Hong Kong and Macao Affairs Office and Xinhua News Agency Hong Kong Branch Directors, Lu Ping and Zhou Nan, samples of hysterical articles decrying the appointments of private sector individuals to the Expert Group. I said, whether the attacks were fair or not, China had to attend to the issue of the potential conflict of interest and assure the public the work and role of the advisors were beyond reproach.

I proposed two ways for the Chinese Government to allay the fears, exaggerated or not. I said advisors from Hong Kong could take an oath, such as that required of Executive Councillors. The wording

Plate 3.17 *The Budget Expert Subgroup of the Sino-British Joint Liaison Group, 1997.*

could be: "I, as advisor to the Chinese Government's expert group in the compilation of the budget estimates, will not disclose in any form sensitive or secret information without the prior permission of the Chinese Government. I will also not benefit myself or any person with the knowledge of sensitive and secret information."

The alternative, which is more difficult to effect, was for the Chinese side not to release to the advisors any document containing secret or sensitive information. In addition, advisors will not participate in discussions that could be construed as conflict of interest.

The Chinese Government heeded the advice and opted to have the four advisors — Nellie Fong, Shao Youbao, Philip Wong and myself — took the oath in April 1995 during the Economic Specialized Group meeting in Beijing before the Chinese Representative of the Joint Liaison Group, Zhao Jihua. Lu, his deputy Zhang Liangdong and a few Chinese officials were also present to witness the simple oath taking ceremony.

Much was discussed in the series of the Expert Group meetings lasting until the Chinese recovery of Hong Kong but none was more memorable than what the Chinese Representative, Chen Zuo'er, blurted out at the press interview after the fifth conclave in Beijing in November 1995. His graphic metaphor and intensity of emotion excited the media as much as the subject that so aroused him. The outburst was cathartic as it was positive too because it showed how sincerely concerned the Chinese side was about protecting the assets and future of the Hong Kong Special Administrative Region.

The Budget Expert Group included, for the record and among others, on the Chinese side: Chen Zuo'er from the JLG, Gao Qiang of the Finance Ministry, Zhu Zushou of the Foreign Ministry, Liu Qiang of the Hong Kong and Macao Affairs Office, plus Wang Lin of Xinhua News Agency of Hong Kong Branch. The British had representing them Hong Kong Government's Treasury Secretary Kwong Ki-chi (now Chief Executive of the Hong Kong Stock Exchange) and his three deputies — Alan Lai, Kevin Ho and Mike Rowse.

At the brief press interview after the meeting, Chen stood side by side with Kwong and made a statement to the astonishment and alarm of everybody present. He said, "The Hong Kong British Government is planning the social welfare expenditure like a reckless driver who is going so fast that he will eventually crash and get killed." He was speaking in response to a reported speech made by the Hong Kong Director of Social welfare, Ian Strachan, at the Kowloon Lions Club on 14 November 1995. Strachan had boosted that welfare expenditure in Hong Kong had increased by 160 per cent in the past five years from HK$5 billion in 1990–91 to $13 billion in 1995–96. He further predicted that based on current rate of expansion Hong Kong's social welfare services would reach the First World standard by year 2000.

Chen was annoyed that the British did not bring the expenditure forecast straddling 1997 for discussion prior to making the public statement. He suspected that the British had a plot to sap the vitality of Hong Kong and present the SAR Government with a bill its treasury could not honour, thus causing social disaffection with the new administration and general alienation. The envoy from the JLG was not speaking from his prepared notes. He extemporized, an utterance that came from the heart.

China had hoped that the British would be more prudent and considerate, which they had promised to be in the spirit of the Joint Declaration. The Colonial Administration had evidently ignored the Chinese plea and, thus, to paraphrase Chen, contrived to drive the car of Hong Kong recklessly.

The Chinese Government Expert Group for the Transitional

Budget commenced its work in March 1995 and continued until the sovereignty transfer on 30 June 1997. During these two years its influence on both the 1996–97 and 1997–98 budgets was really minimal. In the first instance the Hong Kong budgets by themselves are very complicated with all the trend figures and policy ratios that members, including the advisors of the Chinese Expert Group, were not familiar with and could not readily grasp. In addition the Chinese side had no veto power and the British needed not heed its advice and objection. The continual fast expansion of social welfare expenditure after Chen's outburst is a good case in point.

Growth of Welfare Expenditure 1990–99

Fiscal Year	90/91	91/92	92/93	93/94	94/95	95/96
Welfare Exp. ($100 Million)	48.9	61.3	70.3	87.9	105.4	129.6

Average Growth Rate = 21% per annum

Fiscal Year	95/95	96/97	97/98	98/99	99/00
Welfare Exp. ($100 Million)	129.6	167.9	203.4	253.3	272.6
Growth Rate	23%	29%	21%	24%	7%

The Hong Kong SAR Government eventually did slow down the welfare expenditure growth rate in 1999 just as the Asian financial crisis and the resultant Hong Kong recession were raising unemployment. The cut was obviously necessary and painful as it was unpopular.

Victims of the Sino-British Dispute

I have often pondered who were the greatest victims of the wholly needless British and Chinese wrangle in the last years of the transition. Generally speaking, those hurt by the fracas were the ordinary people of Hong Kong, some of whom lost confidence and might have migrated. Still others grew disenchanted with the rancorous political process, especially the constant posturing and bickering that filled the airwaves, the television screens and the news pages. Worst of all, the Sino-British confrontation distracted the public from a worthwhile enterprise, that of developing Hong Kong's longer term economy and society. But they aside, the chief sufferers were individuals who could have gained higher office if Britain and China had co-operated, as envisaged during the early years of the transition.

Back in the mid-1980s when I was the Senior Member of the Executive Council, with the Joint Declaration signed, the Governor in Council had considered constructing a rail for the through train on which the future Chief Executive would first be a passenger, then the conductor. The thinking was that Britain and China in 1995 or 1996 would together nominate a Deputy Governor who would be the under-study of the incumbent. The specification for that was written into the Joint Declaration Clause 3, Sub-clause (4), which reads, "The Chief Executive will be appointed by the Central People's Government on the basis of the results of elections or consultations to be held locally." The Executive Council at that time leaned more towards the consultation method than the election, if only because it appeared less unseemly, more dignified, less contentious, and more in tune with the Hong Kong tradition.

Not only the Deputy Governor would be on the "through train", so too would be the Executive and the Legislative Branches of the Colonial Government with minimum fuss, other than for the necessary oath of allegiance they must pay to the new sovereign on 1 July 1997. Such an effortless, graceful carrying on of business appealed to those of us who simply dreaded any hint of trauma. Businessmen too, local and international, and the foreign community would like this just as much because their interests would not be jeopardized. People would not have to be preoccupied with the succession issue or be forced to take sides. This all seemed so smart, so sensible.

I retired as the Senior Member of EXCO in September 1988. Dame Lydia Dunn succeeded me and Allen Lee in turn succeeded her as the Senior Member of the Legislative Council as well as remained in the EXCO to bridge the two Councils. Lee subsequently told me that, after my exit, the EXCO continued to mull over a candidate for the Deputy Governor. The majority opinion was just like the emerging consensus in the "Cabinet" when I had been its Senior Member.

Should Sino-British co-operation continued as amicable as in the mid-1980s, it was likely that one of the senior mandarins of ethnic Chinese descent and steeped on administrative experience, such as the Chief Secretary or the Financial Secretary, would be appointed to the new post of Deputy Governor prior to 1997 with the blessing of both the British and Chinese Governments. Thereafter in accordance with the Article 45 of the Basic Law, the Deputy Governor would be selected through consultations held locally and appointed by the Central People's Government as the first Chief Executive of the Hong Kong SAR.

But, alas, this tidy and almost seamless transition was not to be, whoever's fault this might have been. The perfect solution dissolved when Britain changed its policy towards China and, thereupon, undermined trust and co-operation. The rancour also undermined the ambition of the incumbent Chief Secretary at the time (Anson Chan, now retired) or the incumbent Financial Secretary at the time (Sir Donald Tsang, now Chief Secretary) to ride on the "through train" ascending to the top office of the first Chief

Executive of the HKSAR. I believe any of those candidates was a casualty of the clash of sovereigns and at least one of them rues that to this day.

Chapter 4

The Hong Kong SAR

The Preparation

Provisional Legislative Council

The Provisional Legislative Council was the reluctant alternative to the "through train" which Chris Patten had derailed with his unilateral reform programme. The Chinese Central Government had co-operated with the British Government through the Joint Declaration and, later, the Basic Law, in which a "through train" was designed for the serving legislators in 1997. These efforts were made to ensure minimum disruptions to the running of Hong Kong as it evolved from a British colony to a Special Administrative Region of China. This sensible, unique approach was initiated by the British in 1988 when I was the Senior Member of the Executive Council. It had, very unfortunately, come undone during the five years of the last Governor who had another agenda.

The Preliminary Working Committee, of which I was a member, had to cope with the derailment. In the first quarter of 1990, Britain and China had reached a consensus on political reform that would allow serving legislators to continue onward, except for a requisite stop on the tracks to pledge allegiance to the new SAR of China and adherence to the Basic Law. When Chris Patten succeeded in getting his political reform package through the Legislative

Council, avoiding being amended by one vote, in June 1994, the derailment was certain. The PWC had then to step in at the eleventh hour to find a way to get all the necessary pieces of the legislation passed and the transitional work related to the legislature done for the ushering in of the new era on 1 July 1997 legally and with dignity.

Five vital steps involving the Legislative Council, provisional or not, must have been taken before the SAR could turn from promise into fact and vision into reality. These were:

(1) The Legislative Council, according to Article 90 of the Basic Law, must endorse the SAR Chief Executive's appointment of the judges of the Court of Final Appeal and the Chief Judge of the High Court.

(2) The National People's Congress in promulgating on 4 April 1990 the Basic Law specified the setting up of the Basic Law Committee with six Mainland members and six Hong Kong members. The latter had to be nominated jointly by the Chief Executive, the President of the Legislative Council and the Chief Justice.

(3) The SAR Legislative Council must be operative at or immediately after mid-night on 30 June 1997 to debate and pass the Reunification Bill.

(4) The SAR Legislative Council must meet as soon as possible after the transition at mid-night on 30 June 1997 to amend and/or revoke any existing legislation that contravened the Basic Law and also any existing legislation not acceptable to the SAR Government.

(5) The SAR Legislative Council must debate and pass the first SAR financial budget for 1997–98 as soon as possible after 1 July 1997.

Quite plainly there must have to be a functioning Legislative Council of some sort latest by 1 July 1997 to fill any legal void. Preferably the Council should be operative before 1 July 1997 to perform the tedious preparatory work. This was the guiding principle taken by the PWC Political Affairs Group in its discussions on contingencies to deal with the end of the Sino-British co-operation. After some lengthy deliberations it was clear that there were two main schools of thought. The first was to establish a Provisional Legislative Council that would exist for a relatively short duration prior to the formation of the substantive Legislative Council. The other was to rush in to form the first substantive legislature.

The second alternative was based on the Basic Law Article 68 which stipulated that the SAR legislature must be constituted by election and in accordance with that prescribed in its Annex II. Annex II stated that the SAR Legislative Council would comprise 60 members, and for the first Legislative Council it should be formed in accordance with the decisions of the National People's Congress. Some PWC members felt the better answer would be to have the NPC amend its own resolution adopted on 4 April 1990 to let the Selection Committee, which was to pick the Chief Executive, also elect the first SAR Legislative Council as well. They figured this option was better than a provisional legislature with a short operating life and with dubious legitimacy that would most likely be challenged in the Hong Kong courts.

The first alternative and the more popular of the choices, was to have a Provisional Legislative Council as the interim solution. The thinking was that such an assembly would handle all the mandatory works for the transition while leaving the first SAR Legislative Council more or less exactly as the NPC had envisaged it when it approved the Basic Law in 1990. Even then, with this tacit agreement, the debate continued. China's legal experts believed the Preparatory Committee, which was to succeed the PWC, had the prerogative to shape the Provisional Legislative Council and favoured having the Selection Committee nominate the 60 legislators along with the Chief Executive.

Members also noted that, in either case, the resultant legislature could not comply with the rules specified in the Basic Law Annex II, regarding the parts about voting procedures for bills and resolutions.

Eventually, after a lot more deliberation, the PWC decided to have a Provisional Legislative Council lasting no longer than twelve months from 1 July 1997 and be succeeded by the first SAR Legislative Council in 1998 under the terms and conditions of the Basic Law.

The PWC of course anticipated the legal challenge, especially from the Democratic Party and its allies. The Democrats did the predictable — and predictability is their trait — in 1997 prior to the sovereignty transfer by seeking a judicial review of the Provisional Legislative Council only to be rebuffed by the High Court on 12 June 1997. There will be more on this in a later section.

The SAR Selection Committee of 400 members, which held its meetings in Shenzhen under the jurisdiction of the People's Republic of China, duly on 21 December 1996 nominated 60 members of the Provisional Legislative Council with Rita Fan as its President. On 28 May 1998 the election was carried out in the HKSAR in accordance with the Basic Law to form the first SAR Legislative Council, which came into being on 1 July 1998, replacing the Provisional Legislative Council and putting behind it the whole Chris Patten reform saga.

Plate 4.1 *The End-of-Term Dinner of the Provisional Legislative Council, 1998.*

The Guessing Game

The idea of converting a British colony into an autonomous region of another country was grand and unprecedented but the details that the process entailed were tedious and complex. Those of us involved in making the notion go were bogged down in a hundred conundrums. But in some ways the most intriguing aspect of our enterprise was identifying the right Chief Executive. The difficulty in the endeavour was that Hong Kong had never had the opportunity to pick its own leader throughout the period of foreign rule in which the Governor was always the beneficiary of one person, one vote, the person being the British Prime Minister of the day.

I did not think too much about being a Chief Executive candidate myself, even though others had periodically tipped me to be a possible choice probably because of my experience in politics and administration. I was flattered, yes, but I was not keen about the pursuit of the post when I was well into my 70s and lacking the vim and vigour. Even if the heart was there, the legs were not.

Back in 1994 the usually informative *Mirror* magazine reported the remarks made by the former Chairman of the National People's Congress, Wan Li, about nominations received in Beijing for the first Chief Executive. One of the names on his list was Chung Sze-yuen, myself. The octogenarian mused aloud that, whilst I was then 76, age should not be an obstacle because what counted to him was competence and ability in capitalist administration. He also mentioned the other nominations received, including Justice Simon Li, the then Chief Justice Sir Ti-liang Yang, former civil servant John Chan, Wheelock conglomerate Chairman Peter Woo and property consultant Leung Chun-ying. Li, Yang and Woo subsequently did bid for the post.

Since the *Mirror* article, which I did not take too seriously, my name constantly cropped up in talks about the future Chief Executive. Fanny Wong in the *South China Morning Post* on 23 November 1995 even claimed that I was the odd one favourite to take up the post because of what she perceived to be my combinations of attributes. She also described a speech I made on 21 November at the Annual Fellows Dinner of the Hong Kong Management Association about the tasks ahead for the Chief Executive as a platform oration. This of course was not the speech's intended purpose. She was off the mark with her interpretation of my delivery and yet she was pretty right about how some people thought what the qualifications were for the job. Some Hong Kong members of the Preliminary Working Committee and the Preparatory Committee, such as Dr. Raymond Wu, Tsui Sze-man, and Professor Patrick Ho, had at times prompted me to vie for the post. I politely dismissed their entreaty.

I recalled the time when I retired from the Executive Council in 1988 when I was already older than 70. At the time with another nine years before 1997, my most fervent wish in 1988 was to live long enough to witness the national reunification under the terms of the Joint Declaration. I did not contemplate being the Chief Executive much until the concept, or temptation, crept briefly into my head when the Chinese Central Government appointed me in 1992 as its Hong Kong Affairs Advisor, and the following year to the newly formed PWC. These appointments together with encouragement from some of my friends stimulated my interest. But then I also realized the limits of time, as I looked at my hair either turning grey or falling off my head. I was basically fit, as robust as could be expected for a person of my age, but just did not have the stamina to campaign for and take on the punitively exacting job. I had a choice between preserving my health or risking it for the service to Hong Kong and also for vanity. I chose the saner course and at one time joking with Dr. Wu that "Your asking me to run for the CE is like wanting me to bid for a state funeral."

While I parried off the PWC and PC colleagues' suggestion, I had to do the same to one from the Hong Kong and Macao Affairs Office Director, Lu Ping. During a quiet talk with him in a hotel room at the Hong Kong Macao Centre in Beijing in 1995, he queried me out of the blue whether I was keen for the Chief Executive's post. I demurred, saying to Lu that if had not been 78 but rather 20 years younger, I would consider running. But now at this stage of my life I could not face the rebuff from the electorate if I lost, or up to the most demanding job if I win. This was what I would call a no win situation.

Bumps and Ruts on the Road

The task of preparing Hong Kong to be a Special Administrative Region of China was hard but made harder by the hostility and pettiness of the Colonial Government that resented any parallel or challenge, real or imagined, to itself even in its waning months. Those called upon to fulfil their civic or patriotic duty never deluded themselves that the British would co-operate as long as Governor Chris Patten remained at the helm since he was the pilot who had steered the ship into troubled waters. But some did expect a little more civility or graciousness only to find out that asking for a little was already asking for too much.

I, one of the victims, felt the Hong Kong Government's wrath as far back as 1995 for trying to do in my personal capacity what Britain had been committed to by treaty to work with China to effect a smooth transition. I gave on 21 November 1995 a speech at the Annual Fellowship Dinner of the Hong Kong Management Association in the Regent Hotel in Kowloon.

The talk, entitled "The Most Crucial Year in the Transition" was quite innocuous in my estimation since it merely laid out on a map the route of the final 12 months of the transition for the SAR Government in waiting. I foresaw the first SAR Chief Executive would be chosen in the latter half of 1996 and he would fashion his administration according to the doctrine of the Basic Law and his own vision. Half a year was the least time he needed to select and drill his team for the very detailed undertaking. Even with the best of the British and Chinese intentions the task would be Herculean but, as I spoke, the British intentions were hostile and the Chinese were sincere but without the clearest directions. Such a Chief Executive Elect, under tremendous public pressure and press scrutiny, must pick his Executive Council, his Cabinet, which would have to be inclusive but not too big and ungainly. He would then have to nominate his principal officials for appointment by the Central Government. He would have to inspire or at least be able to focus the peoples' attention on the future policies and oversee a dignified transfer of sovereignty. He would have to repeal and replace, with the assistance of his Executive Council and legislature, laws which are contrary to either the Basic Law or to the interest of the future SAR. He had to do all this while outside a mob of "democrats" and demagogues, roused by mischief-makers, besieged and beseeched him about preserving the unilateral reforms that had been implemented by the British.

I predicted in my speech that the Chief Executive Elect would set up a temporary office staffed by a few hundred persons ranging from clerks to senior advisors by the end of 1996. Such an essential establishment, though, would irk some paranoid groups and the recalcitrant British Hong Kong Government, which would be afraid of an alternative source of power and disliked being portrayed as a "lame duck" administration. I said such a shadow government was inevitable before Hong Kong's reunification with China and that it should not be lamented but rather appreciated.

I then cited the example of the United States, a superpower of today. The Americans, I stressed, elect their new President once every four years during the first week of November but would not inaugurate him until 20 January the following year, nearly three months later. During the interval the President Elect will have to assemble his team of over one thousand political appointees, who together form in essence a shadow government. I implored the people not to rush to condemn but to collaborate, ignoring the calumnies and excitements of those who did not want the transition to succeed.

Whereas the change in the United States is a regular change of ruling parties, that in Hong Kong in 1997 was one of change of sovereignty which was unusual and a one off operation. Our work was complex, sensitive and tedious and with results which must be right for the six and a half million people before the eyes of the world. But the enterprise was worthwhile because what was to happen was unprecedented in history — a peaceful return of one parcel of land with all the people living on it from one state to another. I urged all to contribute over the final stage to the process that would culminate in an elaborate ceremony, ignore the over-lapping bounds of authority, and be rational rather than emotional.

Immediately after the delivery of my speech which analysed the scenario impassively and objectively, the Hong Kong British Government and the biased wing of the media rounded on me and attempted to mislead the people. Nonetheless the vindication was mine and it was sweet when indeed the Selection Committee of 400 selected the first Chief Executive in December 1996. He in turn established his office, known as the Office of the Chief Executive, Hong Kong SAR, The People's Republic of China, at the Asia Financial Centre on Garden Road, opposite to the new Bank of China Tower, which was designed by the famous Chinese American architect, I. M. Pei.

The Chief Executive Elect, Tung Chee-hwa, eventually brought in a crew of some 80 people, most were seconded from the Hong Kong Government and some were from his own shipping company, Oriental Overseas. Heading the Tung Chee-hwa team was Michael Suen, now the Secretary for Constitutional Affairs, and the Office Administrator was Fanny Law, now the Secretary for Education and Manpower. The legion laboured under tremendous strain and yet they maintained enough composure to ward off vicious and constant barbs as well as innuendoes from the Sinophobic media.

Tung, as the Chief Executive, commiserated with me after the transfer of sovereignty how the Hong Kong British Government had frustrated him and denied him more staff assistance. He was still innocent, not realizing how it was not to the interest of the last occupant of the Government House to let him, a perceived rival, succeed or have a smooth sailing.

Even though the Chief Executive Elect was in the saddle in December 1996, he could not run on without a legislature — the Provisional Legislative Council, which had to be assembled by early 1997 at the latest. Thus for half a year Hong Kong would have two legislatures, the colonial one fading out and the SAR provisional one preparing to get in. This duality would pose many unavoidable problems because the British had derailed the "through train" for those legislators elected in 1995 under the British Administration. Some of the confusion could be cleared away if both the embryonic SAR Government and the end of the line Colonial Administration would explain the predicament to the public. This, however, the Colonial Government, led by Chris Patten, refused to do and, instead, scorned the Provisional Legislative Council and stopped officials from co-operating with it. I did my bid spelling out the need for and the role of such a provisional legislature.

But right after my speech Attorney General Jeremy Mathews, the only British mandarin left behind at that time, attacked me in the letters column of the *South China Morning Post*. The trained solicitor contended that some groups were bound to contest the legitimacy of the Provisional Legislative Council all the way to the SAR Court of Final Appeal. Some politicians took the cue and goaded the public to resist and boycott such a legislature. Matthews then predicted that if the appeal succeeded, then not only this institution would have to be disbanded but also all the laws it had passed would be invalidated, thus causing legal chaos. The two of us were joined in the epistolary fray by a lawyer named Lam Kam, an Oxford graduate, who thought my case was stronger than Matthew's was. The row went on until the end of the British Hong Kong and the return to the United Kingdom of the last colonial Attorney General.

Whilst recognizing the need for the Provisional Legislative Council to operate prior to 1 July 1997, some Chinese officials, members of the Preliminary Working Committee as well as the Preparatory Committee had worries about its operation under the British jurisdiction. Whereas the Attorney General bristled at the legitimacy of the assembly, the others were more concerned with its mundane logistics. They figured the Hong Kong Government would not welcome the institution meeting in its jurisdiction because that would add insult to injury. Some also fretted over groups antagonistic towards China or "Sinophobes" rallying against the Provisional Legislative Council. The Hong Kong Government would also interfere. Those anti-China media would be no less intrusive and injuring.

I had earlier suggested to some Chinese officials and members of the PC that the Provisional Legislature could hold its meetings in the nearby Chinese territory such as Zhuhai, next to Macao on the west bank of Pearl River, or Shenzhen, north of the Hong Kong border. This way the Provisional Legislature would be beyond the reach of the Hong Kong British Government, the shouting range of the rabble rousers and yet close enough to ensure ample press and TV coverage. I remember vividly on one summer day in 1996 Sir Quo-wei. Lee and I had lunch in the Hang Seng Bank penthouse with the visiting PC member Li Chuwen from Shanghai. Li was the Deputy Director of Xinhua Hong Kong Branch during the 1980s and advisor to the

Shanghai Municipal Government in the 1990s. He had expressed the same concern as some other Chinese officials but was quite relieved after hearing my suggestion.

Eventually the Provisional Legislative Council met in Shenzhen from January to June 1997 despite causing some inconvenience to its members. Mathews was right, however, about the Democrats suing the institution. An elderly Democrat, Ng King-luen, became the proxy through which his party challenged the Provisional Legislature in the High Court in 1997 prior to the sovereignty transfer. In the judgement given by Justice Sears on 12 June 1997, it said, *inter alia*:

> "(1) It may well be Mr. Ng was specifically chosen because he qualified for legal aid and therefore the public are funding this application.
> (2) There was nothing unlawful which the Provisional Legislature had done.
> (3) The Court's jurisdiction was only over what took place in Hong Kong."

Finally Justice Sears said, "The conclusion therefore I have come to is that this application is bound to fail. It has no chance of success at all and I would be wrong to permit further public expenses and further judicial time being spent on it. The application is refused."

After the sovereignty transfer and in July 1997, in the case of HKSAR *v.* David Ma and others in the Court of Appeal, Solicitor-General Daniel Fung was acting for the HKSAR and Gladys Li (former Chairman of the Bar Association and daughter of retired Justice Simon Li) for the defendants. The main issue argued was whether the Common Law survived through the change of sovereignty on

1 July 1997. A side issue was the legality of the Provisional Legislative Council.

On the main issue the Court of Appeal concluded that upon a true construction and interpretation of the relevant provisions of the Basic Law, the laws previously in force in Hong Kong, including the Common Law, were adopted and became the laws of the HKSAR on 1 July 1997, the judicial system together with the principles applicable to court proceedings had continued, and indictments and pending criminal proceedings continued to be valid.

As to the side issue the Court held that the Provisional Legislative Council was legally established by the NPC through the Preparatory Committee pursuant to the authority and powers conferred upon it. The NPC, being the sovereign of the HKSAR, the validity of its acts in establishing this interim body could not be challenged in the HKSAR courts.

The Hong Kong British Government knew from the very beginning that it could not prevent China from having a provisional legislature to repeal and replace laws its colonial legislature had passed that violated the Basic Law, contradicted terms of the Joint Declaration, and against the interest of the SAR. No present legislature can bind the hands of the future assembly even within the same sovereign, let alone the succeeding state. But in lieu of power the departing Administration had the posture. The whole purpose of the exercise was to irritate China, agitate the innocent people, and undermine confidence in the incoming SAR Government. It was as spiteful as regrettable.

Vanguard of the Hong Kong SAR

The third session of the Seventh National People's Congress held on

4 April 1990 decided to establish a Preparatory Committee in 1996. This Committee would be responsible for the founding the Hong Kong Special Administrative Region on 1 July 1997. The first task of the PC would be to assemble the Selection Committee, which would recommend the candidate for the first Chief Executive of the SAR through consultation or election. The recommendation would first go to the PC and then, if accepted, be submitted to the Central People's Government for appointment.

The singular task of the SC became more complex, however, when the British in 1994 reneged on their promise in early 1990 to co-operate with China to construct a political "through train" for the legislators from the colonial era to the SAR one. The Selection Committee, therefore, had to nominate not only the CE but additionally assemble members for the Provisional Legislative Council.

This additional task was understood by the Preparatory Committee which gathered for its first plenary session on 16 January 1996 in Beijing to establish the Selection Committee Group with 43 members. Convening this Group were Xiao Weiyun, a law professor at Peking University, Tam Yiu-chung, a Hong Kong labour unionist, and myself. We were entrusted with the urgent responsibility of identifying the types of people eligible for the Selection Committee and we had to do that based on the criteria defined in Annex 1 of the Basic Law and the resolution of the third session of the Seventh National People's Congress on 4 April 1990. We, the Selection Committee Group, therefore became the vanguard of the Hong Kong SAR.

Both the Basic Law and the NPC resolution divided the Selection Committee, an Electoral College in essence, into four broad categories comprising one hundred constituents each. The first category would come from the industrial, commercial and financial

Plate 4.2 *The Chinese leaders and members of the Hong Kong SAR Preparatory Committee, 1996.*

sectors. The second would be from the professional sector, including those drawn from the various guilds or associations representing doctors, engineers, lawyers, accountants, academics, so on and so forth. The third would be constituted by affiliates of labour, religious, grassroots and similar groups. The fourth would compose of local delegates of the National People's Congress, members of the Chinese People's Political Consultative Conference and former political figures, such as retired legislators and Executive Councillors.

The PC Selection Committee Group convened its inaugural meeting in Beijing on 15 February 1996 and decided to form under it four sub-groups, each responsible for one of the four broad categories in the Selection Committee. We then got down to the tedious but necessary detail of pinpointing individuals and organizations most worthy of inclusion in a very exclusive electorate, which was not easy since those who qualified were many but places were scarce. We unavoidably had to be judicious and did not wish to offend or favour any one. We all know the famous book *Making Friends and Influencing People* and, if we stumbled, we could end up "losing friends and alienating people".

We then decided that each sub-group should have two convenors, one from Hong Kong and one from the Mainland. These convenors were, for the record:

(1) The first sub-group for industrial, commercial and financial sectors:

Wilfred Wong, an ex-civil servant and investor of infrastructural projects on the Mainland.

Huang Diyan, a senior executive with the Bank of China, Hong Kong Branch.

(2) The second sub-group for professionals:

Nellie Fong, a senior partner with Author Andersen, a large accounting firm.

Sun Nansan, a division chief at Hong Kong Xinhua News Agency.

(3) The third sub-group for labour, religious and grassroots:

Lo Shuk-ching, a local leader in community services.

Chen Zuo'er, a Chinese representative of the Sino-British Joint Liaison Group.

(4) The fourth sub-group for political figures:

Lee Cho-jat, a leading publisher in Hong Kong.

Ke Zashuo, former senior Chinese representative of the Sino-British Joint Liaison Group.

Rather than drafting a haphazard or arbitrary list of candidature, the Selection Committee Group decided to consult the Hong Kong public over a period of three days — from 13 to 15 April 1996. With results in hand the Selection Committee Group held its fifth meeting in Beijing on 14 May 1996 and decided on the following four major recommendations for the Preparatory Committee to consider:

(1) Selection Committee members must be at least 18 years old and permanent Hong Kong residents, irrespective of their nationality. Under the British Hong Kong law, foreign nationals residing in Hong Kong continuously for seven years or more would still not be eligible for the permanent Hong Kong resident status. However with the application of the Article 24(4) of the Basic Law, foreign nationals such as the activist Elsie Tu and the former Chief Secretary Sir David Akers-Jones would become permanent Hong Kong residents and be eligible for membership of the Selection Committee.

(2) Candidates for the first three categories must be nominated by their own organizations through the Hong Kong Communication Office of the Preparatory Committee.
(3) The fourth, that is the political, category should comprise the following:
  (a) 26 NPC delegates who were concurrently permanent Hong Kong residents;
  (b) 34 representatives of the CPPCC delegates;
  (c) 40 chosen from former legislators, Executive Councillors and government officials.
(4) The Chairman and the nine Vice Chairmen of the Preparatory Committee would be responsible for screening and compiling a list of candidates of not less than 120 per cent of the seats available for election by the PC members. As to the 34 representatives of the CPPCC delegates, the method of selection would be decided by the CPPCC delegates themselves.

The process so recommended, though rather complicated, was competitive so as to dispel the notion that the Selection Committee was a sham or subterfuge for another trite round of appointments.

The Preparatory Committee at its fourth plenary in Beijing on 9 August 1996 accepted in total the recommendations of the Selection Committee Group. It was also announced that nominations would be received by the Selection Committee Group through the Communication Office of the Preparatory Committee in China Building, 29 Queen's Road Central, Hong Kong from 15 August to 14 September 1996.

Eventually a total of 5,791 applications were received with the following breakdowns for each of the four categories:

Category 1: Business (100 places)	1,272.
Category 2: Professionals (100 places)	1,209.
Category 3: Labour, etc. (100 places)	3,162.
Category 4: Political (40 places)	148.

The Preparatory Committee at its fifth plenary in Beijing on 4 October 1996 conducted the final election by secret ballots and decided on the 340 names of the Selection Committee. On the same day, members of the Chinese People's Political Consultative Conference also held their own election for their 34 representatives on the Selection Committee.

With the formation of the 400-member Selection Committee the scene was set for the selection of the first Chief Executive and the election of the Provisional Legislative Council of the Hong Kong SAR.

Plate 4.3 *Meeting of the Selection Committee Group of the Preparatory Committee in Beijing, 1996.*

Support for Tung Chee-hwa

Ever since the signing of the Sino-British Joint Declaration in December 1984, many in the media had speculated on whom might be the likely first Special Administrative Region Chief Executive, a job for which there would be no shortage of applicants. The press had carried on a game, much as the race sheet would on horses, about identifying the candidates and spotting their changing odds based on a number of factors. Among some of the criteria used for rating the probability of any prospect were not only his or her personal merits and latest accomplishments but the state of British and Chinese co-operation and whether such a leader should emerge from the civil service or the private sector. I admit that I did some of that divining myself as I tallied the attributes that such a person must possess and measured these against the people I knew.

The process turned from the frivolous to the serious in April 1990 when the National People's Congress not only promulgated the Basic Law but also decided on creating the Preparatory Committee for the SAR six years later. The Preparatory Committee would be responsible for forming the Selection Committee of 400 individuals from the four broad categories of trades, professions and groups who would in turn have to vote for the Chief Executive.

The Preliminary Working Committee, which was established about two and a half years before the PC, recommended to the Central Government that the PC should compose of 150 members and that more than half of them should come from Hong Kong. The Chinese Government agreed and on 28 December 1995 the NPC Standing Committee announced its appointment of the 150-member PC with 96 of them from Hong Kong. The Government also appointed the Vice Premier and Foreign Minister Qian Qichen as the Chairman and nine Vice-Chairmen. The deputies to Qian were NPC Vice-Chairman Wang Hanbin, Chinese People's Political Consultative Conference Vice-Chairmen Ann Tse-kai and Henry Fok, Director of Hong Kong and Macao Affairs Office Lu Ping, Xinhua News Agency Hong Kong Branch Director Zhou Nan, Deputy Foreign Minister Wang Yingfan, PWC Vice-Chairman Simon Li, PWC Group Convenor Leung Chun-ying and the British Hong Kong Executive Councillor Tung Chee-hwa. The gallery was full and it was generally thought that one of those individuals from Hong Kong would be in the running for the coveted Chief Executive's post. The Central Government also designated Lu Ping as Secretary General for the PC. Assisting him would be Xinhua Hong Kong Deputy Director Qin Wenjun, Hong Kong and Macao Affairs Office Deputy Director Chen Ziying and Chief Executive of the Hong Kong One Country Two Systems Research Centre Shiu Sin-por.

All eyes scanning the roster eventually paused and pondered the name "Tung Chee-hwa", a previously rather obscure heir of a renowned shipping family of C. Y. Tung. He was born in Shanghai in May 1937 and had studied at Liverpool University as a marine engineer and served a stint with General Electric in the U.S.A. before returning to his family business in 1969. He had been a Basic Law Consultative Committee member and was in the first batch of the Hong Kong Affairs Advisors. Governor Chris Patten appointed him in October 1992 to his realigned Executive Council, and China named him in February 1993 to the Eighth CPPCC. These appointments when announced at the time did not alert anyone to his qualifications for the post of the SAR Chief Executive. He was genial yet generally shy and reserved, at least in public. Whilst I had known Tung and his wife since the early 1970s, it was mainly through his shipping magnate father. Back then in 1973 patriarch Tung had invited Lady

Clague and my wife to launch one of his latest container ships in Kobe, Japan. Betty, his daughter in-law and wife of Chee-hwa, was very courteous for she accompanied four of us on the flight to Japan and looked after us extremely well. My wife was so taken by Betty's grace that she commended her to the father in-law who had nodded in agreement.

Shortly after the NPC released the list for the Preparatory Committee on 28 December 1995 I got a phone call from Tung inviting me to meet him at his Oriental Overseas office on 4 January 1996. To prepare him for the talk I sent him a copy of my speech I had delivered on 21 November 1995, "The Most Crucial Year in the Transition", thinking the subjects raised therein would crop up in our scheduled conversation. We met quietly in his office and maundered on the topics raised in my speech. Liking his earnestness and noticing his right age, then 58, I urged him to run for the Chief Executive's job but he, in turn, suggested that I should run. I told him that I had already declined the suggestion from the Chinese side since I was too old and exhausted, but I promised him that I would help him vie for the post. He declined to commit himself and said he would mull it over very carefully, appreciating the gravity of the office and the demands of the calling on his private life. I went away, convinced that he would overcome his qualms and assume his duty.

The day of reckoning came on 26 January 1996 when the Preparatory Committee held its first plenary session in Beijing and assembled for a photo call at the Great Hall of the People. President Jiang Zemin, escorted by Qian, entered the cavernous room, beaming, and proceeded to shake hands with Mainland officials and the PC Vice-Chairmen in the front row. About half way down the line Jiang suddenly bolted from the procession and walked over to where Tung stood at the far end of the front row to seize his hand in a firm grip and speak to him. The gesture surprised the crowd as the photographers' lights flashed. Everyone assumed at the instance that Jiang had handpicked the Chief Executive. Not all were pleased among Hong Kong's chattering class. Some decried the President for pre-empting or even making a mockery of the election to come. Others were quite relieved that finally, after years of the guessing game, the clues were becoming tangible.

I met Tung quite a number of times after that famous handshake and still he had not decided or would not confide in me on whether or not to run, despite all the signs in his favour. He did tell me that he had conversed with Lu Ping in Shenzhen about his contesting the post. Finally in August 1996 Tung banished all doubts and announced his candidacy. He employed a public relations firm, in addition to a few of us, to help him draft his manifesto and presented it to the public in a speech labelled "Building a 21st Century Hong Kong Together", at the Hong Kong Management Association Annual Dinner on 22 October 1996. Soon thereafter other contenders joined the race in quick succession. Wheelock's former Chairman and the then Hospital Authority Chairman, Peter Woo, declared his bid. Retiring Chief Justice Sir Ti-liang Yang, at the prompting of the CPPCC Standing Committee member, Tsui Sze-man, did the same. Then PC Vice-Chairman Justice Simon Li also made his pitch. They along with a few maverick candidates of unknown quality started their campaigns, even though to the media only one person was really in the running. By then the pundits were saying Tung was "preordained" to be the Chief Executive when only a year ago most of them would not have had a clue about him, except for a vague recognition of his name to the shipping company.

Tung in September formed his campaign team that, among others, included Rita Fan, Dr. Raymond Wu, Professor Chia-wei Woo, Chan Wing-kee, Yu Kwok-chun, Charles Lee, Paul Yip, Annie Wu and myself. We met at least weekly at the Oriental Overseas conference room in the Great Eagle Centre, Harbour Road, to plot our moves and to lobby the Selection Committee. The candidate himself was frantically working the phones with the full-time assistance of his son and own crew from his company, namely, Andrew Lo, Stanley Shen, and secretary Vivian Tam who all were zealous. Lo and Tam later joined the SAR Government working in the Chief Executive's Office.

The 400-member Selection Committee on 15 November 1996 convened for the first time at the Hong Kong Convention and Exhibition Centre, the future site of the sovereignty transfer ceremony, to begin the opening round of the Chief Executive nomination process via secret ballot. Tung easily won by a very wide margin of 206 votes, followed by Yang of 82 votes and Woo of 54 votes, all three of whom having obtained more than 50 votes, qualified for the next round of the runoff election. Simon Li acquired 43 votes and was eliminated together with the other few maverick candidates. By then every trace of suspense had vanished. What was left was the coronation. Despite the odds totally in his favour, he nonetheless stumped furiously, making every call personally. The Chief Executive apparent also toiled over his platform speech to be delivered to the Selection Committee in the last week of November. He also held four rounds of questions and answers sessions with the four categories of voters in the Selection Committee for, not only did he long to win, he wanted to impress all with his diligence and dedication. He also wanted to sway some of those members who did not vote for him in the opening round. The consensus was that Tung was reliable and dedicated which was what Hong Kong needed as a reprieve from a tumultuous transition and a flamboyant Governor.

The Selection Committee on 11 December at its third meeting at the Convention and Exhibition Centre gave Tung, as expected, a landslide of 320 votes or 80 per cent of the total and also a convincing mandate. On the other hand Yang received 42 votes and Woo 36 votes, both were much less than the first round. The next day the Preparatory Committee at its seventh plenary in Shenzhen confirmed the results of the election and recommended that the Central Government endorse Tung for his five-year term commencing on 1 July 1997. While some continue to question the democratic credentials of Tung, elected by a body of 400 "nobles" and "nabobs", there is no denying that he had more votes for the Chief Executive job than all the Governors combined. They, after all, had all been nominated by the British Prime Minister and endorsed by the Monarch.

Democracy and the Civil Service

Elections are by definition common features of democratic societies. Who wins at the polls gets the power to shape policies and can count on the co-operation of apolitical career civil servants for their execution. Accordingly there are two types of officials in the administration of a democratic government. Some are politically appointed while others belong to what is generally known as the civil service. Political appointees come and go with the person or party in power. Yet, members of the civil service remain in their posts despite changes in the government leadership.

There are also three distinct features of the civil service in a democratic government. The first is political neutrality. The second

Plate 4.4 The Convenors of all the Sub-Committees of the Preparatory Committee and members of the Secretariat, 1997.

is continuity and permanency. The third is invisibility or low profile. Political neutrality means that civil servants do not express support for or opposition to any political party or policy. Continuity and permanency mean that irrespective of who or which party is in power, civil servants will remain in their posts and serve their master of the day. Invisibility or low profile means that civil servants never appear in the legislature or public arena to debate and defend the government's policy of the day, whatever their personal views. The work of advocacy is the exclusive responsibility of the political appointees. A competent and compliant civil service out of the firing line is pragmatic and sensible. A senior civil servant, who openly denounces or opposes policies advocated by a rival political party, risks discrediting himself should the rival group attains power and asks him to advance another agenda.

The Hong Kong SAR in its political reform has two basic models drawn from the Western, particularly the English-speaking experience. The one that originated in Britain features a dominant party, which elevates its leader to be the Prime Minister who picks a Cabinet from his colleagues in the Parliament and forms the government. The Prime Minister and his team shape the policies based often, though not always, on their campaign platform and expect civil servants to implement the programmes, however radical a departure these might be from the previous agenda. The neutral, professional mandarins (the most senior of whom are called the "Permanent Under-Secretaries of State" as to distinguish them from political appointees identified as "Secretaries of State") are usually reliable and loyal to the Crown. They ensure continuity in government despite the constant political tumult and keep out of the limelight. In return the civil service is respected and enjoys sinecure whereas often the politicians are despised and days in the sun relatively short.

Politicians debate whereas officials execute, and never do the roles blur. As the Prime Minister's party always controls the Parliament, the incumbent is basically given an absolute power without much checks and balances from the Parliament.

The other basic model of the English-speaking democracy is the American and it wedges apart the legislature from the executive with punctilious care. The United States Constitution does not tolerate the mixing of the two branches, which are supposed to check and balance each other, ostensibly to prevent tyranny or conspiracy. Voters get to choose their President and Parliamentarians separately and at different times. The President Elect, as the chief executive, picks his Cabinet from the private sector, academics and also the fraternity of retired politicians — including former governors, congressmen and senators. He has a relatively free hand, except for the loyal stalwarts he must please, the egos of campaign contributors he must flatter, and those who are ideologically his kindred spirits. The President may even take sterling professionals — economists, constitutional experts, decommissioned generals, and so on — from outside his own party to strike the non-partisan pose and to secure the best expertise, whatever the politics. These Cabinet nominees then submit themselves to congressional vetting, which may be partisan and at times embarrassing. Once accepted to the inner sanctum of the presidency, the policy secretaries sign on for the duration of the first term, lasting for four years, at the pleasure of the chief executive who could dismiss them for reasons of performance, popularity or politics. Their job done they sidle back to the private sector, preferably in professions that do not raise doubts about their integrity or hackles over any conflict of interest.

The President is able to receive political advice from people he trusts and who are committed to the administration's programmes. He is also able to influence policy making and execution by appointing senior advisors and even some middle management positions in each department. The system combines the experience and continuity of the permanent civil service with the new ideas and fresh approach of temporary political appointees.

But, nonetheless, the system of recruitment causes friction between the permanent civil servants and the outsiders, who are immediately placed in senior positions while knowing little or nothing about the practical working of the department. There is also the problem of dislocation and confusion when there is a change of President. Further, there are possibilities of corruption, which inevitably exist where temporary appointees have contact with former business associates.

During the Sino-British negotiations, the Chinese Government preferred the American system to the British one, presumably to limit the impact of political parties and avoid the integration of power between the executive and legislative branches. The British ironically also preferred the American system, hoping an openly elected legislature could deter the Chief Executive from taking orders from Beijing.

I expressed these views in a speech, first at a public affairs lecture on 7 May 1996 at the Hong Kong University of Science and Technology, and then again at the annual dinner on 24 September 1996 of the Association of Former Senior Civil Servants. On the second occasion there were in attendance not only retired but also incumbent principal officials of the civil service. Certain senior Chinese officials from the Hong Kong Xinhua News Agency were also present at the banquet. Those current officials were advised to give careful thought to and prepare themselves for this possible change after 1 July 1997. During the following months I did speak to some senior government officials about their reaction to the introduction of political appointees in the Hong Kong SAR Government. About half of them would be prepared to retire from the civil service, take their pension, and then accept political appointment by the incoming Chief Executive.

The Chief Executive Designate, Tung Chee-hwa, was informed of my speech in early 1997 and tacitly accepted in principle the need for such political appointees in a democratic government. He was, however, reluctant to implement the system during the early years of the SAR Government for fear of undermining the morale of the civil service. In addition, since he had no intention of becoming the first Chief Executive until the summer of 1996, Tung had no political affiliates, and did not have sufficient time to identify and groom talents from outside the civil service. The Hong Kong public at that time was also in favour of a smooth transition with minimal disruptions. The Chinese Government, in particular, had a high regard for Hong Kong's civil service and preferred minimum change during the transfer of sovereignty.

For these reasons and with the exception for the post of Secretary for Justice (formerly called Attorney General), all the incumbent senior government officials were given the same jobs prior to the transfer. The need for the change of the incumbent Attorney General (Jeremy Mathews) was because he was a British citizen and a member of the British Overseas Civil Service. Mathews was replaced by Elsie Leung Oi-sie, an experienced solicitor conversant with both English and Chinese laws.

The Basic Law does not recognize such a post as "Chief Secretary". The post of the Chief Secretary (formerly known as "Colonial Secretary") in the British Administration was supposed to be replaced by the post of Administrative Secretary in the Chinese

SAR, as written in Article 53 of the Basic Law. The Chinese Government, nonetheless, acquiesced to the retention of the title of "Chief Secretary" at the insistence of, I was told, Anson Chan who felt that such a change of nomenclature could imply the down-grading of her august rank.

The Ceremonies

Final Hours of the British Rule

The transition lasted more than 12 years but the farewell ceremonies concluded in just over eight hectic hours of elaborate fests and fetes from 4 o'clock in the afternoon of 30 June 1997 to 12 minutes after midnight. The bleak weather cast the whole historic event in sombre mood befitting its significance, its magnitude. The rain, which held off for half a day despite the gathering clouds and the stifling humidity, finally poured coinciding with the first of the afternoon rites, one so meticulously scripted, except for the soaking weather.

The last Governor Chris Patten, who had been the storm centre for the five years he had been in the Colony, stared through tears the lowering of the Union Jack for the last time in the Government House. He watched as the master of the guards lowered the pennant and folded it before handing it to him as he drooped his head to acknowledge less the weight of the flag than the occasion. Patten then waved to the throng of mainly his household staff gathering to bid farewell and entered the Daimler limousine with his family for a slow ride three times around the ellipse before going through the main gate.

The downpour never relented thereafter prompting some to say it was heaven grieving the British departure and others to say it was the divine scrubbing clean of the colonial legacy. The British, promptly at the scheduled time of 6.15 p.m., persisted with the second act of their farewell with "Beating the Final Retreat" out in the open, giving a literal meaning to the saying about "rain on the parade". The United Kingdom, which had decades of practice in packing off from its colonies, remained steadfast. The gunners rang out a 21-gun salute to hail Charles, the Prince of Wales, accompanied by Patten. Assembled under the marquee was the whole ensemble of figures from the United Kingdom who had contributed to the exit, past and present. Among them were of course Prime Minister Tony Blair, Foreign Secretary Robin Cook, and the past Prime Minister Margaret Thatcher, all stoic in the Tamar open grounds buffeted by the gust and the slashing rain. Most of the other less august guests were left without cover to brave both the rain and the wind. Most unfortunate was Jardines taipan Henry Keswick, who slipped and fell over the wet curb, injuring one of his legs.

The last reveille done, the British began the second round of their celebration, which this time resembled more of the carnival rather than the wake. The British military band struck up their routine with the thud of drums and the skirl of bagpipes. There was jigging, singing and marching. But still the rain dampened the performance, forcing many guests to flee the stand for their hotels and homes to change clothes and dry out for the next event — an indoor banquet.

At 9.30 p.m. the British, for the third round, hosted a farewell feast at the Convention and Exhibition Centre on the waterfront. During the pre-dinner reception I chatted to some of the guests from the Chinese side. Everybody said the downpour had really blighted the United Kingdom's retreat ballyhoo and some revealed that the British were somewhat the authors of their own misfortune.

Plate 4.5 *The new wing of the Convention and Exhibition Centre at night, 1997.*

I was told that the Sino-British Joint Liaison Group had actually discussed how to co-ordinate their festivities so that neither side would clash with the other's show. The British insisted on having their magnificent farewell ceremony performed at an outdoor site as it could accommodate a much larger crowd. The Chinese, however, were reluctant to go in the open air in the middle of the typhoon season. They had checked with the Royal Hong Kong Observatory on the meteorological patterns of 30 June and 1 July over the past dozen or so years and noticed a preponderance of foul weather. Whereas the British insisted on the open ground at Tamar for their show, the Chinese requested the Hong Kong Trade Development Council going flat out, round the clock, to ready the new wing of the Convention and Exhibition Centre for their various ceremonies. In this instance Chinese caution prevailed over British bravado.

The Sovereignty Return

The eyes of the world focussed in the late hours of 30 June and the wee ones of 1 July 1997 on Hong Kong, whose Convention and Exhibition Centre basked in lights, flash, klieg and strobe. The British and Chinese Governments, their rancour behind them or suppressed, assembled their own lights, leading luminaries, in the fifth floor hall in the Centre's new wing, whose window panes stared out to the shimmering harbour awash with yachts and almost washed out by the rain. This wing was brand new and built on a man-made island off the north shore line of the Hong Kong Island linking the old wing by an enclosed bridge. The construction work has been going on day and night non-stop for the past year in order to ensure the new wing completed just weeks before the hand-over ceremony.

By 11.30 p.m. more than 4,000 guests, including heads of state and government, senior diplomats from over 40 odd countries and the United Nations General Secretary Kofi Annan, filed into the hall. Never had so many international dignitaries gathered in Hong Kong, arguably the most international city in Asia, to await history making its own grand entrance. I was leading the SAR Executive Councillors who sat on the stage, on the Chinese side, in the uppermost row for the proceedings.

The climatic ceremony commenced at 11.42 p.m. as the British and Chinese ceremonial trumpeters entered the hall and stood on each side of the stage. Exactly at 11.46 p.m. as the trumpets were sounded, representatives of both countries concurrently walked in serial rank into the hall respectively from the two side entrances. At the beginning the British played the host and the Chinese the guest, a role to be switched at the stroke of midnight. The Chinese side was led by the national leader Jiang Zemin. He was followed by Premier Li Peng, Vice Premier and Foreign Minister Qian Qichen, Deputy Commander of the Military Commission Marshal Zhang Wannian in full regalia, and finally the SAR Chief Executive Elect Tung Chee-hwa. The British side featured HRH the Prince of Wales representing the Queen, Prime Minister Tony Blair, Foreign Secretary Robin Cook, departing Governor Chris Patten, and the Chief of Staff, General Sir Charles Guthrie. The two parties then sat in two separate rows on the two sides of the centre stage, at the back of which were two huge national flags hanging on the wall.

After the ritual gun salute, Prince Charles walked to the British rostrum and delivered a speech, citing British achievement in securing a prosperous and stable Hong Kong and wishing the coming Special Administrative Region continual success under the "One Country Two Systems" concept. He pledged full British support for the 1984 Sino-British Joint Declaration.

At 11.56 p.m. the British and Chinese flag guards then marched into the hall and readied themselves at the foot of the flag poles for the finale. Most notably the Chinese guards brought with them the national and the SAR flags folded whereas the British guards were empty handed. There were four flag poles with two, one slightly taller than the other, on each side of the stage. On the British side the British national flag was fluttering on the taller pole next to that of the Hong Kong colonial banner in the fan-generated breeze near the rafter.

No less conspicuous was a simpering and shimmering Chief Secretary, Anson Chan, in an all bright red dress seated in a spot, alone like a throne, at the exact middle point between the British and Chinese platforms, personifying the very spirit of the transition. I was surprised that the SAR Chief Executive Designate Tung Chee-hwa was not aware of this arrangement until a bemused Singapore Prime Minister, Goh Chok Tong, later mentioned this to him.

At 11.59 p.m. sharp the British, with the playing of "God Save the Queen", lowered their national flag from their pole along with the colonial pennant to be returned to the United Kingdom by HRH Prince Charles. This signified the end of 156 years of British rule. At this point of time the whole hall of over 4,000 people was absolutely quiet waiting for the final climax to come. At exactly the zero hour and zero minute of 1 July 1997, the Chinese National Anthem was played and at the same time the Chinese flag guards ran the national and SAR flags simultaneously up the two poles on the Chinese side of the stage. The flag with five golden stars next to the one with a white bauhinia, both against a crimson background, were flapping gently in an artificially generated breeze. The whole audience clapped vigorously along with the Chinese leadership in an ovation that lasted for several minutes. Thus, that was that, the sovereignty peacefully returned to its original and rightful owner, erasing the shame of the Opium Wars in the 19th century.

Plate 4.6 *The Sovereignty Return Ceremony on 1 July 1997.*

Expectedly, I was overwhelmed with mixed emotions, reflecting first on the three years of hard bargain not for the return but for the terms of reunification, and then the twelve and a half long years of transition, through thick and thin, that by then seemed like a flash in time. I did not immigrate to the British Hong Kong. I had no choice as I was born and raised in Hong Kong in the midst of British Administration. I led my UMELCO colleagues to urge the British to negotiate with the Chinese Government for the reunification in accordance with the views, wishes and interests of the majority of the Hong Kong people whom I had never ever betrayed. All along, I aimed for a just and practical solution to the Hong Kong problem, bearing in mind the dignity and sovereignty of China, the grace of the United Kingdom, and the aspirations of the people of my native city. Somehow, with ups and downs, elations and agonies, I helped to accomplish more or less what I set out to do for Hong Kong, for which I have no regrets and will have none for the remain of my day. We, the prodigal Chinese of the territory, were now home again with autonomy and also a responsibility to help modernize our country.

Outside the hall on the streets and in public squares, tens of thousands roared as the neon lights lit up the night as the rain stopped for the moment and an incandescent mist hanged over the waters and between the high-rises. Cars halted along the Causeway Bay corridor and other thoroughfares elsewhere honking horns added to the cacophony. A new era was born.

After the clapping ended President Jiang Zemin walked to the Chinese rostrum and proclaimed the establishment of the Hong Kong Special Administrative Region of the People's Republic of China. He said the date of 1 July 1997 was a great day in the Chinese history and that history would remember the great statesman Deng Xiaoping,

Plate 4.7 *People gathering at Time Square for the sovereignty transfer count-down on 30 June 1997.*

the architect of the novel concept "One Country Two Systems". Jiang also spoke about Hong Kong's future being brighter than its past and about closing one chapter and opening another. The Chinese President also assured the people of Hong Kong that his Government would uphold faithfully the basic concepts of "One Country Two Systems", Hong Kong people ruling Hong Kong, and a high degree of autonomy. He further pledged to preserve Hong Kong's free society, capitalists system, way of life and Common Law practice. Jiang's speech was interrupted five times by prolonged applause.

That ended the ceremony for sovereignty transfer. Thereafter the official delegates of both the Chinese and British Governments walked to the centre of the stage, shook hands and posed for photographs at 00.12 a.m. on 1 July 1997. Hong Kong had been recovered symbolically at the Convention Centre.

At the same time about 20 miles to the north, the People's

Plate 4.8 *People gathering in a community centre watching the sovereignty transfer on 1 July 1997*

Liberation Army elite armoured columns totalling about 4,000 were filing across the Lowu border in the rain. The soldiers remained rod-straight as their cavalcade wended through the roads of the New Territories to throngs of tens of thousands of people welcoming their entry. The navy was already on the way and the airforce helicopters likewise headed south. The rapturous reception the PLA received and the utter professional demeanour of the troops belied all the apocalyptic warnings of the Sinophobes and the Democratic Party as well as its allies. The only regret on the occasion was the absence of the late Deng Xiaoping, the architect of "One Country Two Systems", who unfortunately died in February 1997, just four months short of the return of Hong Kong. I still remember vividly today our greatly publicized meeting with Chairman Deng in the Great Hall of the People in Beijing on 23 June 1984. He had then expressed his fervent hope to see the restoration of the lost territory and the boost to Chinese national pride. I believe hundreds of millions of Chinese, in Hong Kong, on the Mainland and elsewhere, were thinking of him as they watched on the TV screens the return of the lost territory and the inauguration of the Hong Kong SAR, and believing he was content in what he had seen in the other world — a mission one third accomplished on 1 July 1997. In December 1999 Macao was likewise returned to China, thus leaving Taiwan as the only unfinished business of national reunification.

Final British Retreat

HRH Prince of Wales departed the former British colony together with the now former Governor Chris Patten the same way their ancestors had first arrived in Hong Kong, on the waves. Soon after the ceremony returning the sovereignty to China had concluded at the Convention and Exhibition Centre, the representative of HM the Queen, Prince Charles, and Patten, once more a civilian, slipped away and arrived at the waterfront of the Tamar Naval Base via slow-moving motorcade along the esplanade at 00.25 a.m. They were to board the HMS *Britannia* that had been in moorage for days.

Hundreds thronged the nearby roadside for a parting glimpse of the future monarch and also the departing Governor. Most of those waiting at the Tamar were, understandably, sentimental expatriates. In the midst of the farewell crowd stood the loyal household staff members who had served the Patten family at the Government House for the past five years. Late in joining the procession were senior officials, who had been groomed and promoted by the last Governor during his years of office, plus the immediate past Executive Councillors, all tediously polite. As a matter of protocol, Vice Foreign Minister, Wang Yingfan, representing the Chinese Central Government, saw off the hosts-turned guests shortly after the stroke of midnight.

After all the hand shakes, embraces and kisses the British party eventually boarded the *Britannia* at 00.40 a.m. Ten minutes later, the HMS sounded a forlorn wail as she slowly left the dockside under the escort of a Royal Navy frigate and the Hong Kong Marine Police launches, destination the Philippines. A number of Fire Services boats were already in the harbour bidding them *bon voyage* with a ceremonial water spray as tears gushed from sentimental eyes and the rain resumed. This ended the last page of the final chapter of the 156 years of British rule in Hong Kong.

Founding of the Hong Kong SAR

After the British had acceded in 1984 to relinquishing its sovereign and administrative control of Hong Kong at the appointed time of 1 July 1997, the Chinese began preparing for their recovery of the territory. The National People's Congress on 4 April 1990 decided to found the Hong Kong Special Administrative Region on 1 July 1997 with a series of ceremonies.

The very first ceremony after the sovereignty return was the swearing-in scheduled at 1.30 a.m. It took place on the seventh floor in the new wing of the Convention and Exhibition Centre, large enough to accommodate more than four thousand guests plus a huge stage. The ceremony went exactly, except for the rain, according to script. President Jiang Zemin at the threshold declared to the live audience, including foreign dignitaries from more than forty countries and 4,000 guests plus billions watching on television in and outside China, that "The Chinese People's Republic Hong Kong Special Administrative Region is now established."

***Plate 4.9** The Establishment Ceremony of the Hong Kong SAR on 1 July 1997.*

President Jiang of the People's Republic of China then went back to his seat on stage whereas Premier Li Peng walked to and stood at the centre of the stage. The scene was then set for the swearing-in. The first person to stroll to the rostrum facing the Premier was the Chief Executive Designate Tung Chee-hwa, who had been selected by the Selection Committee of 400 and confirmed by the Central People's Government. Tung swore allegiance to the HKSAR of the PRC, the uphold of the Basic Law, and the accountability to both the CPG and the HKSAR, as stipulated by the Basic Law. He was followed in his stead by Chief Secretary Anson Chan who led 23 principal secretaries in swearing allegiance to the HKSAR of the PRC, the uphold of the Basic Law, and the accountability to the HKSAR.

I, as the Convenor of the Executive Council, subsequently walked up with my 14 colleagues in tow to owe our fidelity to Tung, now the Chief Executive proper. Rita Fan, President of the Provisional Legislative Council, conducted the same with her 59 associates. Then finally, Chief Justice Andrew Li proceeded to the stage with 36 other judges, ethnic Chinese and expatriates alike, to take their oath, in this case, first in Chinese and then English.

All the swearing-in completed exactly by 1.53 a.m. Premier Li Peng then went to the rostrum and delivered his address thanking all those guests for their presence as well as acknowledging the work of the members of the Preparatory Committee, the members of the Selection Committee and all those who had supported the reunification of Hong Kong. He then gave encouragement to all the office bearers of the HKSAR and wished them success in maintaining continual prosperity and stability of the territory. Li said Hong Kong had then entered a new era in its history and reaffirmed his confidence that Hong Kong would have a better tomorrow.

Plate 4.10 *The Swearing-in Ceremony for members of the Hong Kong SAR Executive Council, 1997.*

The next speaker was the first Chief Executive Tung Chee-hwa who said Hong Kong after separating from its motherland for 156 years eventually reunited on 1 July 1997. From then on, he continued, we would be masters of our own house and be able to decide our own destiny. He pledged the HKSAR Government would do its utmost to preserve our way of life, maintain our free and open economy, uphold the rule of law, develop a democratic government, build a caring society, and strengthen Hong Kong as a world class cosmopolitan city. Tung also said he was aware of the needs and wishes of the people and recognized the importance of co-operation and unity. He undertook to lead the 6.5 million enterprising citizens under the concept of "One Country Two Systems" marching forward for a better future.

The Swearing-in Ceremony ended at 2.20 a.m. Thereafter we

were ushered into a nearby hall where all the members of the executive, legislative and judicial branches of the newly born HKSAR posted for a historic group photograph with President Jiang, Premier Li and other leaders of the CPG. Chief Executive Tung was seated on the front row whereas Chief Secretary Anson Chan and myself, as Convenor of the Executive Council, were both standing right behind President Jiang who was seating in the very middle of the front row.

Whilst most of us were going home or back to hotel for a few hours of sleep before attending the next programme scheduled at

Plate 4.11 *The HKSAR Chief Executive, Mr. Tung Chee-hwa, shook hands with the author, the Executive Council Convenor, after the Swearing-in Ceremony on 1 July 1997.*

10.00 a.m., the Provisional Legislative Council held its first meeting after the establishment of the SAR at 2.45 a.m. President Rita Fan and all her 59 members of the PLC plus some 18 senior government officials including Financial Secretary Donald Tsang and Secretary for Justice Elsie Leung were assembled in Meeting Room 201 of the Convention Centre. One of the major items debated and passed was the Reunification Bill, which dealt with various important and urgent matters related to the transition. The first meeting lasted for 75 minutes.

Just before 10.00 a.m. about 4,500 guests were assembled again in the new wing of the Convention and Exhibition Centre ready for the Establishment Ceremony. When the clock struck ten the National Anthem was played and then President Jiang addressed the audience. He reiterated the Central People's Government's faithful implementation of the policies of "One Country Two Systems", Hong Kong people ruling Hong Kong, and a high degree of autonomy for the next 50 years.

Chief Executive Tung then spoke. He first paid tribute to the late Chairman Deng Xiaoping for his great vision of and contribution to the open-up and modernization of China from the late 1970s. Deng's widow was present and seating next to President Jiang in the front row facing the stage. At the end of Tung's tribute Deng's widow, helped by both Jiang and Tung's wife, stood up and acknowledged the prolonged applause.

When the hall was quiet again Tung resumed his oration and depicted his plan of administering Hong Kong. He touched on four major areas of housing, education, elderly and economy. After Tung was done with his speech Vice Premier and Foreign Minister Qian Qichen, representing the CPG, presented to Tung a cheque amounting to HK$197 billion which was accumulated from half of the land

Plate 4.12 *Chinese leaders and members of the executive, legislative and judicial brnahces of the HKSAR, 1 July 1997.*

sales proceeds in Hong Kong during the 12-year long transition. This amount contributed to the high fiscal reserve of nearly HK$500 billion as against HKSAR's annual total public expenditure of about $300 billion in year 2000.

After the cheque presentation the revelries and revues followed and did not stop until about 12 noon.

The Mandarin Hurdle

Prior to the Second World War Hong Kong was a Cantonese society with 99 per cent of the Chinese population speaking Cantonese, the local dialect of Canton (Guangzhou), the capital of Guangdong Province. There were only a few hundred northern Chinese from Shandong Province employed as policemen, probably because they are generally taller and sturdier built than their southern compatriots. The influx of Shanghainese and other northerners only began in the late 1940s when Communists took control of the Mainland. During the early stage most of these arrivals resided in North Point, then known as "Little Shanghai". From then on there were more and more local people speaking what was then generally known as Mandarin.

During the Japanese occupation of Hong Kong I fled to the Mainland and worked in the provinces of Jiangxi and Hunan. People there spoke Mandarin but with heavy local accents and slang. Nonetheless I managed to get by with my rudimentary Mandarin with Cantonese accents. After the Pacific War I neither had the need nor the opportunity to polish my Mandarin until the imminent return of Hong Kong to China and later my membership in the Preliminary Working Committee of the Chinese Government.

I was not alone in my appalling Mandarin (now known as Putonghua which means common language) because this shortcoming was prevalent among the relatively elderly population in Hong Kong. The joke was on me at last in the morning of 29 June 1997 when we rehearsed our taking the oath of office from Chief Executive Designate at the Convention and Exhibition Centre. Tung, a native Shanghainese and speaks fluent Putonghua, was usually the most becalming person but even he could not stop from laughing at my reading the pledge of allegiance in what I figured was Putonghua and what others thought was mumble jumble.

After the rehearsal the attractive and attentive, then Director of Radio and Television of Hong Kong, Cheung Man-yee, took pity on me, or on the audience of 1 July, and took the trouble in sending me a box of cassette tapes on basic "pinyin" or phonetics. My helpful Executive Council colleagues Nellie Fong and Antony Leung gave me urgent tutelage to correct decades of my Mandarin abuse. They were coaching me on 1 July even during the one-hour interval between the sovereignty transfer ceremony and the swearing-in ritual to ensure that I would not be the comic relief.

With a stout heart and a great gulp of air, I said my line meticulously, trying not to bungle a single word as I swore my oath in front of Tung. After the Swearing-in Ceremony I was surprised to hear many people saying to me that the Chief Justice Andrew Li's Putonghua was even worse than mine.

During the rehearsal on 29 June as I had turned into the focus of attention and the expected butt of jokes, no one had really listened closely and paid sufficient attention to how Chief Justice Andrew Li's Putonghua. To be totally objective, he was not much better than mine. Whereas I had later practised, Li did not, slinking away for tea with friends during the interval when he could have joined me in boning up on our Putonghua. Since the reunification Li took regular Putonghua lessons and now speaks it much better.

After the ceremony all the principal secretaries, Executive Councillors, Provisional Legislators and judges alike filed into the nearby hall to prepare for a photo session with the Chinese leaders. When we all were in our designated positions the first to enter were President Jiang Zemin and Premier Li Peng. The affable Jiang sidled next to me and said perhaps in jest, and certainly in Cantonese, "I understand your Putonghua," to which I replied in Putonghua "President Jiang, your Cantonese is better than my Putonghua," to the laughter of everyone so glad to get on with celebrating the national reunion and get away from my linguistics.

New Era, New Honours

Hong Kong returned to China on 1 July 1997 and so entered a new, historic era. The SAR Government wanted to encourage civil spirit, affirm social values, salute role models for the society, and enhance cohesion of the community. The Authorities, thereby, decided to introduce a new honour system to replace the British awards used during the colonial days.

The new honour system came into effect on 1 July 1997, with the Grand Bauhinia Medal (GBM) as the highest honour that could be bestowed by the SAR Government. The first medal presentation ceremony was held on 2 July, a day after the ceremonial Chinese recovery of Hong Kong at the Government House, Upper Albert Road. The first Chief Executive of the SAR, Tung Chee-hwa, presented the medals under the gaze of Vice Premier and Foreign Minister, Qian Qichen, and in the presence of over 400 invited guests.

The first Grand Bauhinia Medal was awarded to a dozen Hong Kong citizens in recognition of their individual contributions to the establishment of the Special Administrative Region. They were, in

Plate 4.13 *The First Grand Bauhinia Medal Presentation Ceremony on 2 July 1997.*

the order of number of strokes in the Chinese character of their surname:

Ann Tse-kai	Lee Quo-wei	Simon Li Fook-sean
Elsie Tu	Cha Chi-ming	Tsui Sze-man
Chuang Shih-ping	Wong Ker-lee	Tsang Hin-chi
Henry Fok Ying-tung	Chung Sze-yuen	Lo Tak-shing.

In January 1998 the SAR Government formally announced the new honours and awards system for the Hong Kong citizens:

(1) The Order of the Grand Bauhinia
This Order has only one class. The Grand Bauhinia Medal (GBM) is the highest award under the new honours and awards system. Recipients of the GBM may use the title "The Honourable" as prefix before and the abbreviation "GBM" as suffix after their names in English.

(2) The Order of the Bauhinia Star
This Order consists of three classes, namely,
(a) The Gold Bauhinia Star (GBS);
(b) The Silver Bauhinia Star (SBS);
(c) The Bronze Bauhinia Star (BBS).

(3) The Order of the Medal of Honour
This Order is in one class only — the Medal of Honour (MH).

(4) The Order of the Medal for Bravery
This Order consists of three classes, namely,
(a) The Medal for Bravery (Gold) (MBG);
(b) The Medal for Bravery (Silver) (MBS);
(c) The Medal for Bravery (Bronze) (MBB).

(5) The Chief Executive's Commendation
There are two types of awards under this category, namely,

Plate 4.14 *The author and his friends at the Government House after receiving the GBM Award on 2 July 1997.*

(a) The Chief Executive's Commendation for Government Service;

(b) The Chief Executive's Commendation for Community Service.

Whilst the Hong Kong SAR introduced its new honour system, nonetheless it retains the Western Justice of the Peace (JP). I remember that the Political Affairs Group of the Preliminary Working Committee had discussed a few times whether the SAR should retain or replace the JP system. Most members of the Group preferred the retention of the JP system, stressing that JPs not only existed in Britain and the British Commonwealth countries but also in the United States of America. We, nonetheless, thought the Chinese title was not very appropriate and did ponder for sometime substitutes but could not conjure up a better Chinese terminology that could reflect quite the tradition and familiarity of the *status quo*. Consequently we accepted the full retention of the previous Justice of the Peace system.

The Threshold

The Paradigm Shift

The British and Chinese Governments signed the Joint Declaration in December 1984 based on a common vision. They agreed that Hong Kong the British Colony would transform into a Special Administrative Region of China on 1 July 1997 under the "One Country Two Systems" formula coupled with Hong Kong people ruling Hong Kong and a high degree of autonomy. The epoch was not only for the people of Hong Kong alone but for the whole world in whose gaze the dream would become a reality, proving a bitter legacy could be put right by peaceful means.

Hong Kong through the transition of more than a dozen years had faced a paradox of trying to preserve many features of a very prosperous, free, modern and enlightened society, but at the same time striving to effect changes either as stipulated in the Basic Law or to ensure that the community did not stagnate.

On the political front, the territory would go from an autocratic, archaic colonial regime in which the Governor, invariably a Briton, would appoint his Executive and Legislative Councillors to a more open system in which law-makers and also the Chief Executive would all be elected. Article 45 of the Basic Law, Hong Kong SAR's constitution, is very explicit. In the beginning the Chief Executive of the Hong Kong SAR shall be selected by election or through consultation held locally and be appointed by the Central People's Government.

This initial process will be developed step by step and the ultimate aim is the selection of the CE by universal suffrage upon nomination by a broadly representative nominating committee in accordance with democratic process. Article 68 specifies that the Legislative Council shall be constituted by election. The method of forming the legislature shall be in accordance with the principle of gradual and orderly progress. The ultimate aim is the election of all the members by universal suffrage.

Economically the Joint Declaration encouraged an integration or symbiosis of the SAR and the Mainland. Even as the finishing touches were put to the British and Chinese accord this process was already accelerating. Hong Kong manufacturers made an exodus northward the way they had migrated southward a generation earlier. The trickle north of the late 1970s, when China started to carry out its economic reform and open door policy initiated by Deng Xiaoping, had turned into a veritable tidal wave by 1984. Back then, despite the emptying out of some factories, Hong Kong manufacturing still employed a million people, roughly a third of the labour force. By 1997, fewer than 300,000 still earned their keep from manufacturing and even those so employed were engaged mainly in adding value to products from the Mainland. Hong Kong-owned businesses have so established themselves in the Pearl River Estuary — in hinterland cities such as Shenzhen and Dongguan — that they now hire more than five million people across the border. The Mainland is now Hong Kong's competitive edge and the primary reason for foreign investments. One of my recent papers "Reflections on Manufacturing" summarized the rise and fall of manufacturing in Hong Kong during the past 50 years and was published in the *50th Anniversary Transactions of the Hong Kong Institution of Engineers* in December 1997.

Plate 4.15 *President Jiang Zemin presented his calligraphy scroll "Hong Kong Faces a Better Future" to the HKSAR, received by the HKSAR Chief Executive, Mr. Tung Chee-hwa , 1997.*

Hong Kong exports, and particularly re-exports, have surged, making an already busy port into the most intensely used in the world. While the Mainland has concentrated on light to medium industries, the territory has focussed on retail, re-export, capital finance and banking plus, more recently, information technology and telecommunication. The service industries, which really began to grow in the 1970s, are now dominant. The know-how and sophistication of Hong Kong's finance, transport, commerce and tourism have turned the SAR into the primary service hub of Asia. What Hong Kong does best, however, is service to the Mainland. Should Hong Kong continue with the development in this direction, it would achieve its aspiration being the New York and London of an economically powerful, resurgent China.

The co-operation between Guangdong Province and the Hong Kong SAR is approaching seamless. The division of specialties as both sides make the best of their advantages has also narrowed their cultural differences, which may not always be wonderful news to many Hong Kong women betrayed by their philandering husbands with businesses and concubines on the other side. At this rate of development, as the Pearl River Delta experiences continuous double-digit growth, this region shall mature, in my assessment, in another two decades into one of the foremost industrial and commercial centres in the world, probably rivalling the Philadelphia-New York-Boston Axis, the Kyoto-Tokyo Corridor, and the German Rhine Basin. As early as in 1992 in my speech titled "Hong Kong's New Destiny" delivered at the 20th Anniversary of the Hong Kong Polytechnic, I had already predicted this eventuality.

Despite the vow of "50-years unchanged", Hong Kong has metamorphosed through the transition and into the 21st century. The differences between the colonial period and that of the SAR have been dramatic as new concepts, ideas, ways of doing business, and dealings with the rest of the world burst out of the chrysalis. The SAR has assumed a new identity to go with its new era.

Initially, that is during the 1980s, many people were apprehensive about their prospects in the SAR, terrified by their own and their parents' bleak experiences on the Mainland and wary of the promises from the Chinese leaders who could not eschew completely enough the whimsical excesses of their predecessors. As a result tens of thousands in their phobia emigrated from Hong Kong, mostly to the West. However as time past and as China continued to progress, more and more people were coming to accept the Chinese sovereignty, having banished the doubts that some popular politicians had planted in them. They began to have confidence in the future SAR, despite the Sino-British confrontation during the last years of the transition.

The surge of confidence translated into spectacular, and speculative, gains in the property and stock markets for the period from 1995 to the time of reunification. The Hang Seng Index had reached 10,000 points in December 1995 and this had soared to 16,500 points in August 1997. The upward spiral of the bourse was more than matched by the skyrocketing of property value. At the peak A-grade offices and residential real estate were fetching at an unsustainable, a crazy $24,000 per square foot. By the middle of 1997 Hong Kong had inflated a bubble economy and the pin that would burst the thinning membrane was inevitable. The question that no one could answer at that time, was when?

The Initial Experience

People kept up their celebrations on 2 July 1997, a day after the

Chinese recovery of Hong Kong, now known as the Special Administrative Region. While they continued to rejoice, few noticed the Thai Government had let the Baht, its currency, float only to see it sink. Thus the worst Asian financial crisis in recent memory began with much of Hong Kong oblivious to its impact and implications. For weeks thereafter economists and other experts were confident that Hong Kong would not be seriously affected because of its "strong fundamentals". The Hong Kong Government, probably more for political reasons than others, joined other Asian economies in extending to Thailand its share of an emergency loan of one billion American dollars.

By the middle of October that financial tidal wave had smashed into Taiwan after having ravaged Thailand, Indonesia and Malaysia, countries that in recent years had done so well out of the boom in investments and exports to North America and the European Union. The Government of Lee Teng-hui opted not to use its enormous reserves to back the new Taiwan dollar, which greatly devaluated.

Hong Kong was not spared, regardless of its enormous exchange fund and fiscal prudence, which routinely caused rating agencies to praise its economy as among the most flexible and competitive anywhere. The people finally realized that their bubble economy would burst just like those in the Southeast Asia. The bleakest day was Black Thursday, 23 October 1997, when speculators, who had already devastated Southeast Asia, assaulted the Hong Kong dollar, despite its peg to the greenback. The inter-bank rate shot up to 280 per cent in a flash to deter money draining out of the territory, which did not have or wish to have other control mechanisms such as the ones Malaysia was to adopt. The Hong Kong Monetary Authority, husbanding an exchange fund which included a fiscal reserve of more than HK$630 billion (US$80 billion) at that time, could not stem the fear, the sheer irrational terror.

The interest rates went up and up and the stock market crashed with the Hang Seng Index dropping 6,000 points, from 16,000 in July to 10,000 in October 1997, or nearly a third of its value. The property market, which had caused the bubble economy in the first place, fell and unemployment rose and rose. During the following months the economy that had once been short of labour, despite a guest worker scheme, was now in serious recession with the jobless rate reaching over six per cent, the highest in recent Hong Kong history. The gross domestic product shrank after years of steady growth and once double-digit inflation had gone into reverse, into deflation. Banks that had over-extended their property loans fretted. Assets were now liabilities and optimism changed to despair.

The conspiracy against Asian economies deepened. The heavily leveraged hedge fund marauders attacked the Hong Kong bourse in August 1998 to further drive down stock prices. The Hong Kong Government eventually reacted by having the Monetary Authority commit more than HK$100 billion to the defence of the stock market, routing the conspirators and returning confidence first to the financial institutions and then to the rest of the economy. The recovery so began in late 1998, thanks in part to the Government's (if much maligned by the foreign media) market intervention and to China declining to devalue its own currency.

By year 2000 the once weary economy was again robust, recording a GDP growth rate of over 10 per cent and showing improved employment prospects. The revolution in information technology, surging exports and China's imminent accession to the World Trade Organization spurred on the recovery, which, however, is not complete. Many people, especially those from the manual trades, who had lost their jobs, could not find new ones because their skills were no longer relevant in the knowledge economy. The Government has to grapple with this at a time when austerity is forcing it to tighten the budget and prune expenditure, including the education grants.

Hong Kong is not unfamiliar with the boom and bust cycles. One of the worst was the prolonged recession of the early 1970s. The Hang Seng Index back in those days before the stock market unified had plummeted to 150 points in 1975 from its then peak of 1,750 in 1972. Unemployment increased and investments decreased.

While such a heaving and hefting of the economy is as expected as the changing of the seasons, there is a fundamental difference between the cycle now and that in the past. Back in the 1970s the Hong Kong economy throve on labour-intensive manufacturing and exports. At the time of the oil crisis of the early 1970s, which triggered the recession, manufacturing accounted for a third of the GDP and 40 per cent of the employment. Our products were sold to about 200 countries and territories. Indeed not a corner of the planet seemed not to have toys, plastics, fabrics, shoes, and whatever without the label of "Made in Hong Kong". In short, Hong Kong's economy at that time was global.

Nowadays Hong Kong mainly re-exports items produced on the Mainland, some of which were touched up, value added and repackaged in the territory. The economic symbiosis between the SAR and the Mainland is so structured that the major cost of production line is across the border and the minor cost of administrative, financing and servicing works done right here. Today, year 2001, manufacturing is responsible for less than five per cent of the Hong Kong GDP and ten per cent of the work force — a percentage diminishing even as I write. The last strike for those local manufacturers who are hanging on is approaching as between 2005 and 2010 the garment quota that has given Hong Kong textile businesses a reprieve will be phased out. What is left of our once proud and prosperous manufacturing sector would be in shreds.

The future of Hong Kong as a service centre is now very clear since 85 per cent of the current GDP is already derived from related industries. Finance alone contributes to 25 per cent of the GDP, hotel catering and retail another 25 per cent, and personal and social services some 20 per cent. Hong Kong's role is to serve the Mainland and the rest of Asia. The financial crisis of 1997 to 1998 actually highlighted and accelerated the economic transformation of Hong Kong as the strength of the local currency made the last of its manufacturing even less competitive relative to that in the rest of Asia. In short, Hong Kong's economy is now basically regional and not, as in its manufacturing days, global.

But economic restructuring is not the only daunting change. The other is political change that also, of course, signals changes in society, a society much more assertive and aware of personal rights (rather less so of obligations) than ever before. The days of deference to authority are over and so are those of the people doing what they could for themselves rather than clamouring for the authorities to do more for them.

Hong Kong in colonial time was a "utopia" for the Governor, by whatever name, who had the Legislative Council to support his decisions and the rest of the civil service to implement them without demur. The Governor, with a mandate from the British Monarch, drafted and advanced policies in the overall and perceived interest of Hong Kong without much resistance from pressure groups. These pressure groups back in those days consisted mainly of disparate, and disorganized, activists and lobbyists who had no platform and no constitutional power to air their objections, let alone to block government policies and disapprove public expenditure.

But governing the SAR is a totally new ball game. This is basically caused by the introduction of an elected legislature coupled with a Chief Executive without a party to support him in the Legislative Council and a team of senior officials sharing his vision, trusting each other, acting in solidarity to assist him in the Administration. The Government is constantly under pressure and scrutiny, having to assist the needy with one hand and subsidize small and medium enterprises with the other. People previously treated the services they received — healthcare, welfare, and housing — as a privilege and now they regard these as their entitlements. Gratitude has been replaced with easily aroused dissatisfaction. Citizens demand more and better services but refuse to pay for these improvements with new taxes and higher fees and charges. Some even object to the introduction of declaration for those persons who consider themselves not affordable to pay higher charges for hospital services. The SAR must resolve this impasse and one of the means to do so is the application of the universal system of party politics, like a kind of franchise in the commercial world to run the SAR. This will be one of the subjects in the next section.

The Future

Party Politics

Party politics is essential to any democratic society because it is the proven way to govern effectively and accommodate differing views and interests. A political party is basically an organization with the object of securing consent of the people through democratic election to manage a country or territory in accordance with its manifesto for a specified period of time. This may seem obvious but is worth reciting here because in Hong Kong a political party may aspire to but does not yet to govern.

A political party therefore has to recruit members and develop their talents, determine and publicize its political manifesto, and run for election. Even when a party loses, it can reflect, regroup and reinvent for the next election. Such a party can act as the checks and balances, that is, the royal opposition, which discusses and attempts to amend or reject bills, block new taxes, and vet expenditure proposed by the administration. If won, the party will provide a team of different talents to administer the government in accordance with its manifesto for the specified period with a view to acquiring endorsement of the people and winning a re-election.

The alternative to such an orderly arrangement would be free for all, in which case there would be anarchy, or dictatorship. The Hong Kong Special Administrative Region has spelt out for itself a democratic future in the Basic Law but has not mapped out the contour of politics. This aversion or ambivalence towards political parties reflects history. The Chinese have had a checkered experience with political parties, most notably the Communist Party and the Nationalist Party (Kuomintang) which, between them, have fought, collaborated and fought some more.

Hong Kong, in accordance with its Basic Law, is committed to an executive-led government with a democratically-elected legislature acting as its checks and balances. But for such a system to work, and work effectively, the Chief Executive has to have his senior officials who are able, share his vision, trust each other, act in solidarity as well as come and go together as a team. The Chief

Plate 4.16 *The HKSAR Chief Executive, Mr. Tung Chee-hwa, addressing at his first press conference, 1997.*

Executive also needs a political party, which nominates him, assists him in the election, stands by him, and helps him shape, explain, advocate, defend and implement policies both inside and out of the Legislative Council. Ideally he should be able to recruit from his party loyal and competent colleagues to serve as his senior officials (ministers). This support was woefully lacking when the Government botched many responsibilities through the SAR's teething period during which no party rallied to the Administration or to the innocent Chief Executive who was taking the blame for his subordinates' bungles. The politicians and the press castigated Tung Chee-hwa, even though he had inherited the mandarins, the policies as well as the structure and style of administration from his predecessor. If he had a party to champion his case, he would not have appeared so vulnerable and isolated, and hapless in what had been the most critical and determining phase of his initial term when impressions mattered so much.

There are some people opposing to such a system of political parties. They long for those colonial days in which the governing process was so tame, easy and elitist. Those days are gone. Hong Kong has to join the modern democratic world rather than experiment with a system that has no precedent, no parallel, no future. What we need urgently is a political party law and a policy for developing politics that would nurture our democracy and answer the requirements and aspirations of our people.

Executive Council Reform

In colonial days the Governor and his senior administrators were, until the early 1990s, invariably foreigners who typically spoke hardly any Cantonese and lived in splendid isolation. If the Governor wanted

Plate 4.17 *The Hong Kong SAR Executive Council, 1997.*

to know whether he was doing a decent job or his policies were appropriate, he consulted his civilian appointees, labelled in mangled English "Unofficials", in his Executive Council. Whilst some of these Unofficial Members were also British expatriates, they tended to be company taipans who were veteran residents of the territory, familiar with the turf and its occupants. These advisors were invaluable to the Government for they helped the authorities feel the public pulse and prescribe the right policies, at least much of the time.

In those days such a Chinese counsel to the Governor was addressed aptly as the "Representative of the Chinese Community", and the senior one was of course revered as the "Senior Representative of the Chinese Community". I know because I was bestowed with both titles in succession. Such titles of course conferred status but at the same time also imposed very serious obligations on their holders who had to be answerable to both the ruler and his subjects. There was no free rides.

But from 1 July 1997 onward there was a basic change on the essential function of the Executive Council. I was the Senior Member of the Executive Council during the British rule in 1980 until my retirement in 1988 and I rejoined the Council after the sovereignty transfer in 1997 as its Convenor. The title "Senior Member" was used throughout the British administration until 1994 when Baroness Lydia Dunn retired and Dame Rosanna Wong succeeded her. The title was then changed to Convenor. By then most of the principal secretaries including the Chief Secretary were already Chinese possessing full knowledge of local conditions. The change was not only a name but a sense of history, of tradition, of circumstances.

When Hong Kong became the SAR the Chief Executive who supplanted the Governor was not only a local but had to have lived

Plate 4.18 *The Unofficial Members of the Hong Kong SAR Executive Council at Tiananmen, 1999.*

for 20 consecutive years in Hong Kong. His principal officers also had to be Chinese nationals who had claimed the territory as their home for 15 consecutive years. While the Executive Councillors of the SAR had to be permanent residents as well, they nonetheless need not have lived here continuously for more than 7 years, which is the residential requirement for permanent residency.

What all this means today is that the Chief Executive is already aware of the conditions in society and could consult his own senior officials, if he felt he had the need. Unlike the Governor, he is not beholden to his Executive Councillors for advice about the policies that could go down well with the public. The counsel of the old is now virtually redundant.

During the time of the British rule the Governor excluded the "Unofficials" of the Executive Council from policy formulation, a jealously guarded government prerogative. The Cabinet often did no more than analyse and approve (some critics say "rubber stamp") executive decisions. For years, even before my time and certainly during my time, the Executive Councillors pleaded for more direct input into policy formulation but were politely rebuffed. The Governor parried off the request with the excuse that his advisors were not full-time and had their own full careers and interests in the private sector. The direct and intimate participation in policy formulation could involve conflict of roles and interests. The Governor also considered that the public at large would not accept such a change or at least that was the excuse.

The issue cropped up again soon from my "unofficial" colleagues after the SAR Cabinet was established. I told them my experience but we still made a half-hearted effort to get involved in the formulation of policies. The Administration simply ignored us. In my own experience the only exception to the rule was in the period 1982 to 1984 during the British and Chinese talks on the future of Hong Kong. While the countries negotiated, the British Government did brief the Executive Council from time to time about the progress, or the lack of it, in the parley, and invite our participation in formulating strategy for the talks. In the beginning the British were reluctant to include us in their confidence for fear that sensitive information might be, inadvertently or not, leaked out but we never relented in applying pressure on the Prime Minister. Eventually we were trusted because no one in both the British and Hong Kong Governments could replace us for this function. At the end, the Unofficial Executive Councillors openly recommended the Joint Declaration to the people of Hong Kong after ensuring that the public interests and aspirations were met.

But now the Hong Kong SAR is growing more democratic. The

Plate 4.19 *Happy retirement card for the author from members of the mass media, 1999.*

sort of country club Executive Council of old no longer suffices in the present climate. The solution is to create a proper Cabinet comprising about 15 individuals, directly responsible to the Chief Executive. There could be about a dozen members who are concurrently senior officials with specific responsibilities and command over civil servants. The remaining three or so should also be full-time members though without portfolios, acting as Chief Executive's special advisors or "Cabinet Ministers without Portfolio". Such a system is preferable to the present amorphous arrangement, in which the EXCO members have voting right on policy decisions but no executive power and no accountability. The mirror opposite of this is the senior officials (policy secretaries) who have executive power and accountability but no voting right on policy decisions. The proposed reform will transform the Executive Council into a real Cabinet comprising full-time members with authority to formulate, approve and execute policies as well as accountability for their success and failure.

SAR's Economic Future

When Hong Kong was a British colony it was an isolated entity and attempted to be self-sufficient and to confine its development within its own 1,000 square kilometres. For this reason importers of rice, Hong Kong's staple food, were licensed and required to stock up to 6-months' consumption as a contingency. In the early 1970s Hong Kong had built one of the world's largest seawater desalting plants to safe guard its fresh water supply in case the Chinese Government did not co-operate as it had once happened in 1967. Hong Kong in those days also benefited from turmoil on the Mainland, which justified the isolation and the inward looking mentality.

After reunification with China as its SAR, Hong Kong can only benefit from a stable, increasingly prosperous, and rapidly modernizing Mainland. There is no longer any obsessive need for sufficiency on its own and for confining developments to within its physical boundaries.

The businessmen are very visionary and daring in this paradigm shift. Hong Kong-funded factories in the Pearl River Delta currently employ about five million people, mainly working on production lines. But still the professional manpower and infrastructure required to complement and support these factories in the areas of marketing and sales, product development and design, corporation administration and financing, etc. remain in Hong Kong. Hong Kong has the know-how, the experience, the contacts and the savvy. The Hong Kong SAR is in fact the brain and heart of the manufacturing activities in the Pearl River Delta, which will likely become one of the major manufacturing centres of the world.

Plate 4.20 *The BPF Forum on Hong Kong SAR's Economic Future, 1999.*

This division of labour within a large industrialized country is quite common. Many multinational industrial companies, based say, in the United States, have their headquarters located in New York City for corporate financing, accounting and administration, as well as international relations and marketing. Their shop floor operations may be located in sub-urban districts or out of state, even out of the country as the companies tap the best and most cost effective, wherever the sources. There is no reason why the Hong Kong SAR should not continue to follow this pattern to benefit from the synergetic combination of Hong Kong and the Mainland, particularly the Pearl River Delta region.

Even the siting of Hong Kong's new international airport at Chek Lap Kok serves this purpose, intended or otherwise, as it sits astride the estuary of the Pearl River. With the future construction of a bridge connecting Shekou in Shenzhen and Castle Peak in the north and eventually another one linking Zhuhai on the Pearl River's western shore and possibly Chek Lap Kok, the Hong Kong International Airport will become the apex for international air-travel and air-freight in the vast area of the Pearl River Basin.

For both economic and environmental benefits, the case for relocating the container port at Kwai Chung to either northwest of Lantau Island or west of Castle Peak, away from the densely populated areas, is compelling. Such a transfer should facilitate container movements in and out of the Pearl River Delta without getting traffic in the way of the people. Like the resiting of the Kai Tak Airport, the moving out of the Kwai Chung container port will free a large and valuable parcel of flat industrial land at Kwai Chung in the midst of the Kowloon urban peninsula for commercial, residential and recreational development.

There is a further suggestion that the Hong Kong SAR should

in the longer term development establish a second metropolis in the northeast area of Lantau Island where, based on the present government plan, further land will be reclaimed for building four more container terminals. With the future construction of a new strategic submerged highway linking Green Island on the Hong Kong Island West to the northeast point of Lantau, the use of this area for a second metropolis makes far better sense on longer-term macro-economic and environmental benefits than the four container terminals.

Up to now industrial developments in the Pearl River Delta are concentrated in the eastern bank due to more efficient land transport with the SAR, leaving the western coast much less developed. The lands in the counties of Zhongshan, Jiangmen, Shunde and Doumen on the western bank are in fact much larger, flatter and less expensive than the now over-developed Dongguan, Baoan and Shenzhen to the east. The less developed western coast is mainly the result of lack of direct and efficient land transport with the SAR. With the eventual construction of the Ling Ding Bridge linking Zhuhai, north of Macao and at the middle of the western coast, with Chek Lap Kok of the SAR, it could change the whole dynamics as it will open up the whole area on the western coast of the Pearl River Delta. By then the amenities and acumen of the Hong Kong SAR will serve a population of about 30 million on its hinterland, which is half as many as in Britain, more than that in Taiwan and larger than some countries in the European Union.

All these elements are the ingredients of a bright economic future for the Hong Kong SAR and should be the subject for the Commission for Strategic Development presided over by the Chief Executive. I have no doubt that Hong Kong's destiny is hitched to the emergence of the Pearl River Delta as one of the most, if not the most, promising areas in the global economy.

The idea of developing the Hong Kong cum Pearl River Delta region is not new. I first mentioned it in my public lecture titled "Hong Kong's New Destiny" on 26 October 1992 during the 20th Anniversary of the Hong Kong Polytechnic. The suggestion of establishing a second metropolis was also raised in my public speech at the Annual Dinner of the Hong Kong Institution of Engineers on 6 March 1998.

Rather than be totally preoccupied with the physical infrastructure, the so-called hardware, Hong Kong should not neglect the service industries, arts and culture (the software) without which the city would be a very sterile place. Hong Kong's banking, high finance, insurance, tourism, shipping, entertainment and so forth must serve the whole Delta region, the rest of China, and East Asia.

Hong Kong is a cosmopolitan, polyglot place with Chinese characteristics. Hong Kong people have in them the potential to be multi-talented and multi-lingual, fluent in written English and Chinese and conversant in English, Putonghua and Cantonese. But, sadly, some here have since reunification muffled English when, ironically, on the Mainland the Chinese are clamouring and chattering in the language of universal commerce, science and the arts.

None alarms me in the erosion of this linguistic advantage than in some public utilities and government departments which once printed their bills and notices in both English and Chinese and which now nonchalantly, indifferently, ask their customers to choose the English or Chinese option. This is a retrograde step and will hinder the progress of Hong Kong as a world city. The Canadians for the sake of national unity are enforcing a bilingual community and a multicultural society. The Belgians likewise have made both Dutch and French official languages. Unless Hong Kong is diligent, it can be surpassed linguistically by Singapore and even Shanghai, whose citizens feel no complex about acquiring languages.

The Chief Executive has extolled Hong Kong's prospects and exhorted people to emulate their counterparts in New York and London, which we support. But we are facing with a very difficult problem, which did not exist in New York and London during their process of change. When their manufacturing industries moved out into their hinterland and even other states and counties, their industrial workers moved out together with their factories without the restrictions, legal and psychological, of "One Country Two Systems". The people of the SAR lack that sort of instant mobility, even though thousands of Hong Kong people are doing work inside the Mainland, most as managers and professionals. The unskilled, or even the semi-skilled, have to stay at home and watch their jobs vanish, a plight affecting an estimated half a million of redundant former industrial workers.

The Government and employers here have to create jobs or retrain the people for new ones. This challenge shall daunt and dog the SAR for the next two decades or more — indeed could be a whole generation — since locals, whose wages are five or more times those on the Mainland just north of the border, are no longer competitive. The Government has been braced for this, accepting the days of full employment are behind it and counting on a modernizing China to be its source of growth. But Hong Kong has always adjusted with a resiliency that has been its defining characteristic and it will have to do that magic again.

Appendixes

1. Chronology of Events

1	Oct 1949	Establishment of the People's Republic of China.
	Apr 1964	Arrival of Sir David Trench as the 24th Governor of Hong Kong.
	May 1967	The Cultural Revolution in China spilled over into Hong Kong.
	Nov 1971	Arrival of Sir Murray MacLehose as the 25th Governor of Hong Kong.
8	Jan 1976	Death of the Chinese Premier Zhou Enlai.
9	Sep 1976	Death of the Chinese Chairman Mao Zedong.
	Jul 1977	Re-emergence of Deng Xiaoping and subsequently the NPC's approval of his economic reform plan and open door policy in February 1998.
	Mar 1979	Visit of Governor MacLehose to Beijing.
	May 1982	Arrival of Sir Edward Youde as the 26th Governor of Hong Kong.
	Sep 1982	The First UMELCO Delegation to London.
	Sep 1982	Prime Minister Thatcher talked with the Chinese leaders in Beijing on the future of Hong Kong .
	Mar 1983	Thatcher's secret letter to Premier Zhao Ziyang.
	May 1983	Visit of young professionals to Beijing.

4 Jul 1983	The First UMEXCO Mission to London.
12 Jul 1983	The first round of the Sino-British negotiations.
24 Sep 1983	The "Black Saturday" in Hong Kong with the HKD dropping to 9.60 per USD.
6 Oct 1983	The Second UMEXCO Mission to London.
17 Oct 1983	Pegging HKD7.80 to USD1.00.
19 Oct 1983	The fifth round and second phase of the Sino-British negotiations.
Dec 1983	Britain decided to return the sovereignty and administration of Hong Kong to China on 1 July 1997.
16 Jan 1984	The Third UMEXCO Mission to London.
25 Jan 1984	The eighth round and third phase of the Sino-British negotiations with new chief negotiators on both sides.
14 Mar 1984	The Lobo Motion Debate in the Legislative Council.
6 Apr 1984	The Fourth UMEXCO Mission to London.
20 Apr 1984	British proclamation to return Hong Kong to China in 1997 by Foreign Secretary Sir Geoffrey Howe in Hong Kong.
May 1984	The Second UMELCO Delegation to London.
Jun 1984	The UMELCO Delegation to Beijing.
19 Sep 1984	The Fifth UMEXCO Mission to London.
26 Sep 1984	The Sino-British Joint Declaration initialled in Beijing.
Dec 1984	The Third UMELCO Delegation to London.
19 Dec 1984	The signing of the Sino-British Joint Declaration in Beijing by Premier Zhao and Prime Minister Thatcher.
Jan 1985	The Fourth UMELCO Delegation to London.

12 Jun 1985 The registration of the Joint Declaration at the United Nations.

Jul 1985 The formation of the Basic Law Drafting Committee by the Chinese Government.

Oct 1985 The introduction of the functional constituency election into the Legislative Council.

Dec 1985 The formation of the Basic Law Consultative Committee by the Chinese Government.

6 Dec 1986 Death of Governor Sir Edward Youde in Beijing.

Apr 1987 Arrival of Sir David Wilson as the 27th Governor of Hong Kong.

Jul 1988 The Joint Liaison Group established its principal base in Hong Kong.

Jun 1989 The Tiananmen Incident in Beijing.

Oct 1989 Announcement of building a new airport on Lantau Island.

Dec 1989 Britain granted the right of abode to 50,000 Hong Kong families.

4 Apr 1990 The NPC approved the Basic Law of Hong Kong.

3 Sep 1991 Signing of the Memorandum of Understanding Concerning the Construction of the New Airport by John Major and Li Peng.

Oct 1991 Introduction of direct election into the Legislative Council.

Mar 1992 The Chinese Government appointed the first 44 Advisors on Hong Kong Affairs.

Jul 1992 Arrival of Chris Patten as the 28th and last Governor of Hong Kong.

Oct 1992	Announcement by Governor Patten on his political reform.
22 Apr 1993	Sino-British talks on Patten's political reform began.
16 Jul 1993	Establishment of the HKSAR Preliminary Working Committee by the Chinese Government.
27 Nov 1993	Breakdown of the Sino-British talks on Patten's political reform.
29 Jun 1994	Patten's political reform package passed in the Legislative Council.
Mar 1995	Formation of the JLG Expert Group on the transitional budgets by the Chinese Government.
26 Jan 1996	Establishment of the HKSAR Preparatory Committee by the Chinese Government.
4 Oct 1996	Formation of the HKSAR Selection Committee.
11 Dec 1996	Election of Tung Chee-hwa as the first HKSAR Chief Executive.
21 Dec 1996	Formation of the HKSAR Provisional Legislative Council.
24 Jan 1997	Formation of the HKSAR Executive Council.
20 Feb 1997	Death of Deng Xiaoping in Beijing.
1 Jul 1997	Britain returned Hong Kong's sovereignty to China and the establishment of the Hong Kong SAR.
Oct 1997	The Asian financial crisis spread to Hong Kong.
23 Oct 1997	The "Black Thursday" in Hong Kong with the inter-bank rate shot up to 280 per cent.
1 Jul 1998	Formation of the HKSAR First Legislative Council.

2 Jul 1998	Official opening of the new International Airport at Chek Lap Kok by President Jiang Zemin.
Aug 1998	The HKSAR Government spent HKD120 billion to defend the stock market.
26 Jun 1999	Interpretation by the NPC Standing Committee on Articles 22(4) and 24(2)(3) of the Basic Law.

2. List of Chinese Names with Their English Equivalents

ANN, Tse-kai 安子介

CHA, Chi-ming 查濟民
CHAN, Anson 陳方安生
CHAN, John 陳祖澤
CHAN, Kam-chuen 陳鑑泉
CHAN, Sui-kau 陳瑞球
CHAN, Tou-suen 陳道宣
CHAN, Wei 陳偉
CHAN, Wing-kee 陳永棋
CHAN, Ying-lun 陳英麟
CHAU, Sir Sik-nin 周錫年
CHEN, Dr. Edward 陳坤耀
CHEN, Shou-lum 陳壽霖
CHEN, Ziying 陳滋英
CHEN, Zuo'er 陳佐洱
CHENG, Hon-kwan 鄭漢坤
CHENG, Dr. Y. S. 鄭宇碩
CHEONG, Stephen 張鑑泉
CHEUNG, Man-yee 張敏儀
CHEUNG, Sir Oswald 張奧偉
CHEUNG, Yan-lung 張人龍
CHEUNG, Yung-hing 張蓉馨
CHIANG, Kai-shek 蔣介石
CHOW, Selina 周梁淑怡
CHUANG, Chung-wen 莊重文
CHUANG, Shih-ping 莊世平
CHUNG, Dora 鍾多娜
CHUNG, Gilbert 鍾基博
CHUNG, Lily 鍾麗蓮

DENG, Xiaoping 鄧小平
DUNN, Baroness Lydia 鄧蓮如

FAN, Rita 范徐麗泰
FANG, Sir Harry 方心讓
FOK, Henry Ying-tung 霍英東
FONG, Nellie 方黃吉雯
FUNG, Daniel 馮華健

GAO, Qiang 高強
GAO, Shangquan 高尚全

GOH, Chok Tong 吳作棟

HO, Edward 何承天
HO, Dr. Kam-fai 何錦輝
HO, Kevin 何鑄明
HO, Prof. Patrick 何志平
HO, Shing-him 何承謙
HU, Chiazhao 胡嘉詔
HU, Fa-kuang 胡法光
HU, Weimin 胡會丞
HU, Yaobang 胡耀邦
HUA, Guofeng 華國鋒
HUANG, Diyan 黃滌岩
HUI, Yin-fat 許賢發

IP, Simon 葉錫安
IP, Yuk-lam 葉若林

JI, Pengfei 姬鵬飛
JIANG, Enzhu 姜恩柱
JIANG, Zemin 江澤民

KAN, Sir Yuet-keung 簡悅強
KE, Hua 柯華
KE, Zashuo 柯在鑠
KWAN, Sir Cho-yiu 關祖堯
KWAN, Dr. Simon 關善明
KWOK, Albert 郭志匡
KWOK, Dr. Philip 郭志權
KWONG, Ki-chi 鄺其志

LAI, Alan 黎年
LAI, King-sung 黎景宋
LAM, Kam 林灼淦
LAU, Prof. Siu-kai 劉兆佳
LAU, Wong-fat 劉皇發
LAW, Fanny 羅范椒芬
LEE, Allen P. F. 李鵬飛
LEE, Charles 李業廣
LEE, Cheuk-yan 李卓人
LEE, Cho-jat 李祖澤
LEE, Dick 利銘澤
LEE, Martin 李柱銘
LEE, Mary 李丁金
LEE, Sir Quo-wei 利國偉
LEE, Teng-hui 李登輝
LEONG, Christopher 梁家鏘
LEUNG, Antony 梁錦松
LEUNG, Bowen 梁寶榮
LEUNG, Chun-ying 梁振英
LEUNG, Elsie Oi-sie 梁愛詩
LEUNG, Kwok-kwong 梁國光
LI, Andrew 李國能
LI, Chuwen 李儲文
LI, David K. P. 李國寶
LI, Fook-wo 李福和
LI, Gladys 李志喜
LI, Hou 李後
LI, Hungqiang 李鴻章
LI, Ka-shing 李嘉誠
LI, Peng 李鵬

LI, Qiang 李強
LI, Simon Fook-sean 李福善
LI, Xiannian 李先念
LI, Zhongying 李鍾英
LIAO, Chengzhi 廖承志
LIU, Qiang 劉強
LO, Andrew 路祥安
LO, Shuk-ching 羅叔清
LO, Tak-shing 羅德丞
LO, Vincent 羅康瑞
LU, Ping 魯平

MA, Lin 馬臨
MAO, Junnian 毛鈞年
MAO, Zedong 毛澤東

NG, Hong-mun 吳康民
NG, Pauline 伍周美蓮
NGAI, Shiu-kit 倪少傑

PANG, Chun-hoi 彭震海
PEI, I. M. 貝聿銘
POON, Steven K. L. 潘國濂

QI, Feng 祈峰
QIAN, Qichen 錢其琛
QIAO, Zonghuai 喬宗淮
QIN, Wenjun 秦文俊

SHAO, Tianren 邵天任
SHAO, Youbao 邵友保
SHAW, Sir Run-run 邵逸夫
SHEN, Stanley 沈志澄
SHIU, Sin-por 邵善波
SIU, Gordon 蕭炯柱
SO, Andrew 蘇國榮
SONG, V. K. 宋文魁
SUEN, Michael 孫名揚
SUN, Nansan 孫南生
SUN, Yat-sen 孫中山

TAM, Maria 譚惠珠
TAM, Vivian 譚慧雲
TAM, Yiu-chung 譚耀宗
TANG, Ping-yuan 唐炳源
TIEN, Francis 田元灝
TIEN, James 田北俊
TSANG, Sir Donald 曾蔭權
TSANG, Hin-chi 曾憲梓
TSANG, Wah-shing 曾華勝
TSAO, Peter 曹廣榮
TSUI, Sze-man 徐四民
TSUI, Wilfred 徐志強
TU, Mrs. Elsie 杜葉錫恩
TUNG, Betty 董趙洪娉
TUNG, C. Y. 董浩雲
TUNG, Chee-hwa 董建華

WAN, Li 萬里
WANG, Bingzhang 王炳章

WANG, Hanbin 王漢斌
WANG, Kuang 王匡
WANG, Lin 王林
WANG, Qiren 王啓人
WANG, Shuwen 王叔文
WANG, Yingfan 王英凡
WONG, Andrew 黃宏發
WONG, Fanny 黃麗君
WONG, Joseph 王永平
WONG, Kam 黃鑑
WONG, Ker-lee 黃克立
WONG, Lam 王霖
WONG, Peter C. 王澤長
WONG, Dr. Philip 黃宜弘
WONG, Po-yan 黃保欣
WONG, Dame Rosanna 王葛鳴
WONG, Wilfred 王英偉
WOO, Prof. Chia-wei 吳家瑋
WOO, Peter 吳光正
WU, Alex 吳樹熾
WU, Annie 伍淑清
WU, James 胡文翰
WU, Jianfan 吳建璠
WU, Dr. Raymond 鄔維庸
WU, Xueqian 吳學謙

XI, Zhongxun 習仲勛

XIAO, Weiyun 蕭蔚雲
XIONG, Shihui 熊式輝
XU, Jiatun 許家屯

YANG, Qi 楊奇
YANG, Sir Ti-liang 楊鐵樑
YAO, Guang 姚廣
YE, Jianying 葉劍英
YEUNG, Po-kwan 楊寶坤
YIP, Paul 葉國華
YOUNG, Howard 楊孝華
YOUNG, Dr. John 楊意龍
YU, Kwok-chun 余國春
YUEN, Dr. Natalus 阮中鎏
YUEN, Susan 原劉素珊

ZHANG, Junsheng 張浚生
ZHANG, Liangdong 張良棟
ZHANG, Wannian 張萬年
ZHAO, Jihua 趙稷華
ZHAO, Ziyang 趙紫陽
ZHENG, Yi 鄭義
ZHOU, Enlai 周恩來
ZHOU, Nan 周南
ZHU, Zushou 朱祖壽
ZHUANG, Xin 僮辛
ZHUGE, Liang 諸葛亮

3. Biography of the Author

Sze-yuen Chung (鍾士元) has played an important role in Hong Kong's political, economic, educational and social development for over four decades. He joined the Legislative Council in 1965 and became its Senior Member during 1974–78. He was appointed to the Executive Council in 1972 and served as its Senior Member from 1980 to 1988. During this period he demonstrated his outstanding leadership in helping to bring the Sino-British negotiations on Hong Kong's political future to a successful conclusion. As a result, Hong Kong was able to achieve a peaceful and smooth transition from the British to the Chinese sovereignty on 1 July 1997.

He has contributed significantly to the prosperity of Hong Kong, having been the chairman of many key organizations, including the Federation of Industries (1966–70), the Productivity Council (1974–76), the Asian Productivity Organization (1969–70), the HK/US and the HK/Japan Economic Co-operation Committees (1983–88), and many others, spreading over three decades. He has led many trade missions overseas helping to put Hong Kong on the world map.

Shortly after his return from England, he established in 1953 Sonca Industries Limited, which has since become the world's largest manufacturer of electric flashlights, with products exporting to more than one hundred countries and an employment of nearly 5,000 people. He retired from the company in 1989 as its Executive Chairman.

On higher education, he probably has created a world record for being responsible to establish over a period of 30 years three tertiary educational institutions: the Hong Kong Polytechnic (now a university) in 1972, the City Polytechnic (now also a university) in 1984, and the Hong Kong University of Science & Technology in 1991. He has served as the Founding Chairman of the Governing Council of all these three tertiary institutions and is at present the Pro-Chancellor of the Hong Kong University of Science & Technology.

Sir Sze-yuen is a distinguished professional engineer and has played a leading role in the development of the engineering profession in Hong Kong. He was the President of the Engineering Society of Hong Kong during 1960–61. In 1976 when he was the Senior Member of the Legislative Council, he introduced the bill to transform the Engineering Society into the statutory Institution of Engineers. In 1994 he founded the Hong Kong Academy of Engineering Sciences and was its Founding President until 1997.

In 1988, he took up the challenge of re-engineering the 40 government and subvented hospitals in Hong Kong with over 40,000 staff. He created and chaired the Hospital Authority from 1990 to 1995, integrating all the hospitals into a unitary system with a new corporate culture and decentralized scientific management. These public hospitals now provide much improved services to about 92 per cent of the local 6.5 million population.

During the 1990s he played a very active part in Hong Kong's political transition. The Chinese Government appointed him as a Hong Kong Affairs Advisor in 1992–97, to the Preliminary Working Committee in 1993–95 and to the Preparatory Committee in 1996–97 which dealt with Hong Kong's transitional matters. In January 1997, he came out from his retirement and accepted the appointment by the Chief Executive of the Hong Kong Special Administrative

Region to be the Convenor of the Executive Council. Once again, he played a crucial role in the final stage of the transition and in the formative years of the new HKSAR Government. He retired again in July 1999.

He received his Ph.D. degree in Engineering in 1951 from Sheffield University, England, after furthering his studies there. He now holds five honorary doctorates and many honorary fellowships. He was appointed a Justice of Peace in 1963, received two knighthoods (Knight Bachelor in 1978 and GBE in 1989) from the British Government, was made an Order of Sacred Treasure in 1983 by the Japanese Government, and was awarded the first Grand Bauhinia Medal in 1997 by the HKSAR Government.

Illustration Credits

Plate 2.10 — reprinted from *The UMELCO Annual Report 1982* (Hong Kong: Office of the Unofficial Members of the Executive and Legislative Councils, 1983). Courtesy of the HKSAR Government.

Plates 2.12, 2.14, 2.23,* and *3.1 — reprinted from *The UMELCO Annual Report 1984* (Hong Kong: Office of the Unofficial Members of the Executive and Legislative Councils, 1985). Courtesy of the HKSAR Government.

Plates 3.6* and *3.7 — Courtesy of The Hong Kong University of Science and Technology.

Plate 3.8 — reprinted from *The OMELCO Annual Report 1987* (Hong Kong: Office of Members of the Executive and Legislative Councils, 1988). Courtesy of the HKSAR Government.

Plate 3.10 — reprinted from *Hong Kong 1990* (Hong Kong: Government Information Services Department, 1991). Courtesy of the HKSAR Government.

Plate 3.12 — reprinted from *Hong Kong 1998* (Hong Kong: Government Information Services Department, 1999). Courtesy of the HKSAR Government.

Plate 3.14 — reprinted from *Hong Kong 1992* (Hong Kong: Government Information Services Department, 1993). Courtesy of the HKSAR Government.

Plates 4.5–4.11, 4.15* and *4.16 — reprinted from *Entering a New Era: The Establishment of the Hong Kong Special Administrative Region of the People's Republic of China* (Hong Kong: Government Information Services Department, 1997). Courtesy of the HKSAR Government.

The maps on the endpapers — reproduced with permission of The Director of Lands, © Government of Hong Kong SAR, Licence No. 36/2001.

Index

1997 issue:
  awareness, 25
  China willing to discuss with UMELCO, 96
  councillors' reaction, 29
  Deng's deadline to solve HK issue, 70, 112
  EXCO's debate, 73
  general viewpoints, 34, 49–51, 61–62
  MacLehose's meeting with Deng, 30–31
  official initiation of discussion, 31, 37, 39
  UMELCO's debate, 35–36, 45, 49
  see also confidence, Sino-British Joint Declaration
"50 years unchanged", 73, 83, 100, 111, 285, 296

activist, 35, 254, 301
Advisory Committee on Diversification, 22, 29, 31–33
Africa, 10, 23
African, 18, 86, 94
Airport Authority, 187–88
  Provisional, 187, 222
Airport Railway Corporation, 187
Airport Steering Committee, 189
Akers-Jones, Sir David, 23, 148, 254
anarchy, 162, 303
Ann, Tse-kai:
  as Basic Law drafter, 218
  bestowed GBM, 291
  joined Advisory Committee on Diversification, 29, 32
  joined CPPCC and as Vice-Chairman, 41–43, 258
  pondered HK's future, 27
Annan, Kofi, 272
Arculli, Ronald, 191, 211
Argentina, 43
Ashton, John, 220
Asia Financial Centre, 246
Asia Week (magazine), 152
Asian:
  economies, 298–99
  financial crisis, 233, 298
Association of Former Senior Civil Servants, 266

Atkins, Humphrey (*later* Sir), 39
Australia, 34
Australian, 4
Author Anderson (accounting firm), 254
autonomy:
  colonial, 164
  given to HKSAR, 73, 100, 111, 276, 293
  Jiang's assurance, 278, 285
  PRC's proposal for Taiwan, 37
  promised in Joint Declaration, 140
Auxiliary Transport Services, 4

Bank of China, 139, 246, 253
Bank of East Asia, 51, 222
banking, 29, 32, 296, 299, 315
Baoan, 314
Baptist College (*later* Hong Kong Baptist University), 50–51
Barrow, Martin, 210–13
Basic Law:
  Annexes I and II, 227, 239–40, 251
  Articles 45 and 74, 227, 235, 293
  committees:
    Basic Law Consultative Committee (BLCC), 159, 163, 168–69, 178, 258
    Basic Law Drafting Committee (BLDC), 159, 168
    Committee for the Basic Law of the HKSAR, 106
  drafters, 159, 161–63, 218
  grey areas, 204
  Hong Kong:
    and Patten's reform, 204–207, 210–11
    government's role in the drafting process, 161
    position on LEGCO reform, 176, 196, 198–99
    promulgation, 161, 257
    public responses to the drafts, 159
    UMELCO:
      concern on its interpretation and implementation, 125, 145
      position paper to London, 83–84
      proposals to Beijing and its public support, 104–108
    UMEXCO's stance, 120
    vital legislations before sovereignty transfer, 238
  HKSAR:
    executive-led principle and CE, 223, 244–45, 303
    paradigm shift and democratic future, 293, 303
    political set up and legislature, 167, 226, 240
    the post of "Chief Secretary", 267–68
    validity of colonial laws and judicial system, 249–50
  prescription to "through train", 145, 237

PWC and SC, 222, 251, 254
Basic Law Legal Committee, 105–106
Beijing (central government):
Britian, relation with:
Ambassadors and Attache, 44, 52, 60, 146, 196
visits:
Atkins, 39
Carrington, 37
Cradock, 183
Heath, 70
Howe, 81, 110
MacLehose, 30–31
Major, 184, 186
Patten, 199
Thatcher, 54, 56, 58–61, 114, 128
Youde, 60
HK delegations:
BPF, 178
delegate of young professionals, 64–65, 74
HK Manufacturers Association, 63
Liberal Party, 211
TDC, 63–64
UMELCO, 97–104, 279
HKSAR, relation with:
as central government, 101–102, 242, 266
court of final appeal, 74
representative in, 214
see also China, Tiananmen Square
Belstead, Lord, 60–62
"Black Saturday", 70, 72, *see also* confidence
Black, Sir Robert, 21
"Black Thursday", 298, *see also* confidence
Blair, Anthony, 269, 272
Blair, Tony, *see* Blair, Anthony
brain trust, 30, 191
Britain:
China, relation with:
1990 seven exchange of diplomatic letters, 199
accepted to return HK, 75, 78, 80–81, 111
Ambassador, 208
attitudes towards domestic affairs, 170, 235
on new airport project, 183–85
Zhao Ziyang's visit, 135
see also JLG, Sino-British Joint Declaration, Sino-British Land Commission, Sino-British negotiations on political reform
Conservative Party, 69 70, 138, 192, 203
election and political system, 69, 163–64, 264–65
former colonies and their mass influx to, 86, 94, 164
government:
Commander of the British Forces, 141
Conservative Government, 48

Foreign and Colonial Office, 15, 21
Foreign Office, 44–45, 56, 60, 85–86, 90, 92–93
Foreign Secretary, *see* Carrington, Cook, Howe, Hurd, Pym
Labour Government, 21, 94, 203
Minister of State, 60, 94, 116, 123, 135
Ministry of Intelligence, 118
overseas civil servants, 21, 23
Permanent Under-secretaries of State, 264
Prime Minister, 262, 264–65, *see also* Blair, Heath, Major, Palmerson, Thatcher
Privy Council, 64, 74
Secretaries of State, 264
Whitehall appointees and officials, 23, 54
Hong Kong, relation with:
early position on sovereignty and proclamation of exit, 47, 78, 81
final hours of ruling, 268–69, 271–73, 276, 278–80
moral obligation and commitment, 47, 122, 130, 133, 200
position on political reform, 112, 175–76, 237, *see also* Major, Thatcher
relation with UMELCO, 60
role after 1997, 84–85
see also BDTC, BNO, expatriate, Hong Kong Bill, Hong Kong International Airport, mandarin, Nationality Act, Patten, right of abode
parliament, 68, 84, 94, 135, 166, 175, 264–65
Anglo-Hong Kong and Anglo-China All Party Parliamentary Committees, 86
House of Commons, 47, 83, 125, 133, 164, 209
Foreign Affairs Committee, 123
House of Lords, 83, 126, 162–64, 202
Life Peer, 107, 212
Members of Parliament (MP), 86–88, 92, 133
Parliamentary Ministers, 54
honour system, *see* GBE, Knight Bachelor
JP system, 292
press, 58, 85–86, 128
royal family:
Charles, Prince of Wales, 269, 272–73, 280
Queen Elizabeth, 94, 111, 131–32, 148, 163–64, 166, 223, 272, 280
Queen Victoria, 14
Tories, 68, 203
Britannia (royal yacht), 280

British Commonwealth, 60, 94, 292
British Council, 11–13
British Dependent Territory Citizens (BDTC), 84, 95, 120, 125, 133, 141, *see also* passport
British National (Overseas) (BN(O)), 95, 133, 141, *see also* passport
British Nationality Act, *see* Nationality Act
British nationals, 84, 116, 133, 174
British Overseas Citizens, 94
Brown, William Charles, 80, 85
"buffer" solution, *see* delegate of young professionals
Bush, President George, Senior, 167
Bush, President George W., 166, 167
business:
  community, 29, 212
  in early 20th century, 1
  migration to mainland, 294
  practice, 185, 297
  qualification and quota in SC Category 1, 253, 256
Business and Professional Federation of Hong Kong (BPF), 178, 185, 192
businessmen:
  attended British state banquet, 135
  attitudes towards "through train", 234
  British and Japanese, 66
  British passport beneficiary, 176
  British relayed China's assurance to, 16, 31
  exodus, 27
  participation in politics, 178, 192, 194
  vision in paradigm shift, 312

Canada, 122
Canadian, 4, 315
Canton, 287
Cantonese, 1, 287, 305, 315
  Chinese leaders who speak, 63, 98, 289
capital, 3, 18, 29, 32, 52, 101, 296
capital city, Chinese province, 5, 9, 215–16, 287
capitalism, 73, 77, 80, 111, 161
Carrington, Lord, 37
Castle Peak, 313
Cha, Chi-ming, 216, 291
Chan, Anson, 189, 221, 235, 268, 273, 282, 284
Chan, John, 242
Chan, Kam-chuen, 51, 55, 122
Chan, Sui-kau, 214
Chan, Tou-suen, 20
Chan, Wei, 220
Chan, Wing-kee, 214, 261
Chan, Ying-lun, 81, 85, 123
Charles, HRH Prince, 269, 272–73, 280
Chau, Sir Sik-nin, 21–22, 25–27, 41
Chek Lap Kok, 182, 189, 313–14,

see also Hong Kong International Airport
Chen, Dr. Edward, 49
Chen, Shou-lum, 32, 149
Chen, Ziying, 258
Chen, Zuo'er, 231, 254
Cheng, Hon-kwan, 151, 154
Cheng, Dr. Y. S., 50
Cheong, Stephen, 64, 66, 76, 81, 85, 191
Cheung Kong Group, 222
Cheung, Man-yee, 288
Cheung, Oswald (*later* Sir), 33, 51, 85, 90, 93, 117
Cheung, Yan-lung, 81, 85, 123
Cheung, Yung-hing, 5, 9, 12–13, 19, 93, 259
Chiang, Kai-shek, 7
Chiang Kai-shek University, 8–9
Chief Executive (CE):
- at GBM Presentation Ceremony, 289
- at HKSAR establishment ceremonies, 272–87
- candidates named by Wan Li, 242
- CE Designate and staff, 246–47
  - Office, 246, 261
- dual loyalty, 226
- duties, 106, 227, 238
- forbade political affiliation, 228
- method of election and terms of office, 161–62, 167–68, 234–35, 293
- rounds of elections and results, 261–62
- *see also* Tung Chee-wah

Chief Justice, *see* Court of Final Appeal
China:
- Chinese People's Political Consultative Conference (CPPCC):
  - and Chung, 39, 41, 169, 178
  - and SC, 253, 255–56
  - Standing Committee member, 260
  - Vice-Chairman, 43, 216, 258
- Communists, 11, 13, 15, 174, 287, *see also* CCP
  - found PRC, 13
- Constitution, 63, 66–67, 125, 159, 163, 209
  - Article 31, 50, 73, 111
- democratic reform, 172
- economic reform and open door policy, 28, 36, 80, 149, 294
- Great Hall of the People, 56, 63, 98, 128, 180, 184–85, 218, 259, 279
- Hong Kong, relation with:
  - assurance of future, 73, 102
  - authority to interpret Basic Law, 145
  - liaison office in HKSAR, 208
  - position on electoral arrangements, 201–202
  - potential interference in local affairs, 109, 112, 123–24, 170, 173
  - principles for reunification, 63, 72–73

responsible for foreign affairs and defence, 111
Military Commission, 141, 272
National Anthem, 273, 285
National Day, 112, 219
National People's Congress (NPC):
and CE, 242
decision on HKSAR establishment ceremonies, 281
decision on HKSAR legislature, 239
endorsed Deng's economic reform, 28
established BLCC and BLDC, 159
established PWC, 218, 221
established PC, 250–51, 257–59
plan for reunification with Taiwan, 37
promulgated Basic Law, 106, 161, 238
resolution on SC constitution, 251, 253, 255
national pride, 279
national security, 145
President, *see* Jiang Zemin, Li Xinnian
Special Economic Zone, 36, 149
State Council, 43, 159, 178
Finance Ministry, 231
Foreign Ministry, 196, 199, 201, 231
Hong Kong and Macao Affairs Office:
arrangement to monitor transitional budgets, 228–29, 231
blamed London for failure of negotiations, 200–202
Deputy Director, *see* Chen Ziying, Li Hou, Li Zhongying
Director, *see* Ji Pengfei, Liao Chengzhi, Lu Ping
invitations to join CPPCC, 43
meetings with British delegates, 81
meetings with HK delegates, 63, 66, 98, 102, 104, 178, 185, 211
meetings with Patten, 199
position on direct election, 142, 145
see also Hong Kong Affairs Advisors, PC, PWC
National Security Bureau, 74
Premier, *see* Li Peng, Zhao Ziyang, Zhou Enlai
Vice Premier, *see* Ji Pengfei, Qian Qichen
see also Beijing, CE, Deng Xiaoping, Hong Kong International Airport, JLG, PC, PLA, PWC, Sino-British Joint Declaration, Sino-British Land Commission, Sino-British negotiations on

political reform, Xinhua News Agency
China Light & Power, 87, 212
China News Agency, 104
China Spring (magazine), 174
Chinese Chamber of Commerce, 11
Chinese Communist Party (CCP), 28, 64–65, 71, 74, 122, 170, 175, 210, 303
Politburo, 95, 172
Chinese University of Hong Kong, 50, 95, 151
Chongqing, 5
Chow, Selina:
founder of Co-operative
meeting with Heath, 71
meeting with Lu in Beijing, 211
position on Lobo Motion, 81
Resource Centre and Liberal Party, 64, 191
UMELCO delegation to London, 85, 93, 123
Chuang, Chung-wen, 27
Chuang, Shih-ping, 291
Chung, Dora, 12
Chung, Gilbert, 19
Chung, Lily, 12
Chung, Sir Sze-yuen:
early days:
career shift, 18–20
first voyage to England, 11–12
jobs in 1940s, 3, 7–10
wartime participation and exile, 4–5
economic vision, 296, 311–16
education, 2–3, 11–12
educational contribution, 148–49, 151–54
family:
children (Dora, Gilbert, Lily), 12, 19
parents and siblings, 1–2
wife (Cheung Yung-hing), 5, 9, 12–13, 19, 93, 259
national honours:
GBE, 130
GBM, 289, 291
Knight Bachelor, 131
Order of Sacred Treasure, 331
political loyalty, 180, 276
political nexus:
British government:
attended state banquet, 135
meetings with Thatcher, 51–56, 58, 61–62, 128, 130
Chinese government:
as HK Affairs Advisor, 180–81, 185
as PWC member, 217–18
declined political appointments, 39, 41–43, 169–70, 178
first meeting with Lu, 98
first visit to Beijing, 97–98
meeting with Deng, 98–104
secret meetings with Xu, 95–97, 139–145

colonial government:
as LEGCO and EXCO Senior Member, 33
beginning, 21–22
meeting with Patten, 194–95, 203
relation with Youde, 146–49
retirement, 132, 137, 142
HKSAR:
as EXCO Convenor, 282
refused to vie for CE, 241–43
swearing-in, 282
political views:
Basic Law, 181, 208–209, 227
HK political system, 180–81
HKSAR political development, 209–10, 228, 302–303, 305, 307–309, 311
last year of transition, 244–46
pace of democratization, 162–63
Patten's political reform, 204–205
PWC establishment, 215–17
City Polytechnic (*later* City University of Hong Kong), 149, 155
City University of Hong Kong, 149
Clague, Douglas (*later* Sir), 22
Clague, Lady, 259
class, social, 17, 95, 176, 260, 283
Clinton, President Bill, 167
Cock, E., 3
commerce, 64, 296, 315
Commission for Strategic Development, 314
Common Law, 161, 249–50
confidence, public:
in HKSAR government, 250
in Hong Kong:
crisis, 65–66, 72, 170
Deng's opinion, 101, 103–104
in 1960s, 27–28
in 1970s, 32
in 1980s, 45–47, 69, 100, 297
in 1990s, 176, 182, 297, 299
opinion poll, 108
in Tung's office, 228
see also "Black Saturday", "Black Thursday"
conscription, 125
consultation:
colonial governance strategy, 23
method to elect CE, 111–12, 161, 234–35, 251, 293
of a Green Paper, 142–43
of the bill on Airport Corporation, 188
of the draft Basic Law and public responses, 159
container terminal, 206, 313–14
Contemporary Chinese Architectural Art Exhibition, 158
Convention of 1898, 14, 29, 47
Convention of Peking, 14
Cook, Robin, 269, 272
Co-operative Resource Centre

(*later* Liberal Party), 64, 76, 191
corruption, 172, 266
cosmopolitan, 116, 283, 315
Court of Appeal, 249–50
Court of Final Appeal and judges, 74, 106, 238, 247
Cowperthwaite, Sir John, 24
Cradock, Sir Percy, 56, 77, 183
Cultural Revolution (China), 27–28
currency, 69–70, 298–99, 301

Davies, Derek, 29–30, 32
Daya Bay Nuclear Power, 133
de-colonization, 48, 94
defence (Hong Kong), 4–5, 111
delegate of young professionals, 64, 74–75
  "buffer" solution, 65–66
Democratic Party, 65, 189, 210, 215, 240, 279
democratic reform, 138, 172, 175–76, 200, *see also* Patten, political reform
democratization, 143–44, 177
Deng, Xiaoping:
  assurance of HK's future, 30
  deadline to resolve HK issue, 70, 112
  death, 106, 279
  his widow attending HKSAR establishment ceremonies, 285
  initiation of economic reform, 28, 36, 294
  meetings:
    Heath, 70
    Howe, 81
    MacLehose, 30–32
    Thatcher, 56, 58–60, 128
    UMELCO, 97–104
  position on PLA in HKSAR, 141
Diaoyutai State Guest House, 128
dictatorship, 303
Director of Audit, 154, 157
District Board:
  passed the electoral arrangement reform bill, 201–203
  Patten's reform and China's reaction, 138, 195–96, 198, 208
  support for UMELCO and the draft Joint Declaration, 91, 122–23
Donald, Alan (*later* Sir), 52, 56, 60
Dongguan, 294, 314
Dunn, Lydia (*later* Baroness):
  as LEGCO and EXCO Senior Member, 168, 190, 235
  at Youde's funeral, 148
  declined invitation to join BLCC, 169–70
  "Lady First" incident, 53–55
  led task force to support delegation, 88–89
  meeting with Deng, 97–104
  meetings with Chinese officials, 95, 97, 139–40
  national honours, 107, 175
  retired, 307
  "Soho" incident, 116–17

tendered resignation to Patten and was "re-appointed", 193
UMELCO delegations to London, 51, 123–26

East Asia, 315
economic prosperity, *see* prosperity
economy, 15, 32, 65, 206–207, 234, 283, 285
bubble, 297–99
deflation, 299
inflation, 155, 157, 297, 299
recession, 16, 101, 233, 299–300
recovery, 28, 186, 299
regional, 301
restructuring and transformation, 148, 301
see also global
Election Committee, 198–99, 211, 226, 239–40, 257
electoral:
politics, 191
system:
double-seat, double-vote, 196
first past the post, 164
preferential voting, 164
proportional representation, 164, 209, 210, 215
single-seat, single-vote, 196, 201, 208–10
electorate, 167, 196, 210, 243, 253
emigration, 88
environmental benefits, 313–14
Europe, 36, 43, 93, 209–10
European Union, 298, 314
Evans, Sir Richard, 77, 118
Eveready (American company), 18–19
Executive Council (EXCO):
appointment, 23–24, 111
functions and members' background, 23, 36, 307
meeting with Belstead in HK, 60–61
meeting with Howe in HK, 81, 83, 110
position on:
CE election method, 234
Hong Kong Bill, 133
JLG, 109
Joint Declaration, 75, 113–14
LEGCO direct election, 112, 144
UST, 151
realigned by Patten's reform, 138, 192–94, 205, 258
reaction to 1997 issue, 73
relation with British government, 309
relation with local community, 34, 194
Senior Chinese Member and Senior Member, *see* Chau Sik-nin, Chung Sze-yuen, Lydia Dunn, Kan Yuet-keung, Kwan Cho-yiu
see also UMEXCO
Executive Council (HKSAR):
at Establishment Ceremony, 282, 284, 289

at Sovereignty Return Ceremony, 272, 280
change of functions, 307–308, 311
members' background and requirement, 308
expatriate, 1–3, 23, 34, 280, 282, 307, *see also* mandarin
exports, 15, 20, 296, 299–300
export-oriented and -driven, 16–17, 149, 151
to Russia, Africa, North America, 8, 10, 298

Falklands, 43, 52
Fan, Rita:
as Provisional LEGCO President, 240, 282, 285
as PWC Security Specialized Group Convenor, 218, 222
joined Tung's campaign team, 261
position on Lobo Motion, 81
UMELCO delegation to London, 123
wept when informed of British retreat, 76
Fang, Sir Harry, 80
Far Eastern Economic Review (magazine), 29, 65
Federation of Hong Kong Industries, 22, 26
Federation of Industries, 27, 149
finance, 32, 73, 296, 301, 315
financial crisis, 301
Financial Times (newspaper), 152
Fire Services, 280
Fok, Henry Ying-tung, 216, 218, 258, 291
Fong, Nellie, 187, 218, 231, 254, 288
Ford, Sir David, 220–21
foreign affairs, 59, 111
Foshan, 1
free society, 58
Fung, Daniel, 249

"Gang of Four" (China), 28
Gao, Qiang, 231
Gao, Shangquan, 187, 218
Gavshon, Arthur, 58
General Electric Company, 212–13, 258
German Rhine basin, 296
GKN (British company), 13
global:
market and economy, 17, 21, 300–301, 314
media, 98
problems, 45
Goh, Chok Tong, 273
Gordon, Leslie, 32
Gordon, Sir Sidney, 33
Goronwy-Roberts, Lord, 94
Government Information Services, 78
Grand Bauhinia Medal (GBM), 289, 291
Grantham, Sir Alexander, 21
Gross Domestic Product (GDP), 17, 299–301
Guangdong, 1, 215, 287, 296

Guangzhou, 5, 15, 206, 215–16
guest worker scheme, 299
guilds, 140, 253
Guthrie, General Sir Charles, 272

Haddon-Cave, Sir Philip, 23, 29–31, 45, 80, 86
Hang Seng Index, 70, 297, 299–300
Hangzhou, 219
Heath, Sir Edward, 48, 70–72, 92–93, 112
Heilongjiang, 9
Her Majesty's Government (HMG), *see* Britian
Heung Yee Kuk, 123, 222
High Court and judges, 64, 122, 238, 240, 249
Ho, Edward, 65
Ho, Dr. Kam-fai, 80
Ho, Kevin, 232
Ho, Prof. Patrick, 242
Ho, Shing-him, 98
Hollingworth, Clare, 50
Hong Kong:
  government:
    civil service:
      civil servants, 67, 176, 222, 224, 266, 311
      commitment and "localization" policy, 34
      introduction of political appointment, 267
      political neutrality, 262, 264
      see also expatriate, mandarin
    governance strategy, 23
    "lame duck" administration, 245
    policy of neutrality towards Chinese politics, 138, 170, 174–75
    structure, 23
    see also District Board, EXCO, Hong Kong Governor, Hong Kong Monetary Authority, LEGCO
  history, 13–18, 311
    ceded to Britain, 14
    foreign exchange reserves, 184–86
    Japanese occupation, 4, 14–15
    race relation, 1
    see also HKSAR
  people:
    "anti-Communist" activities, 138, 174
    distrusted Chinese government, 73, 77, 105, 122, 297
    linguistic advantage and its erosion, 315–16
    political worries and demands, 101, 124–25
    social value and its changes, 301–302
    support for Beijing student movement, 172–73
    support for the draft Joint Declaration, 122
    support for UMELCO, 88–92, 107–109

work ethics, 17
see also BDTC, BNO, Nationality Act, passport, right of abode
Hong Kong Affairs Advisors, 180, 193, 216, 228, 243, 258
Hong Kong & Shanghai Banking Corporation, 29
Hong Kong Aviation Advisory Board, 22
Hong Kong Bill (UK), 133, 135
Hong Kong Chinese Bank, 27
Hong Kong Chinese Manufacturers Association, 63
Hong Kong Convention and Exhibition Centre, 261–62, 269, 271, 280, 281, 285, 288
Hong Kong Electric, 149
Hong Kong Governor:
relation with British government and power, 21, 111
see also Black, Grantham, MacLehose, Patten, Trench, Wilson, Youde, Mark Young
Hong Kong Institution of Engineers, 294, 315
Hong Kong International Airport, 313
Memorandum, 183
official opening, 189
published white paper on Airport Corporation, 188
Study Panel on Airport's recommendations, 187–88
time schedule, financial arrangement and cost, 182–85, 187–88
see also Chek Lap Kok
Hong Kong Management Association, 242, 244, 260
Hong Kong Manufacturers Association, 63–64, 66
Hong Kong Monetary Authority, 298–99
Hong Kong Observers, 35, 50–51
Hong Kong One Country Two Systems Research Centre, 258
"Hong Kong people running Hong Kong", 66, 70, 278, 285, 293
Hong Kong Polytechnic (*later* Hong Kong Polytechnic University), 148–49, 296, 315
Hong Kong Prospect Institute, 50
Hong Kong Reform Club, 35, 50
Hong Kong Special Administrative Region (HKSAR):
economic environment and socio-political change, 293–94, 296–302
economic future, 311–16
establishment ceremonies:
Establishment, 285, 287–89
Sovereignty Return, 271–73, 276, 278–79
Swearing-in, 281–84
honour system, 289, 291–93
first GBM Presentation Ceremony, 289, 291
political set up, 167–68
see also CE, EXCO (HKSAR),

LEGCO (HKSAR), Provisional LEGCO
Hong Kong Telephone, 22, 51
Hong Kong Textile Advisory Board, 61
Hong Kong Tourist Association, 210
Hong Kong University of Science and Technology (UST), 151–54, 157, 222, 266
  Campus Project Management Committee, 155
  cost overrun, 154–55, 157
  Governing Council, 158
  University Planning Committee, 155
  UST Planning Committee, 151, 154, 158
Hong Kong's future, question of:
  during Cultural Revolution, 27
  economic future, 311–16
  significance of technology and economic transformation, 158, 301
  see also 1997 issue, confidence
Hong Kong-Japan Business Co-operation Committee, 41
Hospital Authority, 260
housing, 17, 37, 285, 302, *see also* real estate
Howe, Sir Geoffrey:
  announced British retreat, 133
  meetings in London:
    UMELCO, 87–90, 92, 123, 135
    UMEXCO, 72, 116
  visit to Beijing, 81, 110
  visit to Hong Kong, 81, 110
Hu, Chiazhao, 9
Hu, Fa-kuang, 80
Hu, Weimin, 9
Hu, Yaobang, 170
Hua, Guofeng, 28
Huang, Diyan, 253
Hui, Yin-fat, 213
human rights, 125, 138
Hunan, 8, 287
Hurd, Douglas (*later* Baron), 138, 195

immigration, 27, 85–88, 93, 122, 133, 175
Independent Commission against Corruption, 229
India, 11
Indian, 4, 94
Indonesia, 298
industry, 15–16, 19, 22, 32, 151
  migration of, 29, 294
  see also manufacturing, textile
information technology, 296, 299
Innovative Art Award, *see* Contemporary Chinese Architectural Art Exhibition
Institution of Mechanical Engineers (UK), 13, 31
International Covenant on Civil and Political Rights, 138
investments, 101, 298, 300
  foreign, 37, 294
Ip, Simon, 214
Ip, Yuk-lam, 11

"Iron Lady", *see* Thatcher

Jacobs, Sir Piers, 186
Japan, 3, 41, 259
  invasion and occupation, 2–7, 9–10, 14–15, 27, 287
Jardine and Matheson, 29, 66, 211–13, 269
Ji, Pengfei, 39, 81, 98, 104–105, 144–45
Jiang, Enzhu, 208, 218
Jiang, Zemin:
  at HKSAR establishment ceremonies, 272–89
  confirmed SAR model was designed for Taiwan, 50
  "hand-shake with Tung" incident, 259–60
  officiated new airport opening, 189
Jiangmen, 314
Jiangxi, 5, 7–10, 287
Jiejiang University, 219
Jilin, 9
jobless rate, 299, *see also* unemployment
Joint Publishing (HK) Company, 201
judicial system, 250
judiciary:
  Attorney General (*later* Secretary for Justice), 189, 247–48, 267
  Secretary for Justice, 267, 285
  see also Court of Appeal, Court of Final Appeal, High Court
Justice of the Peace (JP), 22, 292–93

Kadoorie, Lord, 87
Kai Tak International Airport, 19, 182, 313
Kan, Sir Yuet-keung:
  accompanied MacLehose to Beijing, 30
  as EXCO Senior Member and retirement, 29, 33–34
  bestowed double knighthood, 132
  chaired TDC and HKJBCC, 41, 64
  complained to London on right of abode proposal, 94
  declined invitation to join CPPCC, 41–42
Ke, Hua, 66
Ke, Zashuo, 254
Keswick, Henry, 66, 212, 269
Knight Bachelor (UK), 131–32
Knight Grand Cross of the Most Excellent Order of the British Empire (GBE, UK), 130–32
knowledge economy, 300
Korean War, 15
Kowloon Lions Club, 232
Kowloon Whampoa Shipyard, 3–4, 7
Kuomintang, 11, 13, 213, 303, *see also* Nationalist Party
Kwai Chung, 313
Kwan, Sir Cho-yiu, 41
Kwan, Dr. Simon, 154

Kwok, Albert, 65
Kwok, Dr. Philip, 65
Kwong, Ki-chi, 232
Kyoto-Tokyo corridor, 296

labour:
  blue- and white-collar workers, 91, 107
  cheap and abundant, 16, 29
  employed in manufacturing, 294
  industrial and unskilled workers, 316
  labour-intensive, 17, 151, 300
  qualification and quota in SC Category 3, 253–54, 256
  unemployment, 299
  see also guest worker scheme
Labour Advisory Board, 214
Lai, Alan, 232
Lai, King-sung, 10, 43, 66–67
Lam, Kam, 248
"lame duck" administration, *see* Hong Kong
land:
  cost and supply, 29, 151, 206 207, 313–14
  granted to new airport, 187
  lease, 47, 52, 121
  propriety and inheritance rights over, 37
  transactions, 30–31, 285
Lantau Island, 182, 314–15
Lau, Prof. Siu-kai, 223
Lau, Wong-fat, 187, 222
Law, Fanny, 246
Lee, Allen:
  as LEGCO Senior Member and resignation, 190, 235
  effort to amend Patten's reform, 207, 211–15
  founder of Co-operative Resource Centre and Liberal Party, 64, 189–92
  leader of the delegate of young professionals, 64, 74
  position on Lobo Motion, 80
  UMELCO delegations to London, 85, 123, 175
Lee, Charles, 261
Lee, Cheuk-yan, 173
Lee, Cho-jat, 254
Lee, Dick, 50
Lee, Martin, 64, 157, 215
Lee, Mary, 65
Lee, Quo-wei (*later* Sir), 29, 32, 95, 97, 123, 139, 291
Lee, Teng-hui, 298
Legg, Dr. Keith, 32
Legislative Council (LEGCO):
  appointment system, 23, 144
  composition, 181, 223–24
  debate on the draft Joint Declaration, 121
  direct election, 112, 142, 144, 154, 175, 189
  duties, 23, 26
  Electoral College, 113, 251
  functional constituencies, 140, 163, 189, 191, 196, 198, 211, 225
  passed 1994 elections reform bill, 203

passed LEGCO reform bill, 204
Senior Member, *see* Oswald Cheung, Chung Sze-yuen, Lydia Dunn, Allen Lee, Lobo
"through train" and derailment, 145, 198–99, 207, 211, 215, 237, 247, 251
Legislative Council (HKSAR):
method of election and terms of office, 113, 167–68, 226
power, 227
private members' bills, 227
voting procedure and system, 163, 168, 227
Leong, Christopher, 65
Leung, Antony, 288
Leung, Bowen, 214
Leung, Chun-ying, 218, 242, 258
Leung, Elsie Oi-sie, 267, 285
Leung, Kwok-kwong, 65
Li, Andrew, 65, 282, 288
Li, Chuwen, 97, 142–43, 248
Li, David Kwok-po, 222
Li, Fook-wo, 30, 32, 51, 55, 109, 117
Li, Gladys, 249
Li, Hou, 66, 98, 104, 145
Li, Hungqiang, 74
Li, Ka-shing, 222
Li, Peng, 180, 184, 272, 282, 284, 289
Li, Qiang, 74
Li, Simon Fook-sean, 122, 218, 242, 249, 258, 260–61, 291
Li, Xiannian, 128
Li, Zhongying, 98
Liao, Chengzhi, 43, 63
Liaoning, 9
Liberal Party, 64, 164, 189, 191, 204, 207, 210–12
liberty, 67–69, 73, 92, 111, *see also* personal freedom
Ling Ding Bridge, 314
Lingnan University (China), 5
"Little Shanghai", 287
Liu, Qiang, 231
Liverpool University, 258
Lo, Andrew, 261
Lo, Shuk-ching, 254
Lo, Tak-shing, 80, 85, 93, 163, 222, 291
Lo, Vincent, 178, 185, 187, 192, 194, 216, 222
lobbyists, 301
Lobo Motion, 78, 80–81, 121
Lobo, Roger (*later* Sir):
bestowed knighthood, 131
retired from LEGCO, 139, 168
UMELCO delegation to Beijing, 96
UMELCO delegations to London 51, 55, 85, 123, 126
see also Lobo Motion
London, *see* Britain
Lowu, 279
Lu, Ping:
a deal with Liberal Party, 211–12
as PWC and PC Vice-Chairman, 218, 258
formed Budget Expert Group, 228–29, 231

interflow with Chung Sze-yuen, 178, 181, 193–94, 204–206, 217, 243
meetings:
BPF, 178, 185
delegate of young professionals, 66
HK Affairs Advisors, 216
Patten, 199
UMELCO, 98, 104
position on direct election, 142
position on reserve for HKSAR, 185–86
Luce, Richard, 116, 123, 135

Ma, Lin, 95
Macao:
China's acts to take back, 48, 93
during Cultural Revolution, 27
during wartime, 4–7, 10, 13
geographic location, 248, 314
one-off identification paper to Britain, 93
returned to China and first SAR anniversary, 50, 279
McLaren, Sir Robin, 196
MacLehose, Sir Murray (*later* Lord):
appointed Chung as EXCO and LEGCO Senior Member, 28
as MP meeting UMELCO, 86–87, 89
meeting with Deng, 30–32
most aware about the beginning of Sino-British negotiations, 25
reformed LEGCO, 224
retired to Scotland, 44
MacWhinnie, Sir Gordon, 155
Major, John:
appointed Patten as HK Governor, 177, 192
endorsed Patten's reform, 138, 195, 204, 212–13, 226
position on PWC, 221
signed new airport memorandum, 184, 186
Malaysia, 23, 298
Manchester, 12–13
Manchuria, 3, 9–10
mandarin, 22–23, 34, 220–21, 223, 235, 247, 264, 305, *see also* expatriate
Mandarin, 287–88, *see also* Putonghua
manufacturer, 20–21, 294
manufacturing, 15–16, 148, 294, 312
export-oriented and -driven, 17, 149
industries, 151, 316
labour-intensive, 151, 300
sector, 148–49, 301
see also industry, textile
Mao, Junnian, 139
Mao, Zedong, 28, 56
mass media:
anti-China stance, 246–48
avoided by politicians, 96
quipped Allen Lee as Chung's chosen heir, 64
reports on transition negotiations, 200, 220, 231

- reports on UMELCO's Beijing visit, 102
- role in local politics, 194
- role in Joint Declaration negotiations, 67, 88–89, 139
- sided with United Democrats, 191
- speculation on CE election, 257, 260
- *see also* press

Mathews, Jeremy, 247, 249, 267
Medical Council, 65
Meeting Point (*later* Democratic Party), 189
metropolis, second, 314–15
military, 59, 111, 269
militia, 141
Ming Pao (newspaper), 73, 148
Mirror (magazine), 242
mobility, 316
multinational industrial companies, 313
municipal councils, 196, 198, 201–203, 208, *see also* Urban Council

Nanchang, 9
Nanjing, 9
National Tea Corporation, 8
Nationalist Party, 303, *see also* Kuomintang
nationality, 122, 132–33, 141, 175, 254
Nationality Act (UK), 34, 92, 94, 138
New York, 45, 296, 313, 316
Newbigging, David, 29, 32
Ng, Hong-mun, 218
Ng, Pauline, 81
Ngai, Shiu-kit, 30, 32, 222
Nixon, Richard, 128
North America, 36, 298
North Point, 287

Observer (newspaper, UK), 58, 60–61
oil crisis, 300
"one country two systems", 137, 272, 278–79, 284–85, 293, 316
opinion poll:
- on 1997 arrangement, 50–51, 77
- on the draft Joint Declaration, 122–23
- on UMELCO's Beijing visit, 107
- on UMELCO's position paper, 91, 116

Opium Wars, 14, 273
Oriental Overseas (shipping company), 246, 259, 261

Pacific War, 287
Palmerson, Lord, 14
Pang, Chun-hoi, 213
paradigm shift, 151, 293, 312
party politics, 167, 302, *see also* political party
passport, 34, 93, 125, 138, 176
- British Citizen, 92
- HKSAR, 141

see also BDTC, BNO, travel document
patriot, 102, 216
patriotic duty, 9, 159, 244
Patten, Alice, 193
Patten, Christopher:
appointed Tung to EXCO, 258
arrival, 186, 192
at Sovereignty Return Ceremony, 271–73
departure, 268–69, 279–80
dissolved UMELCO, 195
family (Lavender, Alice, Laura), 193
lost Bath parliamentary seat, 138, 192
ordered officials not to co-operate with PWC and Provisional LEGCO, 221–22, 247
Policy Address and its late delivery to Beijing, 193, 196, 198
political reform package:
announcement, 186
five main features, 195–96, 198
Liberal Party's effort to amend, London intervened and LEGCO final vote, 210–15
passed 1994 elections reform bill, 203
passed LEGCO reform bill, 204, 207
secured support from London, 195
see also Sino-British negotiations on political reform
political stance, 193
realigned executive and legislative branches, 192–95
refused to act as "caretaker governor", 203
visit to Beijing, 199
Patten, Laura, 193
Patten, Mrs. Lavender, 193
Pearl River Delta (China), 248, 294, 296, 312–15
Pei, I. M., 246
People's Liberation Army (PLA, China), 125, 141, 278
People's Republic of China, *see* China
"Perennial Temporary Legislator", 22, 24
personal freedom, 64, 125, *see also* liberty
Philadelphia-New York-Boston axis, 296
police, 27, 141, 224, 280
Special Branch, 118, 173
political advisor, 30, 77, 174, 220
political party:
embryonic, 35
HKSAR's aversion towards, 303
in a democracy, 181, 191–92, 205, 266, 302–303
law for, 228, 305
relation with civil servants and executive, 264, 305
political reform:
1984 Green Paper, 1985 White

Paper and 1987 Green paper, 142–43
basic models, 264–66
direct election:
China's position, 112, 142, 198, 201
to LEGCO, 112, 144, 154, 163, 175, 189, 194
political review and popular demand, 142–43
representative government, 123, 141
Sino-British consensus on the pace of, 237
trend, 181
White Paper on Representative Government, 175
See also democratic reform, Patten
politicians, 135, 154, 225, 247, 297, 305
poll, *see* opinion poll
Polytechnic Planning Committee, 148
Poon, Steven, 191, 212
Portman Intercontinental Hotel (London), 86, 123
Powell, Sir Charles, 213
Powell, Enoch, 133, 135
Preliminary Working Committee (PWC):
composition, 218
establishment, 186–87, 215–18, 221
legal status in HK, 219–21
liaison office in HK, 219
relation with British and HK governments, 221–22
recommendation on PC's composition, 257
specialized groups and convenors, 218
Economic Specialized Group, 187, 229, 231
Study Panel on Airport, 187
Political Specialized Group:
established Provisional LEGCO, 237–40
decided to retain JP system, 292
position on executive-led government, 223
Preparatory Committee (PC):
applications for SC, 255–56
Chairman and Vice-Chairmen, 257–58
confirmed CE election result, 262
establishment, 215, 217, 250–51
Hong Kong Communication Office, 255
Selection Committee Group and its subgroups, 251, 253–54
recommendation on SC, 254–55
tasks, 251
work acknowledged by Li Peng, 282
press:

conferences, 83, 97, 102–103, 119
interview with Budget Expert Group, 231–32
reports and stance on:
China's invitation of Chung and Dunn to join CPPCC, 169
MacLehose and Youde's Beijing visits, 30, 60
Provisional LEGCO, CE election and Tung, 248, 257, 305
United Democrats and Patten's reform, 190, 205
pressure groups, 301
primary service hub of Asia, 296
Prior, Lord, 212–13
professional association, 140
professionals:
British passport beneficiary, 176
exodus, 27, 101
functional constituencies and political appointment, 192, 194
qualification and quota in SC Category 2, 253, 256
racial composition, 3
working in the mainland, 316
see also delegate of young professionals
propaganda, 66, 69, 72, 77, 87, 199, 204, 220
property, 37, 161, 178
boom, 149, 155
market, 18, 28, 186, 297, 299
prospects, 29, 297, 299, 316
prosperity:
balance between democratization and, 137
dependent on people's confidence, 45, 47
public perception, 124
purpose of Joint Declaration negotiations, 56, 58, 68–69
UMELCO's position and concern, 48, 53, 67, 80–81, 84
Provisional Legislative Council:
at HKSAR establishment ceremonies, 282
election method, 256
logistics arrangement, 249–50
passed Reunification Bill, 285
purpose of establishment and mandatory works, 237–40
question of legitimacy, 240, 247–48
Putonghua, 44, 287–89, 315, *see also* Mandarin
Pym, Francis (*later* Sir), 52, 56

Qi, Feng, 43, 66
Qian, Qichen, 207–208, 218, 257–59, 272, 285, 289
Qiao, Zonghuai, 139
Qin, Wenjun, 220, 258
Qing Dynasty, 74

Radiation Board (HK government), 22
radio, 89

Radio and Television of Hong Kong, 288
Reagan, President Ronald, 44, 167
real estate, 31, 297, *see also* housing
Red Army (China), 13
Red Guard (China), 27
re-exports, 296, 300
refugees (from China), 14, 16, 52, 77, 105
retail, 296, 301
reunion, 37, 53, 289
right of abode (in UK), 94, 122, 176
Roosevelt, President Franklin, 4
Rowse, Mike, 232
Royal Academy of Engineering (UK), 31
Royal Hong Kong Jockey Club (RHKJC, *later* Hong Kong Jockey Club), 152, 154–55, 157
Royal Hong Kong Observatory, 271
"royal opposition", 194, 303
Royal Society for Life Saving, 2
rule of law, 58, 73, 111, 283
"running Hong Kong the Hong Kong way", 67
Russia, 8

Sandberg, Michael (*later* Lord), 29, 32, 85
Sanya, Hainan Island, 228
Sargant, Maurice, 85
Sears, Justice, 249
Second World War, 94, 287
Selection Committee (SC):
- applications and election results, 255–56
- formation, 251, 253–55
- results of CE elections, 282
- task, 246, 251, 256
- work acknowledged by Li Peng, 282

service industries, 296, 315
Shandong, 64, 287
Shanghai, 2, 11, 142, 248–49, 258, 316
- refugees and industrialists from, 16, 18, 21
- TDC delegation to, 64

Shanghainese, 287–88
Shao, Tianren, 218
Shao, Youbao, 187
Shaw, Sir Run-run, 174
Sheffield, 12–13
Sheffield University, 12
Shek Kip Mei fire, 17
Shekou, 313
Shen, Stanley, 261
Shenzhen:
- advantages, 151
- as HK's hinterland, 294, 313–14
- as Special Economic Zone, 36, 149
- meetings:
  - Election Committee, 240
  - PC, 262
  - Provisional LEGCO, 248–49
  - Tung and Lu, 260
- PLA stationed in, 141

Shiu, Sin-por, 258

Shui On Group, 178, 222
Shunde, 314
Sichuan, 5, 44, 98
Singapore, 11, 273, 316
Sino-British Joint Declaration:
  Annexes I and II, 109, 113, 144, 161
  Britian:
    House of Commons' debate, 47
    proclamation of exit, 78, 81
    Thatcher's letter to Zhao Ziyang, 68–69
    visits to Beijing, *see* Beijing
  China:
    initiated the discussion, 37
    objection to UMEXCO's involvement, 62–63
    positions, 47–48, 58–61, 63–64
    principles for securing HK's future, 72–73
    "united front" strategy, 51, 63, 77
  deadline for agreement, 70, 112
  first joint statement on negotiation, 56
  functions and backdrop, 25, 43–44
  initialling ceremony and public release, 118–19
  "microphone diplomacy", 67
  negotiation teams:
    phase 3, 77, 113
    phases 1 and 2, 69, 72
  negotiations:
    phase 1 (rounds 1 to 4), 69, 72, 76
    phase 2 (rounds 5 to 7), 72, 75–76
    phase 3 (rounds 8 to 22), 86, 112–14
  ratifications and tendered to UN, 114
  signing ceremony, 128
  UMEXCO and UMELCO's reaction, 119–26
Sino-British Joint Liaison Group (JLG):
  advice on transition ceremonies, 271
  Budget Expert Group, 229–33
  contribution to Basic Law drafting, 161
  "mirror image" life, 110–11
  purpose of establishment, 81, 101
  terms of reference, 110–11
Sino-British Land Commission, 187
Sino-British negotiations on political reform:
  diplomatic cunning and faith, 200
  negotiations (17 rounds):
    beginning, 200, 204
    breakdown, 201, 207
    China blamed failure on London, 201
    reasons for failure, 201–202
  release of seven exchange of diplomatic letters, 199–200

see also Patten
Sinophobes, 247–48, 279
situation of extreme abnormality, 59
Siu, Gordon, 188
small and medium enterprises, 302
So, Andrew, 80, 123
social protest, 27, 161, 172–73, 175
social stability:
balance between democratization and, 137
dependent on people's confidence, 45, 47
importance of having a strong executive, 210
public perception, 124
purpose of Joint Declaration negotiations, 56, 58, 68–69
UMELCO's position and concern, 48, 53, 67, 80–81, 84
social unrest, 27, 100, 102
Societies Ordinance, 219–21
Soho (London), 117
Sonca Industries, 20
Song, V. K., 18–20
South China Morning Post (newspaper), 91–92, 107, 109, 169, 229, 242, 247
South Sea Textiles, 149
Southeast Asia, 298
sovereignty (over HK):
Britain accepted to return HK, 78, 80–81, 111
China's reassertion of, 59, 61, 100, 102, 113, 145
difference in priority, 67
people's inclinations, 50–52, 76, 297
return, 271, 273, 279, 281, *see also* HKSAR
Thatcher's Beijing visit, 47
transfer, 184, 217, 233, 240, 245, 249, 267, 278
Sovereignty Transfer Planning Committee, 206, 216
see also Provisional LEGCO, PWC, Sino-British Joint Declaration
troop deployment, 141
S S Canton (ocean liner), 11
St. John's Ambulance, 2
St. John's University (Shanghai), 2
St. Paul's College, 2, 11
stock, 31, 70, 186, 297, 299–300
Strachan, Ian, 232
Suen, Michael, 246
Sun, Nansan, 254
Sun, Yat-sen, 173
Survey Research Hong Kong Limited, 50–51, 91, 107, 122
Swaine, John (*later* Sir), 122
Swift, H. W., 12
Swire, 51, 70, 95
Sir Adrian, 66
John, 66
synergetic combination, 313

Ta Kung Pao (newspaper), 80
Taihe, 5, 7
taipan, 29, 269, 307
Taiwan:

deportation of suspected agents, 173
during Asian financial crisis, 298
during civil war, 8, 13, 15
plan for reunification, 37, 50
target of national reunification, 28, 279
Tam, Maria, 81, 85, 93, 110, 123, 133, 222
Tam, Vivian, 261
Tam, Yiu-chung, 222, 251
Tamar Naval Base, 269, 271, 280
Tang, Ping-yuan, 149
telecommunication, 296
Television Broadcast, 174
textile, 16, 21, 61–62, 301
Thailand, 298
Thatcher, Margaret, Baroness:
at HKSAR establishment ceremonies, 269
Argentine attack and popularity, 44
"Lady First" incidence, 53–55
letter to Zhao Ziyang, 68–69
meetings:
Chung in London, 61–62
Chung on the plane, 128
Deng in Beijing, 54, 56, 58–61
UMELCO in HK, 56
UMELCO in London, 51–53, 125, 175
UMEXCO in London, 72, 116
Zhao Ziyang in London, 135
memoirs and stance on HK democratization, 177, 200
think tank, 29, 31, 191, 217
Three Kingdoms period (China), 148
"three legged-stool", 100
Tiananmen Square, 13
incident, 138, 161, 170, 172–75, 182, 184
Tien, Francis, 80
Tien, James, 192
tourism, 211, 296, 315
Townsend, Dr. Henry, 189
Trade and Industry Advisory Board (HK government), 22
Trade Development Council (TDC), 22, 26, 41–42, 63–64, 66, 271
transition, regime:
British retreat and founding of HKSAR, *see* Britain, HKSAR
pre-transitional period:
Deng's comment, 101–102
suggestion to extend the period of, 65
UMELCO's primary concern, 123
see also 1997 issue, Sino-British Joint Declaration
transitional period:
co-operative phase, 137, *see also* Basic Law, JLG
confrontational phase, 139, 192, *see also* Patten, Sino-British negotiations on political reform
period of distrust, 138, 170, *see also* Hong Kong International Airport

shadow government, 245
transport, 296, 314
travel document, 95, 133, 141, *see also* passport
treachery, 207, 212
Treaty of Nanking, 14
Trench, Sir David, 22, 24, 27–28
troop, 102, 125, 141, 173, 279, *see also* PLA
Tsang, Sir Donald, 235, 285
Tsang, Hin-chi, 291
Tsang, Wah-shing, 5
Tsao, Peter, 63
Tsuen Wan, 16
Tsui, Sze-man, 242, 260, 291
Tsui, Wilfred, 85, 98
Tu, Mrs. Elsie, 254, 291
Tung, Betty, 259
Tung, C. Y. 258
Tung, Chee-hwa:
  announced CE candidacy and campaign team, 260–61
  at GBM Presentation Ceremony, 289
  at HKSAR establishment ceremonies, 272–87
  attitudes towards political appointment, 267
  biography, 258–59
  Policy Address, 158
  relation with EXCO, legislature and the administration, 228, 303, 305, 307–308, 309
  won and established CE Office, 246, 261–62
  see also CE
unemployment, 233, 299, *see also* jobless rate
United Democrats (*later* Democratic Party), 189–91
United Kingdom, *see* Britain
United Nations, 15, 48, 93, 114, 272
  Human Rights Commission, 139
United States of America, 18, 64, 106, 313
  American presidential cum congressional paradigm, 164
  Congress, 166–67, 227
    House of Representatives, 166, 209
    Senate, 166, 209, 227
  constitution, 158, 166, 265
  JP system, 292
  political system, 164, 193
  President, 166–68, 227, 245, 265–66, *see also* G. Bush Senior, G. W. Bush, Clinton, Reagan, Roosevelt
  ruling parties, 246
  Supreme Court, 166
University and Polytechnic Grants Committee (*later* University Grants Committee), 151, 157
University Grants Committee, 151, 154
University of California, Berkeley, 95
University of Hong Kong, 2, 5–7, 50, 151, 157
Unofficial Members of the Executive and Legislative Councils

(UMELCO):
advocate for faster democratic reform, 175–77
dissolution, 194
expeditions to London, 51–53, 85–90, 122–26, 132–33, 135
appeal for public support, 88–90
immediacy of reaction to 1997 issue, 29–30
lobby for right of abode package, 175–76
meetings:
Deng in Beijing, 97–103
Heath in HK, 70–72
Howe in HK, 81, 83
Ji Pengfei in Beijing, 103–106
Thatcher in HK, 56, 58
mistrusted by British and Chinese governments, 60, 77
position on 1997 issue, 34–38, 45–49, 60–61
position papers:
a statement with eight concerns and two demands, 124–25
on HK's future, 83–84
on nationality, 132–33
three proposals on HK's future, 100–101, 104–109
role and function, 35–36
self-identity, 77
Unofficial Members of the Executive Council (UMEXCO):
final (5th) expedition to London, 114, 116
position on Sino-British negotiation, 61–63, 69
recommended the draft Joint Declaration to HK, 119–21
second expedition to London, 72
secret meetings with Xu, 95–97, 139–45
unrest, *see* social unrest
Urban Council, 23, 123, 138

Victory over Japan Day, 15

Walker, Prof. Anthony, 157
Wan, Li, 242
Wanchai Vocational School, 4
Wang, Bingzhang, 174
Wang, Hanbin, 258
Wang, Kuang, 95
Wang, Lin, 231
Wang, Qiren, 187
Wang, Shuwen, 218
Wang, Yingfan, 258, 280
Watkins, General Guy, 155
way of life, 25, 37, 64, 73, 76, 80, 111, 283
Wen Wei Po (newspaper), 80
Wesley-Smith, Peter, 50
Westminster model, 162, 164
White Swan Hotel (Guangzhou), 216
Whitworth Prize, 13
Wilson, David (*later* Lord):
as HK Governor, 174, 182
as leader of British negotiation team, 113

as political advisor to MacLehose, 30
recalled by London, 138, 177, 186, 192
Wilson, Harold, 203
Wing On Bank, 65
woman, Chinese, 10–11
Wong, Andrew, 50
Wong, Fanny, 229, 242
Wong, Joseph, 49
Wong, Kam, 63
Wong, Ker-lee, 291
Wong, Lam, 80
Wong, Peter C., 80, 133
Wong, Dr. Philip, 222, 231
Wong, Po-yan, 80, 189, 222
Wong, Dame Rosanna, 307
Wong, Wilfred, 253
Woo, Prof. Chia-wei, 153, 155, 222, 261
Woo, Peter, 242, 260
worker, *see* labour
Working Committee on Productivity, 22
world city, 315
World Light Manufactory, 10, 18
World Trade Organization, 299
Wu, Alex, 80
Wu, Annie, 261
Wu, James, 27, 30, 32, 149
Wu, Jiangfan, 218
Wu, Dr. Raymond, 242, 261
Wu, Xueqian, 81, 135

xenophobe, 86, 133
Xi, Zhongxun, 64–65, 74
Xiao, Weiyun, 218, 251
Xingquo, 9
Xinhua News Agency, Hong Kong Branch:
as de facto Chinese embassy in HK, 39, 95, 219
Beijing appointed HK Affairs Advisors to support, 180
Deputy Director, *see* Li Chuwen, Qi Feng, Qin Wenjun, Zhang Junsheng
Deputy Secretary General, *see* Chan Wei, Yang Qi
Director, *see* Wang Kuang, Xu Jiatun, Zhou Nan
invitations:
Allen Lee to lead young professionals to Beijing, 64
Kan, Ann and Chung to join CPPCC, 39, 41–43
UMELCO to Beijing, 95–97
membership in:
Budget Expert Group, 231
PC, 258
PC Selection Committee Group, 254
PWC, 217
refused to register PWC office in HK, 219–21
secret meetings with UMELCO, 95–97, 139–45
social protest at HK headquarters, 172
Stanley Villa, 143
Xiong, Shihui, 9
Xu, Jiatun:

dispute with UMELCO on Deng's comment, 98, 103
fled to USA, 77, 106
host dinner for UMELCO, 80
invited Chung and Dunn to join BLCC, 169
secret meetings with UMELCO, 95–97, 139–45

Yang, Qi, 97–98
Yang, Sir Ti-liang, 195, 242, 260
Yangtze, 5
Yao, Guang, 72, 77
Ye, Jianying, 37
Yeung, Po-kwan, 81
Yip, Paul, 261
Youde, Sir Edward:
accompanied Thatcher to Beijing, 56, 60
announced British retreat to UMELCO, 75
arrival, 43, 146
as British negotiation team senior member, 58, 69
biography, 44
called UMELCO to discuss Thatcher's Beijing visit, 47–48
death and funeral, 146–48
economic vision and established UST, 148, 151, 153–54, 158
inexpressive to UMELCO's conflict with Heath, 72
led UMELCO delegations to London, 51–55, 85, 114, 118, 135
on Chung's GBE award, 130, 132
reformed LEGCO, 224
suggested UMELCO to form delegation, 49
trips to London and Japan, 48, 95, 126
Youde, Lady Pamela, 44, 146
Young, Howard, 211
Young, Dr. John, 50
Young, Sir Mark, 15
Yu, Kwok-chun, 261
Yuen, Dr. Natalus, 65
Yuen, Susan, 22, 27

Zhang, Junsheng, 219
Zhang, Liangdong, 231
Zhang, Wannian, 272
Zhao, Jihua, 231
Zhao, Ziyang, 39, 56, 68–69, 81, 128, 135, 172
Zheng, Yi, 218
Zhongshan, 314
Zhou, Enlai, 28
Zhou, Nan:
as Chinese team chief negotiator, 77
as PC Vice-Chairman, 258
as PWC Vice-Chairman, 218
as Xinhua News Agency's Director, 181, 193–94, 204–205, 229
attended British state banquet, 135
initialled the draft Joint Declaration, 118–19

met HK Affairs Advisors in Guangzhou, 216–17
invited Chung to join PWC, 217

Zhu, Zuzhou, 231
Zhuang, Xin, 74
Zhuge, Liang, 148

GUANGZHOU
TIANHE
BAIYUN SHAN
HUANGPU
Huangpu Port
Guangzhou Econ. & Tech. Dev. Zone
Huangpu New Port
Zhu Jiang
SANSHUI
FOSHAN
NANHAI
GAOMING
HESHAN
PANYU
SHUNDE
DONGGUAN
JIANGMEN
XINHUI
ZHONGSHAN
ZHUHAI
DOUMEN
MACAU
TAIPA
COLOANE
TAISHAN
SHIZITOU
WUGUI SHAN
DAGUDING
HUANGSHANLU
Nansha Econ. & Tech. Dev. Zone
HU MEN
HONGQI MEN
HENG MEN
LINGDINGYANG
ZHUJIANG KOU
MODAO MEN
JITI MEN
YA MEN
Shiziyang
Xi Jiang
Tan Jiang
Yamen Shuidao
Shunde Shuidao
Shawan Shuidao
Hongqili Shuidao
Jiaomen Shuidao
Xiaolan Shuidao
Jiya Shuidao
Shiqi Shuidao
Rongqi
Xiaolan
Dongfeng
Guzhen
Tanzhou
Sanxiang
Tangjia
Qianshan
Gongbei
Jiuzhou Port
Gaolan Port
Gaolan Liedao
Gaolan Dao
Sanzao Dao
Hengqin Dao
Qi'ao Dao
Neilingding Dao
Dajiu Zhou
Wanshan
Dawanshan Dao
Xiaowanshan Dao
Longxue Dao
Hengmen Dao
Changjiang Shuiku
SCALE
km 0 5 10 20 30 40
113°00'E
113°30'

HONG KONG IN ITS REGIONAL SETTING
LEGEND
Railway
Main road
Secondary road
Built-up area / Cultivation
Airport / Major port
Power station
702 Peak (in metres)
Contours (vertical interval 200 metres with supplementary contour at 100 metres)
Sea depth in metres
NOTE : Data compiled from different sources. The publisher cannot guarantee absolute accuracy of all data shown herein.
Series AR/18/IRS
Edition 6 2001
Survey and Mapping Office, Lands Department
© Copyright reserved —— reproduction by permission only
114°00'
114°30'E
SOUTH CHINA SEA
HUIZHOU
BOLUO
HUIDONG
HUIYANG
LONGGANG
SHENZHEN
FUTIAN
BAO'AN
HONG KONG
KOWLOON
Hong Kong Island
Lantau Island
DAYA WAN
MIRS BAY
DEEP BAY
DANGAN SHUIDAO
Dong Jiang
Xizhi Jiang
TOLO HARBOUR
VICTORIA HARBOUR
TUEN MUN
YUEN LONG
TIN SHUI WAI
TSUEN WAN
SHA TIN
TAI PO
FANLING
LO WU
SAI KUNG
MA ON SHAN
TSEUNG KWAN O
TUNG CHUNG
TAI MO SHAN
LANTAU PEAK
VICTORIA PEAK
KOWLOON PEAK
CASTLE PEAK
WUTONG SHAN
BAIYUNZHANG
QINIANG SHAN
BAIKENG SHAN
HEZHANG SHAN
URMSTON ROAD
WEST LAMMA CHANNEL
EAST LAMMA CHANNEL
TATHONG CHANNEL
Lamma Island
Cheung Chau
Peng Chau
Soko Islands
Po Toi Islands
Ninepin Group
Wanshan Qundao
Dangan Liedao
Sanmen Liedao
Jiapeng Liedao
Tuoning Liedao
Zhongyang Liedao
Gangkou Liedao
Boundary of Special Administrative Region